Old-Fashioned
FAVORITE
RECIPES OF ALL TIME

Publications International, Ltd.

Favorite Brand Name Recipes at www.fbnr.com

Pictured on the front cover: *(clockwise from top left):* Fruit 'n Juice Squares *(page 336)*, Italian Rustico Soup *(page 69)*, Spaghetti Sauce *(page 141)* and Apple-Raisin Cobbler Pie *(page 303)*.

Pictured on the back cover *(top to bottom):* Italian-Style Meatloaf *(page 122)*, Blueberry Muffins *(page 49)* and Velveeta® Easy Pasta Primavera *(page 222)*.

Microwave Cooking: Microwave ovens vary in wattage. Use the cooking times as guidelines and check for doneness before adding more time.

Preparation/Cooking Times: Preparation times are based on the approximate amount of time required to assemble the recipe before cooking, baking, chilling or serving. These times include preparation steps such as measuring, chopping and mixing. The fact that some preparations and cooking can be done simultaneously is taken into account. Preparation of optional ingredients and serving suggestions is not included.

CONTENTS

p. 24

p. 136

p. 262

p. 322

APPETIZER FAVORITES

❦

Spice up your entertaining and start any party or casual gathering with mouthwatering finger foods, creamy spreads and zesty dips. Select from these popular, crowd-pleasing snacks— perfect for nibbling and impossible to resist.

Deluxe Fajita Nachos (page 6)

Deluxe Fajita Nachos

1 tablespoon vegetable oil
4 boneless, skinless chicken
    breast halves (about
    1 pound) thinly sliced
1 package (1.27 ounces)
    LAWRY'S® Spices &
    Seasonings for Fajitas
⅓ cup water
8 ounces tortilla chips
1¼ cups (5 ounces) shredded
    Cheddar cheese
1 cup (4 ounces) shredded
    Monterey Jack cheese
1 large tomato, chopped
1 can (2¼ ounces) sliced black
    olives, drained
¼ cup sliced green onions
    Salsa

In medium skillet, heat oil. Add chicken and cook over medium-high heat 5 to 8 minutes. Add Spices & Seasonings for Fajitas and water; mix well. Bring to a boil over medium-high heat; reduce heat to low and simmer 7 minutes. In large shallow broilerproof platter, arrange chips. Top with chicken mixture and cheeses. Place under broiler to melt cheeses. Top with tomato, olives, green onions and desired amount of salsa.   *Makes 4 appetizer or 2 main-dish servings*

Substitution: 1¼ pounds cooked ground beef can be used in place of shredded chicken.

Beer-Boiled Shrimp with Cocktail Sauce

1 (12-ounce) bottle beer
1 pound raw shrimp peeled
    and deveined except for
    tails

COCKTAIL SAUCE
1½ cups ketchup
2 tablespoons prepared
    horseradish, drained
1 tablespoon Worcestershire
    sauce
2 teaspoons fresh lemon juice
1 teaspoon TABASCO® brand
    Pepper Sauce

Fill large pot half full with water and beer; bring to boil over medium-high heat. Add shrimp, cover and turn off heat. After 4 minutes, drain shrimp and rinse with cold water.

For cocktail sauce, combine all sauce ingredients in small bowl. Cover and refrigerate 1 hour. Arrange shrimp, tails up, on serving platter around bowl of cocktail sauce.   *Makes 20 to 30 shrimp*

Hot Artichoke Dip

Hot Artichoke Dip

Prep Time: 5 minutes
Bake Time: 30 minutes

- 1 envelope LIPTON®
  RECIPE SECRETS®
  Onion Soup Mix*
- 1 can (14 ounces) artichoke
  hearts, drained and
  chopped
- 1 cup HELLMANN'S® or BEST
  FOODS® Mayonnaise
- 1 container (8 ounces) sour
  cream
- 1 cup shredded Swiss or
  mozzarella cheese (about
  4 ounces)

*Also terrific with LIPTON® RECIPE SECRETS®
Savory Herb with Garlic, Golden Onion, or Onion
Mushroom Soup Mix.*

1. Preheat oven to 350°F. In 1-quart casserole, combine all ingredients.

2. Bake uncovered 30 minutes or until heated through.

3. Serve with your favorite dippers.
Makes 3 cups dip

Cold Artichoke Dip: Omit Swiss cheese. Stir in, if desired, ¼ cup grated Parmesan cheese. *Do not bake.*

Hint: When serving hot dip for a party, try baking it in 2 smaller casseroles. When the first casserole is empty, replace it with the second one, fresh from the oven.

Velveeta® Con Queso Dip

Prep Time: 5 minutes
Microwave Time: 5 minutes

> **1 pound (16 ounces) VELVEETA® Pasteurized Prepared Cheese Product, cut up**
>
> **1 can (10 ounces) diced tomatoes and green chilies, drained**

Microwave Directions: Microwave VELVEETA and tomatoes and green chilies in 1½-quart microwavable bowl on HIGH 5 minutes or until VELVEETA is melted, stirring after 3 minutes. Serve hot with tortilla chips.   *Makes 2¼ cups*

Spinach Dip

Prep Time: 10 minutes
Chill Time: 2 hours

> **1 package (10 ounces) frozen chopped spinach, thawed and squeezed dry**
>
> **1 container (16 ounces) sour cream**
>
> **1 cup HELLMANN'S® or BEST FOODS® Mayonnaise**
>
> **1 can (8 ounces) water chestnuts, drained and chopped (optional)**
>
> **1 package KNORR® Recipe Classics™ Vegetable Soup, Dip and Recipe Mix**
>
> **3 green onions, chopped**

• In medium bowl, combine all ingredients; chill at least 2 hours.

• Stir before serving. Serve with your favorite dippers.
Makes about 4 cups dip

Yogurt Spinach Dip: Substitute 1 container (16 ounces) plain low-fat yogurt for sour cream.

Spinach and Cheese Dip: Add 2 cups (8 ounces) shredded Swiss cheese to dip.

Finger Lickin' Wings

> **2 dozen chicken wings, washed and dried**
>
> **3 tablespoons LAWRY'S® Seasoned Salt**
>
> **¼ cup butter or margarine**
>
> **1 jar (12 ounces) orange marmalade**

Sprinkle wings with Seasoned Salt to cover. In large heavy skillet, heat butter. Add chicken wings and cook over medium-high heat 3 minutes on each side. Spoon marmalade over chicken. Reduce heat to low and cook an additional 15 minutes.
Makes 6 to 10 servings

Serving Suggestion: Serve from skillet or from lettuce-lined platter. Garnish with orange twists.

Spinach Dip

Hotsy Totsy Spiced Nuts

Hotsy Totsy Spiced Nuts

Prep Time: 5 minutes
Cook Time: 45 minutes

    1 can (12 ounces) mixed nuts
    3 tablespoons *Frank's® RedHot®* Cayenne Pepper Sauce
    1 tablespoon vegetable oil
    ¾ teaspoon seasoned salt
    ¾ teaspoon garlic powder

1. Preheat oven to 250°F. Place nuts in 10×15-inch jelly-roll pan. Combine remaining ingredients in small bowl; pour over nuts. Toss to coat evenly.

2. Bake 45 minutes or until nuts are toasted and dry, stirring every 15 minutes. Cool completely.

Makes about 2 cups mix

Ratatouille

    1 large onion, thinly sliced into rings
    2 zucchini, sliced
    2 green bell peppers, cut into strips
    1 small eggplant, peeled and cut into ¾-inch cubes
    ¾ teaspoon LAWRY'S® Garlic Powder with Parsley
    ½ teaspoon (to taste) LAWRY'S® Seasoned Salt
    ½ teaspoon (to taste) LAWRY'S® Seasoned Pepper
    5 tomatoes, seeded and chopped
    1 tablespoon capers (optional)

Microwave Directions: In 3-quart glass casserole, combine onion, zucchini, bell peppers, eggplant and seasonings. Cover with plastic wrap, venting one corner. Microwave on HIGH 8 minutes. Stir in tomatoes; cover and microwave on HIGH 3 to 4 minutes, just until vegetables are tender-crisp and remain colorful. Add capers, if desired.

Makes 12 to 16 appetizers or 6 to 8 main dish servings

Serving Suggestion: Serve hot or cold with warm pita bread wedges as a relish accompaniment or as a vegetable.

Savory Stuffed Mushrooms

Prep Time: 20 minutes
Cook Time: 15 minutes
Total Time: 35 minutes

20 medium-sized mushrooms
2 tablespoons finely chopped onion
2 tablespoons finely chopped red bell pepper
3 tablespoons FLEISCHMANN'S® Original Margarine
½ cup dry seasoned bread crumbs
½ teaspoon dried basil leaves

1. Remove stems from mushrooms; finely chop ¼ cup stems. Discard remaining stems.

2. Cook and stir chopped stems, onion and pepper in margarine in skillet over medium heat until tender. Remove from heat; stir in bread crumbs and basil.

3. Spoon crumb mixture loosely into mushroom caps; place on baking sheet. Bake at 400°F for 15 minutes or until hot.

Makes 20 appetizers

Savory Stuffed Mushrooms

Crispy Bacon Sticks

½ cup (1½ ounces) grated Wisconsin Parmesan cheese, divided
5 slices bacon, halved lengthwise
10 breadsticks

Microwave Directions
Spread ¼ cup cheese on plate. Press one side of bacon into cheese; wrap diagonally around breadstick with cheese-coated side toward stick. Place on paper plate or microwave-safe baking sheet lined with paper towels. Repeat with remaining bacon halves, cheese and breadsticks. Microwave on HIGH 4 to 6 minutes or until bacon is cooked, checking for doneness after 4 minutes. Roll again in remaining ¼ cup Parmesan cheese. Serve warm. *Makes 10 sticks*

*Favorite recipe from **Wisconsin Milk Marketing Board***

Cheese and Pepper Stuffed Potato Skins

Prep Time: 30 minutes
Cook Time: 1 hour 20 minutes

- **6 large russet potatoes (about ¾ pound each), scrubbed**
- **4 tablespoons *Frank's*® *RedHot*® Cayenne Pepper Sauce, divided**
- **2 tablespoons butter, melted**
- **1 large red bell pepper, seeded and finely chopped**
- **1 cup chopped green onions**
- **1 cup (4 ounces) shredded Cheddar cheese**

1. Preheat oven to 450°F. Wrap potatoes in foil; bake about 1 hour 15 minutes or until fork tender. Let stand until cool enough to handle. Cut each potato in half lengthwise; scoop out insides,* leaving a ¼-inch-thick shell. Cut shells in half crosswise; place on baking sheet.

2. Preheat broiler. Combine 1 tablespoon **Frank's RedHot** Sauce and butter; brush on inside of each potato shell. Broil shells, 6 inches from heat, 8 minutes or until golden brown and crispy.

3. Combine remaining 3 tablespoons **Frank's RedHot** Sauce with remaining ingredients. Spoon about 1 tablespoon mixture into each potato shell. Broil 2 minutes or until cheese melts. Cut each shell in half to serve.   *Makes 24 servings*

*Reserve leftover potato for mashed potatoes, home-fries or soup.

Krispie Cheese Twists

- **½ cup grated Parmesan cheese**
- **¾ teaspoon LAWRY'S® Seasoned Pepper**
- **½ teaspoon LAWRY'S® Garlic Powder with Parsley**
- **1 package (17¼ ounces) frozen puff pastry (2 sheets), thawed**
- **1 egg white, lightly beaten**

In small bowl, combine Parmesan cheese, Seasoned Pepper and Garlic Powder with Parsley. Unfold pastry sheets onto cutting board. Brush pastry lightly with egg white; sprinkle each sheet with ¼ cheese mixture. Lightly press into pastry, turn over; repeat. Cut into 1-inch strips; twist. Place on greased cookie sheet and bake in 350°F oven 15 minutes or until golden brown.
Makes 2 dozen twists

Hint: To make 1 dozen, use only one of the two packaged pastry sheets and reduce other ingredients by half.

Cheese and Pepper Stuffed Potato Skins

Mini Cocktail Meatballs

1 envelope LIPTON® RECIPE SECRETS® Onion, Onion Mushroom, Beefy Mushroom or Beefy Onion Soup Mix
1 pound ground beef
½ cup plain dry bread crumbs
¼ cup dry red wine or water
2 eggs, lightly beaten

Preheat oven to 375°F.

In medium bowl, combine all ingredients; shape into 1-inch meatballs.

In shallow baking pan, arrange meatballs and bake 18 minutes or until done. Serve, if desired, with assorted mustards or tomato sauce.

Makes about 4 dozen meatballs

Holiday Meatballs

1½ pounds lean ground beef
⅔ cup dry bread crumbs
1 egg, lightly beaten
¼ cup water
3 tablespoons minced onion
1 clove garlic, minced
½ teaspoon salt
¼ teaspoon pepper
1 tablespoon vegetable oil
1 cup HEINZ® Chili Sauce
1 cup grape jelly

Combine first 8 ingredients. Form into 60 bite-sized meatballs using rounded teaspoon for each.

Place in shallow baking pan or jelly-roll pan brushed with oil. Bake in 450°F oven 15 minutes or until cooked through. Meanwhile, in small saucepan, combine chili sauce and grape jelly. Heat until jelly is melted. Place well-drained meatballs in serving dish. Pour chili sauce mixture over; stir gently to coat. Serve warm. *Makes 60 appetizers*

Hint: For a zestier sauce, substitute hot jalapeño jelly for grape jelly.

Cherry Tomato Appetizers

1 pint cherry tomatoes
Ice water
½ cup sliced green onions
¼ cup LAWRY'S® Lemon Pepper Marinade with Lemon Juice

In large pan of rapidly boiling water, carefully immerse tomatoes 15 seconds. Remove with slotted spoon and immediately submerge in ice water. Peel off and discard skins and stems. In large resealable plastic food storage bag, place tomatoes. Add green onions and Lemon Pepper Marinade; seal bag. Marinate in refrigerator at least 30 minutes.
Makes 4 to 8 servings

Serving Suggestion: Serve as an appetizer with wooden picks or as a side dish.

Bruschetta

Bruschetta

Prep Time: 15 minutes
Cook Time: 30 minutes

> 1 can (14½ ounces)
>   **DEL MONTE® Diced
>   Tomatoes, drained**
> 2 tablespoons chopped fresh
>   basil *or* ½ teaspoon dried
>   basil
> 1 small clove garlic, finely
>   minced
> ½ French bread baguette, cut
>   into ⅜-inch-thick slices
> 2 tablespoons olive oil

1. Combine tomatoes, basil and garlic in 1-quart bowl; cover and refrigerate at least ½ hour.

2. Preheat broiler. Place bread slices on baking sheet; lightly brush both sides of bread with oil. Broil until lightly toasted, turning to toast both sides. Cool on wire rack.

3. Bring tomato mixture to room temperature. Spoon tomato mixture over bread and serve immediately. Sprinkle with additional fresh basil leaves, if desired.

Makes 8 appetizer servings

Note: For a fat-free version, omit olive oil. For a lower-fat variation, spray the bread with olive oil cooking spray.

Pace® Sausage Stuffed Mushrooms and Pepperidge Farm® Stuffed Clams (page 28)

Pace® Sausage Stuffed Mushrooms

Prep Time: 25 minutes
Cook Time: 10 minutes

    24 medium-sized mushrooms (about 1 pound)
    2 tablespoons margarine *or* butter, melted
    ¼ pound bulk pork sausage
    1 cup PACE® Picante Sauce *or* Chunky Salsa, divided
    ½ cup dry bread crumbs
    Chopped fresh cilantro *or* parsley

1. Remove stems from mushrooms. Chop enough stems to make **1 cup** and set aside. Brush mushroom caps with margarine. Place top-side down in shallow baking pan. Set aside.

2. In medium skillet over medium-high heat, cook sausage and chopped mushroom stems until sausage is browned, stirring to separate meat.

3. Add ½ **cup** picante sauce and bread crumbs. Mix lightly. Spoon about **1 tablespoon** stuffing mixture into each mushroom cap.

4. Bake at 425°F. for 10 minutes or until mushrooms are heated through. Top each with **1 teaspoon** remaining picante sauce and cilantro.   *Makes 24 appetizers*

Hint: To make ahead, prepare through step 3. Cover and refrigerate up to 24 hours. Bake as in step 4.

Deviled Shrimp

Devil Sauce (recipe follows)
2 eggs, lightly beaten
¼ teaspoon salt
¼ teaspoon TABASCO® brand
    Pepper Sauce
1 quart vegetable oil
1 pound raw shrimp, peeled
    and cleaned
1 cup dry bread crumbs

Prepare Devil Sauce; set aside. Stir together eggs, salt and TABASCO® Sauce in shallow dish until well blended. Pour oil into heavy 3-quart saucepan or deep-fat fryer, filling no more than ⅓ full. Heat oil over medium heat to 375°F. Dip shrimp into egg mixture, then into bread crumbs; shake off excess. Carefully add shrimp to oil, a few at a time. Cook 1 to 2 minutes or until golden. Drain on paper towels. Just before serving, drizzle Devil Sauce over shrimp.

Makes 6 appetizer servings

Devil Sauce

2 tablespoons butter *or*
    margarine
1 small onion, finely chopped
1 clove garlic, minced
1½ teaspoons dry mustard
½ cup beef consommé
2 tablespoons Worcestershire
    sauce
2 tablespoons dry white wine
¼ teaspoon TABASCO® brand
    Pepper Sauce
¼ cup lemon juice

Melt butter in 1-quart saucepan over medium heat; add onion and garlic. Stirring frequently, cook 3 minutes or until tender. Blend in mustard. Gradually stir in consommé, Worcestershire sauce, wine and TABASCO® Sauce until well blended. Bring to a boil and simmer 5 minutes. Stir in lemon juice. Serve warm over shrimp or use as a dip.

Makes about 1¼ cups

Fiery Chicken Bites

½ cup ketchup
1 tablespoon vegetable oil
2 to 2½ teaspoons hot pepper
    sauce
1½ teaspoons LAWRY'S® Lemon
    Pepper
1½ teaspoons LAWRY'S®
    Seasoned Salt
12 chicken drummettes, wings
    or thighs

In small saucepan, combine all ingredients except chicken. Bring just to a boil over medium-high heat; set aside. Broil chicken 5 inches from heat until no longer pink, about 8 to 10 minutes, turning once during cooking. Brush on sauce mixture; broil additional 2 minutes. *Makes 6 to 8 servings*

Serving Suggestion: Serve on bed of lettuce and garnish with lemon peel.

Lipton® Ranch Dip

Prep Time: 5 minutes

> **1 envelope LIPTON® RECIPE SECRETS® Ranch Soup Mix**
> **1 container (16 ounces) sour cream**

1. In medium bowl, combine ingredients; chill, if desired.

2. Serve with your favorite dippers.

Makes 2 cups dip

Ranch Salsa Dip: Stir in ½ cup of your favorite salsa.

Ranch Artichoke Dip: Stir in 1 jar (14 ounces) marinated artichoke hearts, drained and chopped.

Lipton® Onion Dip

Prep Time: 5 minutes

> **1 envelope LIPTON® RECIPE SECRETS® Onion Soup Mix**
> **1 container (16 ounces) sour cream**

1. In medium bowl, combine ingredients; chill, if desired.

2. Serve with your favorite dippers.

Makes 2 cups dip

Salsa Onion Dip: Stir in ½ cup of your favorite salsa.

Swiss Fondue

> **2 cups dry white wine**
> **1 tablespoon lemon juice**
> **1 pound Wisconsin Gruyère cheese, shredded**
> **1 pound Wisconsin Fontina cheese, shredded**
> **1 tablespoon arrowroot**
> **¼ cup kirsch**
> **Pinch nutmeg**
> **French bread cubes**
> **Apples, cut in wedges**
> **Pears, cut in wedges**

Bring wine and lemon juice to a boil in fondue pot. Reduce heat to low. Toss cheese with arrowroot and gradually add to wine, stirring constantly. When cheese is melted, stir in kirsch. Sprinkle with nutmeg to serve. Serve with French bread, apples and pears.

Makes 6 servings

*Favorite recipe from **Wisconsin Milk Marketing Board***

Top to bottom: Lipton® Ranch Dip & Lipton® Onion Dip

Ortega® 7-Layer Dip

1 can (16 ounces) ORTEGA® Refried Beans
1 package (1.25 ounces) ORTEGA® Taco Seasoning Mix
1 container (8 ounces) sour cream
1 container (8 ounces) refrigerated guacamole
1 cup (4 ounces) shredded Cheddar cheese
1 cup ORTEGA® Salsa Prima Homestyle Mild or Thick & Chunky
1 can (4 ounces) ORTEGA® Diced Green Chiles
2 large green onions, sliced Tortilla chips

COMBINE beans and seasoning mix in small bowl. Spread bean mixture in 8-inch square baking dish.

TOP with sour cream, guacamole, cheese, salsa, chiles and green onions. Serve with chips.

Makes 10 to 12 servings

Note: Can be prepared up to 2 hours ahead and refrigerated.

Spicy Shrimp Cocktail

Prep Time: 6 minutes
Cook Time: 10 minutes

2 tablespoons olive or vegetable oil
¼ cup finely chopped onion
1 tablespoon chopped green bell pepper
1 clove garlic, minced
1 can (8 ounces) CONTADINA® Tomato Sauce
1 tablespoon chopped pitted green olives, drained
¼ teaspoon red pepper flakes
1 pound cooked shrimp, chilled

1. Heat oil in small skillet. Add onion, bell pepper and garlic; sauté until vegetables are tender. Stir in tomato sauce, olives and red pepper flakes.

2. Bring to a boil; simmer, uncovered, for 5 minutes.

3. Chill thoroughly. Combine sauce with shrimp in small bowl.

Makes 6 servings

Crab Cakes

1 egg
2 tablespoons mayonnaise
1 teaspoon dry mustard
1 teaspoon LAWRY'S®
  Seasoned Pepper
½ teaspoon LAWRY'S®
  Seasoned Salt
¼ teaspoon cayenne pepper
4 cans (4¼ ounces each)
  crabmeat, drained, rinsed
  and cartilage removed
3 tablespoons finely chopped
  fresh parsley
2 tablespoons soda cracker
  crumbs
Vegetable oil for frying
  (about ½ cup)

In medium deep bowl, beat egg. Blend in mayonnaise, mustard, Seasoned Pepper, Seasoned Salt and cayenne pepper. Add crabmeat, parsley and cracker crumbs; mix lightly. Divide mixture into eight equal portions; shape each into a ball, about 2 inches in diameter. Flatten each ball slightly; wrap in waxed paper. Refrigerate 30 minutes. In large deep skillet, heat oil. Carefully add crab cakes, four at a time, to skillet and fry over medium-high heat 8 minutes or until golden brown on all sides, turning frequently. With slotted spoon, remove cakes from oil; drain on paper towels. Serve immediately.
Makes 8 cakes

Serving Suggestion: Serve with tartar sauce and lemon wedges.

Spicy Shrimp Cocktail (page 20)

Garlic Pepper Cheese

8 ounces mozzarella cheese,
  cut into 6 wedges
2 tablespoons olive oil
1 teaspoon LAWRY'S® Garlic
  Pepper

In large resealable plastic food storage bag, combine all ingredients; seal bag. Marinate in refrigerator at least 8 hours or overnight. Remove cheese from marinade; discard used marinade.
Makes 6 servings

Serving Suggestion: Serve with crackers or sliced French bread, tomato slices and fresh herbs as an appetizer or as a side dish for sandwiches and vegetable platters.

Beefy Nachos

1 pound ground beef
¼ cup chopped onion
⅓ cup A.1.® Steak Sauce
5 cups tortilla chips
1 cup (4 ounces) shredded
    Monterey Jack cheese
    Dairy sour cream (optional)
1 cup chopped tomato
    (optional)
¼ cup diced green chilies,
    drained (optional)
¼ cup sliced pitted ripe olives
    (optional)

In large skillet, over medium-high heat, brown beef and onion; drain. Stir in steak sauce. Arrange tortilla chips on large heatproof platter. Spoon beef mixture over chips; sprinkle with cheese. Broil, 6 inches from heat source, for 3 to 5 minutes or until cheese melts. Top with sour cream, tomato, chilies and olives if desired. Serve immediately.

Makes 6 servings

Microwave Directions: In 2-quart microwave-safe bowl, combine beef and onion; cover. Microwave at HIGH (100% power) for 5 to 6 minutes or until browned; drain. Stir in steak sauce. In 9-inch microwave-safe pie plate, layer half of each of the chips, beef mixture and cheese. Microwave at HIGH for 2 to 3 minutes or until heated through. Top with half of desired toppings. Repeat with remaining ingredients.

Hot Crab Dip

Prep Time: 10 minutes
Bake Time: 30 minutes

2 packages (8 ounces each)
    PHILADELPHIA® Cream
    Cheese, softened
2 cans (6 ounces each)
    crabmeat, drained, flaked
½ cup KRAFT® 100% Shredded
    Parmesan Cheese
¼ cup chopped green onions
2 tablespoons dry white wine
2 teaspoons KRAFT® Prepared
    Horseradish
¼ teaspoon hot pepper sauce
    PLANTERS® Sliced Almonds,
    toasted (optional)

MIX all ingredients except almonds with electric mixer on medium speed until well blended.

SPOON into 9-inch pie plate or 1-quart shallow casserole.

BAKE at 350°F for 25 to 30 minutes or until very lightly browned. Sprinkle with almonds. Serve with assorted NABISCO® Crackers.

Makes 10 to 12 servings

Variation: Substitute PHILADELPHIA® Neufchâtel Cheese, ⅓ Less Fat than Cream Cheese for cream cheese.

Grilled Baby Artichokes with Pepper Dip

Prep Time: 20 minutes
Cook Time: 13 minutes

    18 baby artichokes* (about 1½ pounds)
    ½ teaspoon salt
    ¼ cup *Frank's® RedHot®* Cayenne Pepper Sauce
    ¼ cup butter or margarine, melted
    Roasted Pepper Dip (recipe follows)

*You may substitute 2 packages (9 ounces each) frozen artichoke halves, thawed and drained. Do not microwave. Brush with Frank's® RedHot® butter mixture and grill as directed below.

1. Wash and trim tough outer leaves from artichokes. Cut ½-inch off top of artichokes, then cut in half lengthwise. Place artichoke halves, 1 cup water and salt in 3-quart microwavable bowl. Cover; microwave on HIGH 8 minutes or until just tender. Thread artichoke halves onto metal skewers.

2. Prepare grill. Combine ***Frank's RedHot*** Sauce and butter in small bowl. Brush mixture over artichokes. Place artichokes on grid. Grill, over hot coals, 5 minutes or until tender, turning and basting often with sauce mixture. Serve artichokes with Roasted Pepper Dip.
        Makes 6 servings

Roasted Pepper Dip

Prep Time: 10 minutes
Chill Time: 30 minutes

    1 jar (7 ounces) roasted red peppers, drained
    1 clove garlic, chopped
    ¼ cup reduced-fat mayonnaise
    2 tablespoons *French's®* Dijon Mustard
    2 tablespoons *Frank's® RedHot®* Cayenne Pepper Sauce
    ¼ teaspoon salt

1. Place roasted peppers and garlic in food processor or blender. Cover; process on high until very smooth.

2. Add mayonnaise, mustard, ***Frank's RedHot*** Sauce and salt. Process until well blended. Cover; refrigerate 30 minutes.
        Makes about 1 cup dip

Grilled Baby Artichokes with Roasted Pepper Dip

Buffalo Chicken Wings

24 chicken wings
1 teaspoon salt
¼ teaspoon ground black pepper
4 cups vegetable oil for frying
¼ cup butter or margarine
¼ cup hot pepper sauce
1 teaspoon white wine vinegar
Celery sticks
1 bottle (8 ounces) blue cheese dressing

Cut tips off wings at first joint; discard tips. Cut remaining wings into two parts at the joint; sprinkle with salt and pepper. Heat oil in deep fryer or heavy saucepan to 375°F. Add half the wings; fry about 10 minutes or until golden brown and crisp, stirring occasionally. Remove with slotted spoon; drain on paper towels. Repeat with remaining wings.

Melt butter in small saucepan over medium heat; stir in pepper sauce and vinegar. Cook until thoroughly heated. Place wings on large platter. Pour sauce over wings. Serve warm with celery and dressing for dipping.

Makes 24 appetizers

Favorite recipe from **National Chicken Council**

Glazed Meatballs

1 pound ground beef
½ cup fine dry bread crumbs
⅓ cup minced onion
¼ cup milk
1 egg, beaten
1 tablespoon chopped parsley
1 teaspoon salt
½ teaspoon Worcestershire sauce
⅛ teaspoon black pepper
2 tablespoons vegetable oil
½ cup bottled chili sauce
1 cup (12-ounce jar) SMUCKER'S® Grape Jelly

Combine ground beef, bread crumbs, onion, milk, egg, parsley, salt, Worcestershire sauce and pepper; mix well. Shape into 1-inch meatballs. Cook in hot oil over medium heat for 10 to 15 minutes or until browned. Drain on paper towels.

Combine chili sauce and jelly in medium saucepan; stir well. Add meatballs; simmer 30 minutes, stirring occasionally. Serve in a chafing dish.

Makes about 5 dozen meatballs

Buffalo Chicken Wings

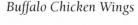

Deviled Eggs

Prep Time: 40 minutes
Cook Time: 20 minutes
Chill Time: 30 minutes

> **12 large eggs at room temperature**
> **1 tablespoon vinegar**
> **Lettuce leaves**

Filling
> **3 tablespoons *Frank's® RedHot®* Cayenne Pepper Sauce**
> **2 tablespoons mayonnaise**
> **2 tablespoons sour cream**
> **½ cup minced celery**
> **¼ cup minced red onion**
> **¼ teaspoon garlic powder**

1. Place eggs in single layer in bottom of large saucepan; cover with water. Add vinegar; bring to full boil. Immediately remove from heat. Cover; let stand 15 minutes. Drain eggs; rinse with cold water. Set eggs in bowl of ice water; cool.

2. To peel eggs, tap against side of counter. Gently remove shells, holding eggs under running water. Slice eggs in half lengthwise; remove yolks to bowl. Arrange whites on lettuce-lined platter.

3. To make Filling, add **Frank's RedHot** Sauce, mayonnaise and sour cream to egg yolks in bowl. Mix until well blended and creamy. Stir in celery, onion and garlic powder; mix well. Spoon about 1 tablespoon filling into each egg white. Garnish as desired. Cover with plastic wrap; refrigerate 30 minutes before serving.

Makes 12 servings (about 1½ cups filling)

Tip: Filling may be piped into whites through large star-shaped pastry tip inserted into corner of plastic bag.

Pecan Cheese Ball

Prep Time: 15 minutes
Chill Time: 1 hour

> **2 packages (8 ounces each) cream cheese, softened**
> **1 package shredded Cheddar cheese (about 8 ounces)**
> **1 envelope LIPTON® RECIPE SECRETS® Onion Soup Mix**
> **2 tablespoons finely chopped fresh parsley**
> **½ teaspoon garlic powder**
> **½ cup finely chopped pecans, toasted if desired**

1. In large bowl, with electric mixer, beat cream cheese until light and fluffy, about 2 minutes. Stir in Cheddar cheese, soup mix, parsley and garlic powder.

2. Wet hands with cold water. Roll cheese mixture into ball. Roll cheese ball in pecans until evenly coated.

3. Refrigerate 1 hour or until set. Serve with crackers.

Makes 1 cheese ball

Mini Sausage Quiches

Mini Sausage Quiches

½ cup butter or margarine, softened

3 ounces cream cheese, softened

1 cup all-purpose flour

½ pound **BOB EVANS®** Italian Roll Sausage

1 cup (4 ounces) shredded Swiss cheese

1 tablespoon snipped fresh chives

2 eggs

1 cup half-and-half

¼ teaspoon salt

Dash cayenne pepper

Beat butter and cream cheese in medium bowl until creamy. Blend in flour; refrigerate 1 hour. Roll into 24 (1-inch) balls; press each into ungreased mini-muffin cup to form pastry shell. Preheat oven to 375°F. To prepare filling, crumble sausage into small skillet. Cook over medium heat until browned, stirring occasionally. Drain off any drippings. Sprinkle evenly into pastry shells in muffin cups; sprinkle with Swiss cheese and chives. Whisk eggs, half-and-half, salt and cayenne until blended; pour into pastry shells. Bake 20 to 30 minutes or until set. Remove from pans. Serve hot. Refrigerate leftovers. *Makes 24 appetizers*

Hint: Pour mixture into 12 standard 2½-inch muffin cups to make larger individual quiches. Serve for breakfast.

Party Stuffed Pinwheels

Prep Time: 10 minutes
Cook Time: 13 minutes

> 1 envelope LIPTON®
>   RECIPE SECRETS®
>   Ranch Soup Mix*
> 1 package (8 ounces) cream
>   cheese, softened
> 1 cup shredded mozzarella
>   cheese (about 4 ounces)
> 2 tablespoons milk
> 1 tablespoon grated Parmesan
>   cheese
> 2 packages (10 ounces each)
>   refrigerated pizza crust

*Also terrific with LIPTON® RECIPE SECRETS®
Savory Herb with Garlic or Onion Soup Mix.*

1. Preheat oven to 425°F. In medium bowl, combine all ingredients except pizza crust; set aside.

2. Unroll pizza crusts, then evenly top with filling. Roll, starting at longest side, jelly-roll style. Cut into 32 rounds.*

3. On baking sheet sprayed with nonstick cooking spray, arrange rounds cut side down.

4. Bake, uncovered, 13 minutes or until golden brown.

Makes 32 pinwheels

*If rolled pizza crust is too soft to cut, refrigerate
or freeze until firm.*

Pepperidge Farm® Stuffed Clams

> 24 cherrystone clams, scrubbed
> 2 slices bacon, diced
> 3 tablespoons margarine *or*
>   butter
> 1 medium onion, chopped
>   (about ½ cup)
> ¼ teaspoon garlic powder *or*
>   2 cloves garlic, minced
> 1½ cups PEPPERIDGE FARM®
>   Herb Seasoned Stuffing
> 2 tablespoons grated
>   Parmesan cheese
> 2 tablespoons chopped fresh
>   parsley *or* 2 teaspoons
>   dried parsley flakes

1. Open clams. Remove and discard top shell. Arrange clams in large shallow baking pan.

2. In medium skillet over medium heat, cook bacon until crisp. Remove and drain on paper towels.

3. Add margarine, onion and garlic powder to hot drippings and cook until tender. Add stuffing, cheese, parsley and bacon. Mix lightly. Spoon on top of each clam. Bake at 400°F. for 20 minutes or until clams are done.   *Makes 24 appetizers*

Party Stuffed Pinwheels

Open-Faced Reubens

1 box (6 ounces) rye melba toast rounds

¼ pound thinly sliced cooked corned beef, cut into ½-inch squares

1 can (8 ounces) sauerkraut, rinsed, drained and chopped

1 cup (4 ounces) finely shredded Wisconsin Swiss cheese

2 teaspoons prepared mustard Caraway seeds

Preheat oven to 350°F. Arrange toast rounds on baking sheets. Top each with 1 beef square and 1 teaspoon sauerkraut. Combine cheese and mustard in small bowl; spoon about 1 teaspoon cheese mixture on top of sauerkraut. Sprinkle with caraway seeds. Bake about 5 minutes or until cheese is melted.

Makes about 48 servings

Microwave Directions: Arrange 8 toast rounds around edge of microwave-safe plate lined with paper towel. Place 2 rounds in center. Top as directed. Microwave, uncovered, on MEDIUM (50% power) 1 to 2 minutes until cheese is melted, turning plate once. Repeat with remaining ingredients.

Favorite recipe from **Wisconsin Milk Marketing Board**

Brandied Apricot Brie

1 wheel ALOUETTE® Baby Brie™, Plain

1 cup apricot preserves

1 tablespoon freshly squeezed orange juice

2 teaspoons brandy

1 teaspoon ground cinnamon

1 loaf French bread, sliced

Microwave Directions: Combine preserves, orange juice, brandy and cinnamon in microwave-safe bowl. Cover with plastic wrap and microwave on HIGH (100% power) 1½ minutes or until sauce begins to bubble. Place ALOUETTE® Baby Brie™ in shallow dish and top with apricot sauce. Microwave, uncovered, on HIGH 30 to 90 seconds or until cheese softens. Serve with French bread.

Makes 6 to 8 servings

❧ *tip* ❧

Brie is a soft-ripened cheese with a creamy texture. The white rind of Brie is edible, so don't discard it when serving as an appetizer.

Chicken Satay

Prep Time: 15 minutes
Marinating Time: 30 minutes
Cook Time: 5 minutes

> **1 pound boneless skinless chicken breast halves**
> **1 recipe Peanut Dip (recipe follows), divided**
> **Cucumber slices**
> **Chopped fresh cilantro**

1. Soak 8 (6-inch) bamboo skewers in hot water 20 minutes. Cut chicken lengthwise into 1-inch-wide strips; thread onto skewers.

2. Place skewers in large shallow glass dish. Pour ½ cup Peanut Dip over chicken, turning to coat evenly. Cover and marinate in refrigerator 30 minutes.

3. Place skewers on oiled grid and discard any remaining marinade. Grill over high heat 5 to 8 minutes or until chicken is no longer pink, turning once. Place on serving platter. Serve with cucumber, cilantro and remaining Peanut Dip.
Makes 8 appetizer or 4 main-dish servings

Peanut Dip

Prep Time: 10 minutes

> **⅓ cup peanut butter**
> **⅓ cup *French's*® Dijon Mustard**
> **⅓ cup orange juice**
> **1 tablespoon chopped peeled fresh ginger**
> **1 tablespoon honey**
> **1 tablespoon *Frank's*® *RedHot*® Cayenne Pepper Sauce**
> **1 tablespoon teriyaki baste and glaze sauce**
> **2 cloves garlic, minced**

Combine peanut butter, mustard, juice, ginger, honey, **Frank's RedHot** Sauce, teriyaki sauce and garlic in large bowl. Refrigerate until ready to serve.
Makes 1 cup dip

Hint: Serve as a dip for assorted cut-up fresh vegetables. Also great as a spread on grilled French bread with grilled vegetables.

Chicken Satay and Peanut Dip

BOUNTIFUL BREADS

❧

From quick-to-make muffins to slow-rising yeast breads, you'll discover all-time favorite breads that have been loved by families for years. Everyone will head to the table in a hurry when they smell the fragrance of freshly-baked bread.

Top Choice White Bread (page 34)

Top Choice White Bread

5½ to 6 cups all-purpose flour, divided
3 tablespoons sugar
2 envelopes FLEISCHMANN'S® RapidRise™ Yeast
2 teaspoons salt
1½ cups water
½ cup milk
2 tablespoons butter or margarine

In large bowl, combine 2 cups flour, sugar, undissolved yeast and salt. Heat water, milk and butter until very warm (120° to 130°F); stir into dry ingredients. Beat 2 minutes at medium speed of electric mixer, scraping bowl occasionally. Stir in 1 cup flour; beat at high speed for 2 minutes, scraping bowl occasionally. Stir in enough remaining flour to make soft dough. Knead on lightly floured surface until smooth and elastic, about 8 to 10 minutes. Cover; let rest 10 minutes.

Divide dough in half. Roll each half to 12×7-inch rectangle. Beginning at short end of each rectangle, roll up tightly as for jelly roll. Pinch seams and ends to seal. Place seam sides down in 2 greased 8½×4½-inch loaf pans. Cover; let rise in warm, draft-free place until doubled in size, about 45 minutes.

Bake at 400°F for 25 to 30 minutes or until done. Remove from pans; cool on wire rack.

Makes 2 loaves

Note: To make Whole Wheat Bread: Substitute 2 cups whole wheat flour for equal part of all-purpose flour.

Pumpkin Bread

1 package (about 18 ounces) yellow cake mix
1 can (16 ounces) solid pack pumpkin
⅓ cup GRANDMA'S® Molasses
4 eggs
1 teaspoon cinnamon
1 teaspoon nutmeg
⅓ cup nuts, chopped (optional)
⅓ cup raisins (optional)

Preheat oven to 350°F. Grease two 9×5-inch loaf pans.

Combine all ingredients in large bowl and mix well. Beat at medium speed 2 minutes. Pour into prepared pans. Bake 60 minutes or until toothpick inserted into center comes out clean.   *Makes 2 loaves*

Hint: Serve with cream cheese or preserves, or top with cream cheese frosting or ice cream.

Pumpkin Bread

Cinnamon Coffee-Crumb Muffins

3 cups all-purpose flour
1 tablespoon baking powder
1 teaspoon ground cinnamon
¼ teaspoon salt
1¼ cups sugar
½ cup (1 stick) SHEDD'S®
    Spread Country Crock
    Spread-Sticks
2 eggs
1 tablespoon instant coffee
    crystals or instant
    espresso
1 teaspoon vanilla extract
1 cup milk
    Crumb Topping (recipe
    follows)

Preheat oven to 400°F. Grease 12-cup muffin pan or line with paper cupcake liners; set aside.

In large bowl, combine flour, baking powder, cinnamon and salt; set aside.

In large bowl, with electric mixer, beat sugar and SHEDD'S® Spread Country Crock Spread on medium-high speed until light and fluffy, about 5 minutes. Beat in eggs, coffee and vanilla, scraping side occasionally. Alternately beat in flour mixture and milk until blended. Evenly spoon batter into prepared pan; sprinkle with Crumb Topping.

Bake 23 minutes or until toothpick inserted into centers comes out clean. On wire rack, cool 10 minutes; remove from pan and cool completely.   *Makes 12 muffins*

Crumb Topping: In small bowl, combine ¼ cup all-purpose flour, 2 tablespoons sugar and ¼ teaspoon ground cinnamon. With pastry blender or 2 knives, cut in 2 tablespoons Shedd's® Spread Country Crock Spread-Sticks until mixture is size of coarse crumbs.

French Toast

1 egg
4 egg whites
¼ cup skim milk
3 tablespoons packed brown
    sugar, divided
½ teaspoon almond extract
¼ teaspoon ground cinnamon
1 teaspoon vegetable oil
6 slices bread
1 ripe banana, sliced

Combine egg and egg whites in large bowl; beat with wire whisk until frothy. Add milk, 2 tablespoons sugar, almond extract and cinnamon. Heat oil over medium-high heat in nonstick skillet. Dip each bread slice in egg mixture. Place bread in skillet; cook each side 2 to 3 minutes until browned. If necessary, spray pan with nonstick cooking spray and continue to cook remaining bread slices. Top each piece with banana slices, sprinkle with remaining 1 tablespoon sugar and serve immediately.   *Makes 6 servings*

Favorite recipe from **The Sugar Association, Inc.**

Streusel Coffeecake

Streusel Coffeecake

Prep Time: 25 minutes
Cook Time: 40 minutes
Cooling Time: 2 hours
Total Time: 3 hours

  32 CHIPS AHOY!® Chocolate Chip Cookies, divided
  1 (18- to 18.5-ounce) package yellow or white cake mix
  ½ cup BREAKSTONE'S® or KNUDSEN® Sour Cream
  ½ cup PLANTERS® Pecans, chopped
  ½ cup BAKER'S® ANGEL FLAKE® Coconut
  ¼ cup packed brown sugar
  1 teaspoon ground cinnamon
  ⅓ cup margarine or butter, melted
  Powdered sugar glaze (optional)

1. Coarsely chop 20 cookies; finely crush remaining 12 cookies. Set aside.

2. Prepare cake mix batter according to package directions; blend in sour cream. Stir in chopped cookies. Pour batter into greased and floured 13×9×2-inch baking pan.

3. Mix cookie crumbs, pecans, coconut, brown sugar and cinnamon; stir in margarine. Sprinkle over cake batter.

4. Bake at 350°F for 40 minutes or until toothpick inserted near center of cake comes out clean. Cool completely. Drizzle with powdered sugar glaze, if desired. Cut into squares to serve.

Makes 24 servings

Buttermilk Doughnuts

Doughnuts
3½ cups unsifted all-purpose flour, divided
¾ cup sugar
2 teaspoons baking powder
1 teaspoon baking soda
1 teaspoon ground cinnamon
¾ teaspoon salt
½ teaspoon ground nutmeg
¾ cup buttermilk
¼ Butter Flavor CRISCO® Stick or ¼ cup Butter Flavor CRISCO® all-vegetable shortening
2 eggs
1 teaspoon vanilla
CRISCO® Oil* for frying

Glaze
1 cup confectioners' sugar
2 tablespoons hot water

Use your favorite Crisco Oil product.

1. For doughnuts, combine 2 cups flour with sugar, baking powder, baking soda, cinnamon, salt, nutmeg, buttermilk, shortening, eggs and vanilla in large mixing bowl. Beat at low speed of electric mixer until blended. Beat at medium speed 2 minutes. Stir in remaining flour. Chill several hours or overnight.

2. Divide dough in half. Sprinkle lightly with flour. Roll each half to slightly less than ½-inch thickness on well-floured board. Cut with floured 2¾- to 3-inch doughnut cutter. Reserve doughnut holes.

3. Heat 2 inches oil to 375°F in deep-fat fryer or deep saucepan. Fry a few doughnuts at a time in hot shortening, 1 minute on each side, or until golden brown. Fry doughnut holes 1 to 1½ minutes total time. Drain on paper towels. Serve plain, dip tops in glaze or cool and shake in plastic bag of confectioners' sugar.

4. For glaze, combine confectioners' sugar and water in small bowl; stir until smooth. Dip tops of doughnuts in glaze. Invert on wire racks until glaze is set.

Makes 1½ to 2 dozen doughnuts and doughnut holes

Cranberry Pecan Wreath

3½ to 4 cups all-purpose flour,
    divided
⅓ cup sugar
1 envelope FLEISCHMANN'S®
    RapidRise™ Yeast
¾ teaspoon salt
½ cup milk
⅓ cup butter or margarine
¼ cup water
2 large eggs
    Cranberry-Pecan Filling
    (recipe follows)
    Orange Glaze (recipe
    follows)

Cranberry Pecan Wreath

In large bowl, combine 1½ cups flour, sugar, undissolved yeast and salt. Heat milk, butter and water until very warm (120° to 130°F); stir into dry ingredients. Stir in eggs and enough remaining flour to make soft dough. Knead on lightly floured surface until smooth and elastic, about 8 to 10 minutes. Cover; let rest 10 minutes.

Roll dough to 30×6-inch rectangle; spread Cranberry-Pecan Filling over dough to within ½ inch of edges. Beginning at long end, roll up tightly, pinching seam to seal. Form into ring; join ends, pinching to seal. Transfer to greased large baking sheet. Cover; let rise in warm, draft-free place until doubled in size, about 45 to 60 minutes.

Bake at 350°F for 40 to 45 minutes or until done. Remove from pan;

cool on wire rack. Drizzle with Orange Glaze. Decorate with additional cranberries, orange slices and pecan halves, if desired.
Makes 1 (10-inch) coffeecake

Cranberry-Pecan Filling: In medium saucepan, combine 1½ cups fresh or frozen cranberries, finely chopped; 1 cup firmly packed brown sugar; and ⅓ cup butter or margarine. Bring to a boil over medium-high heat. Reduce heat; simmer 5 to 7 minutes or until very thick, stirring frequently. Remove mixture from heat; stir in ¾ cup chopped toasted pecans.

Orange Glaze: In small bowl, combine 1¼ cups sifted powdered sugar; 2 tablespoons butter or margarine, softened; 1 to 2 tablespoons milk; and 2 teaspoons freshly grated orange peel. Stir until smooth.

Oreo® Muffins

1¾ cups all-purpose flour
½ cup sugar
1 tablespoon baking powder
½ teaspoon salt
¾ cup milk
⅓ cup sour cream
1 egg
¼ cup butter or margarine, melted
20 OREO® Chocolate Sandwich Cookies, coarsely chopped

1. Mix flour, sugar, baking powder and salt in medium bowl; set aside.

2. Blend milk, sour cream and egg in bowl; stir into flour mixture with butter until just blended. Gently stir in cookie pieces. Spoon batter into 12 greased 2½-inch muffin-pan cups.

3. Bake at 400°F for 20 to 25 minutes or until toothpick inserted in center comes out clean. Remove from pan; cool on wire rack. Serve warm or cold.   *Makes 1 dozen muffins*

Freezer Rolls

1¼ cups warm water (100° to 110°F), divided
2 envelopes FLEISCHMANN'S® Active Dry Yeast
½ cup warm milk (100° to 110°F)
⅓ cup butter or margarine, softened
½ cup sugar
1½ teaspoons salt
5½ to 6 cups all-purpose flour
2 large eggs

Place ½ cup warm water in large warm bowl. Sprinkle in yeast; stir until dissolved. Add remaining warm water, warm milk, butter, sugar, salt and 2 cups flour. Beat 2 minutes at medium speed of electric mixer. Add eggs and ½ cup flour. Beat at high speed for 2 minutes. Stir in enough remaining flour to make soft dough. Turn out onto lightly floured surface. Knead until smooth and elastic, about 8 to 10 minutes. Cover with plastic wrap; let rest 20 minutes.

Punch dough down. Shape into desired shapes for dinner rolls. Place on greased baking sheets. Cover with plastic wrap and foil, sealing well. Freeze up to 1 week.*

Once frozen, rolls may be placed in plastic freezer bags.

Remove from freezer; place on greased baking sheets. Cover; let rise in warm, draft-free place until doubled in size, about 1½ hours.

Bake at 350°F for 15 minutes or until done. Remove from baking sheets; cool on wire racks.
          Makes about 2 dozen rolls

*To bake without freezing: After shaping, let rise in warm, draft-free place, until doubled in size, about 1 hour. Bake according to above directions.

Shaping the Dough for Crescents:
Divide dough in half. Roll each half to 14-inch circle. Cut each into 12 pie-shaped wedges. Roll up tightly from wide end. Curve ends slightly to form crescents.

Oreo® Muffins

Honey Currant Scones

2½ cups all-purpose flour
2 teaspoons grated orange peel
1 teaspoon baking powder
½ teaspoon baking soda
½ teaspoon salt
½ cup butter or margarine
½ cup currants
½ cup sour cream
⅓ cup honey
1 egg, slightly beaten

Preheat oven to 375°F. Grease baking sheet; set aside.

Combine flour, orange peel, baking powder, baking soda and salt in large bowl. Cut in butter with pastry blender or 2 knives until mixture resembles coarse crumbs. Add currants. Combine sour cream, honey and egg in medium bowl until well blended. Stir into flour mixture until soft dough forms. Turn out dough onto lightly floured surface. Knead dough 10 times. Shape dough into 8-inch square. Cut into 4 squares; cut each square diagonally in half, making 8 triangles. Place triangles 1 inch apart on prepared baking sheet.

Bake 15 to 20 minutes or until golden brown and wooden pick inserted into centers comes out clean. Remove from baking sheet. Cool on wire rack 10 minutes. Serve warm or cool completely.

Makes 8 scones

Favorite recipe from **National Honey Board**

Mexican Corn Bread

¾ cup butter
¾ cup sugar
4 eggs
1 can (16 ounces) cream-style golden corn
1 can (4 ounces) diced green chiles
½ cup (2 ounces) shredded Monterey Jack cheese
½ cup (2 ounces) shredded Cheddar cheese
1 tablespoon LAWRY'S® Minced Onion with Green Onion Flakes
1 cup all-purpose flour
1 cup yellow corn meal
4 teaspoons baking powder

In large bowl, cream butter and sugar. Add eggs; mix well. Add corn, chiles, cheeses and Minced Onion with Green Onion Flakes; mix well. In small bowl, combine flour, corn meal and baking powder; add to corn mixture and blend well. Pour into greased and floured 12×8×2-inch baking dish. Place in preheated 350°F oven and immediately reduce heat to 300°F. Bake 1 hour. Cut into squares to serve.

Makes 12 servings

Honey Currant Scones

Challah

1-POUND LOAF
- ½ cup water
- 1 large egg
- 2 tablespoons margarine, cut up
- 1 teaspoon salt
- 2 cups bread flour
- 4 teaspoons sugar
- 1½ teaspoons FLEISCHMANN'S® Bread Machine Yeast
- 1 yolk of large egg
- 1 tablespoon water

1½-POUND LOAF
- ¾ cup water
- 1 large egg
- 3 tablespoons margarine, cut up
- 1¼ teaspoons salt
- 3 cups bread flour
- 2 tablespoons sugar
- 2 teaspoons FLEISCHMANN'S® Bread Machine Yeast
- 1 yolk of large egg
- 1 tablespoon water

Add water, egg, margarine, salt, bread flour, sugar and yeast to bread machine pan in the order suggested by manufacturer. Select dough/manual cycle. When cycle is complete, remove dough from machine to lightly floured surface. If necessary, knead in enough additional flour to make dough easy to handle. (For 1½-pound recipe, divide dough in half to make 2 loaves.)

For each loaf, divide dough into 2 pieces, one about ⅔ of the dough and the other about ⅓ of the dough. Divide larger piece into 3 equal pieces; roll into 12-inch ropes. Place ropes on greased baking sheet. Braid by bringing left rope under center rope; lay it down. Bring right rope under new center rope; lay it down. Repeat to end. Pinch ends to seal. Divide remaining piece into 3 equal pieces. Roll into 10-inch ropes; braid. Place small braid on top of large braid. Pinch ends firmly to seal and to secure to large braid. Cover and let rise in warm, draft-free place until almost doubled in size, 15 to 20 minutes. Lightly beat egg yolk and 1 tablespoon water; brush over braids.

Bake at 375°F for 25 to 30 minutes or until done, covering with foil after 15 minutes to prevent excess browning. (For even browning when baking two loaves, switch positions of baking sheets halfway through baking.) Remove from baking sheets; cool on wire racks.

Makes 1 or 2 loaves

Challah

Country Biscuits

Country Biscuits

2 cups all-purpose flour
1 tablespoon baking powder
1 teaspoon salt
⅓ CRISCO® Stick or ⅓ cup CRISCO® all-vegetable shortening
¾ cup milk

1. Heat oven to 425°F. Combine flour, baking powder and salt in medium bowl. Cut in shortening using pastry blender (or two knives) to form coarse crumbs. Add milk. Mix with fork until dry mixture is moistened. Form dough into a ball.

2. Transfer dough to lightly floured surface. Knead gently 8 to 10 times. Roll out dough to ½-inch thickness. Cut with floured 2-inch round cutter. Place on *ungreased* baking sheet.

3. Bake at 425°F for 12 to 14 minutes or until golden. *Do not overbake.* *Makes 12 to 16 biscuits*

Southern Caramel Pecan Rolls

Topping

- ⅔ cup sifted powdered sugar
- ⅔ cup dark brown sugar
- ½ cup whipping cream
- 1 teaspoon vanilla
  WESSON® No-Stick Cooking Spray
- 1 cup coarsely chopped pecans

Rolls

- 1 cup dark raisins
- ⅓ cup brandy
- 2 (1-pound) loaves frozen sweet or white bread dough, thawed, but not doubled in size
- ¼ cup WESSON® Best Blend Oil
- ½ cup packed dark brown sugar
- 1 tablespoon ground cinnamon
- ½ teaspoon ground nutmeg

Topping

In medium bowl, stir together sugars, cream and vanilla. Spray two 9×1½-inch round cake pans with Wesson® Cooking Spray. Evenly divide mixture between pans and sprinkle with pecans; set aside.

Rolls

In small bowl, soak raisins in brandy for 30 minutes; set aside and stir occasionally.

On floured surface, roll *each* loaf into 12×8×¼-inch rectangle. Generously brush *each* sheet of dough with Wesson® Oil. In small bowl, mix together sugar, cinnamon and nutmeg. Sprinkle over dough; top with soaked raisins. Roll up rectangles jelly-roll style starting with long edge. Pinch dough to seal. Cut into 12 slices. Place rolls, spiral side down, in cake pans. Cover with towels and let rise in warm place for 30 minutes or until nearly double in size. Preheat oven to 375°F. Bake, uncovered, for 15 to 20 minutes. Cover pans with foil to prevent overbrowning and bake an additional 10 minutes. Cool in pans 7 minutes. Invert onto serving plate. Serve warm.   *Makes 24 rolls*

Savory Pull Apart Biscuits

- 2 tablespoons butter or margarine
- 1 tablespoon minced onion
- 2 tablespoons grated Parmesan cheese
- ½ teaspoon TABASCO® brand Pepper Sauce
- 1 (8-ounce) package refrigerated biscuits

Melt butter in small saucepan. Add onion and cook until tender. Stir in cheese and TABASCO® Sauce; remove from heat. Separate biscuits. Dip biscuit tops in butter mixture and arrange biscuits buttered side up in lightly greased 8-inch round cake pan, making sure sides of biscuits touch. Bake 10 to 15 minutes or until golden. Serve warm.

Makes 10 biscuits

Southern Caramel Pecan Rolls

Cranberry Orange Bread

2 cups all-purpose flour
1 cup QUAKER® Oats (quick or old fashioned, uncooked)
¼ cup granulated sugar *or* 2 tablespoons fructose
1 teaspoon baking powder
½ teaspoon baking soda
¼ teaspoon salt (optional)
¾ cup fat-free milk
¾ cup egg substitute *or* 3 whole eggs
⅓ cup unsweetened orange juice
¼ cup vegetable oil
1 tablespoon grated orange peel
½ cup chopped cranberries, fresh or frozen
¼ cup chopped nuts* (optional)

To toast nuts for extra flavor, spread evenly in small baking pan. Bake in 350°F oven 7 to 10 minutes or until light golden brown.

Heat oven to 350°F. Grease and flour 9×5-inch loaf pan. Combine flour, oats, granulated sugar, baking powder, baking soda and salt; mix well. Set aside. Beat milk, egg substitute, orange juice, vegetable oil and orange peel until thoroughly mixed. Add to dry ingredients, mixing just until moistened. Stir into cranberries and nuts. Pour into prepared pan. Bake 60 to 70 minutes or until wooden pick inserted in center comes out clean. Cool 10 minutes; remove from pan. Cool completely. *Makes 16 servings*

Dilly of a Batter Bread

3¼ cups all-purpose flour, divided
2 packages RED STAR® Active Dry Yeast or QUICK•RISE™ Yeast
2 tablespoons sugar
1 tablespoon instant minced onion
2 teaspoons dill seed
1 teaspoon salt
1 carton (8 ounces) plain yogurt
½ cup water
2 tablespoons shortening
1 egg

In large mixer bowl, combine 1½ cups flour, yeast, sugar, onion, dill seed and salt; mix well. Heat yogurt, water and shortening until very warm (120°-130°F; shortening does not need to melt). Add to flour mixture. Add egg. Blend at low speed until moistened; beat 3 minutes at medium speed. By hand, gradually stir in remaining flour to make a stiff batter.

Spoon into greased 1½- or 2-quart casserole. Cover; let rise in warm place until light and double, about 1 hour (40 minutes for Quick•Rise™ Yeast). Bake at 375°F for 35 to 40 minutes or until golden brown. Remove from casserole; serve warm or cold. *Makes 1 round loaf*

Blueberry Muffins

1 cup fresh or thawed frozen blueberries
1¾ cups plus 1 tablespoon all-purpose flour, divided
2 teaspoons baking powder
1 teaspoon grated lemon peel
½ teaspoon salt
½ cup MOTT'S® Apple Sauce
½ cup sugar
1 whole egg
1 egg white
2 tablespoons vegetable oil
¼ cup skim milk

1. Preheat oven to 375°F. Line 12 (2½-inch) muffin cups with paper liners or spray with nonstick cooking spray.

2. In small bowl, toss blueberries with 1 tablespoon flour.

3. In large bowl, combine remaining 1¾ cups flour, baking powder, lemon peel and salt.

4. In another small bowl, combine apple sauce, sugar, whole egg, egg white and oil.

5. Stir apple sauce mixture into flour mixture alternately with milk. Mix just until moistened. Fold in blueberry mixture.

6. Spoon evenly into prepared muffin cups.

7. Bake 20 minutes or until toothpick inserted into centers comes out clean. Immediately remove from pan; cool on wire rack 10 minutes. Serve warm or cool completely.   *Makes 12 servings*

Blueberry Muffins

Banana Nut Bread

8 - **2 ripe, large DOLE® Bananas**
1⅓ **⅓ cup butter**
⅔ cup sugar ✓
2 eggs
2 cups all-purpose flour ✓
2 teaspoons baking powder ✓
½ teaspoon baking soda
½ cup buttermilk
¾ cup chopped nuts

• Purée bananas in blender (1¼ cups). Cream butter and sugar until light and fluffy. Beat in bananas and eggs. Combine flour, baking powder and baking soda. Add dry ingredients to banana mixture alternately in thirds with buttermilk, blending well after each addition. Stir in nuts.

• Pour into greased 9×5-inch loaf pan. Bake at 350°F 50 to 60 minutes or until wooden toothpick inserted near center comes out clean. Cool in pan on wire rack 10 minutes. Remove from pan and cool completely. *Makes 1 loaf*

Irish Soda Bread

4 cups sifted all-purpose flour
1 tablespoon sugar
1½ teaspoons ARM & HAMMER® Baking Soda
1 teaspoon baking powder
½ teaspoon salt
¼ cup unsalted margarine or butter-flavored hydrogenated shortening
1 cup seedless raisins
1½ cups buttermilk

Sift together flour, sugar, Baking Soda, baking powder and salt into large bowl. Cut in butter until crumbly. Stir in raisins. Add buttermilk and stir to make a soft dough. Turn onto lightly floured board and knead to form a smooth ball.

Place dough on greased baking sheet; pat with hands to 1¼-inch thickness. With sharp knife score dough into 4 sections. Bake in 350°F oven 1 hour or until bread is browned and toothpick inserted near center comes out clean. Serve warm with butter. *Makes 1 loaf*

Potato Rosemary Rolls

Potato Rosemary Rolls

Dough

- 1 cup plus 2 tablespoons water (70 to 80°F)
- 2 tablespoons olive oil
- 1 teaspoon salt
- 3 cups bread flour
- ½ cup instant potato flakes or buds
- 2 tablespoons nonfat dry milk powder
- 1 tablespoon sugar
- 1 teaspoon SPICE ISLANDS® Rosemary, crushed
- 1½ teaspoons FLEISCHMANN'S® Bread Machine Yeast

Topping

- 1 egg, lightly beaten
- Sesame or poppy seeds or additional dried rosemary, crushed

Measure all dough ingredients into bread machine pan in the order suggested by manufacturer, adding potato flakes with flour. Select dough/manual cycle. When cycle is complete, remove dough to floured surface. If necessary, knead in additional flour to make dough easy to handle.

Divide dough into 12 equal pieces. Roll each piece to 10-inch rope; coil each rope and tuck end under coil. Place rolls 2 inches apart on large greased baking sheet. Cover; let rise in warm, draft-free place until doubled in size, about 45 to 60 minutes. Brush tops with beaten egg; sprinkle with sesame seeds. Bake at 375°F for 15 to 20 minutes or until done. Remove from pan; cool on wire rack.

Makes 12 rolls

Note: Dough can be prepared in 1½ and 2-pound bread machines.

State Fair Cracked Wheat Bread

State Fair Cracked Wheat Bread

1⅓ cups water
2 tablespoons butter or margarine
1 teaspoon salt
¼ cup cracked wheat
3 cups bread flour
½ cup whole wheat flour
3 tablespoons nonfat dry milk powder
2 tablespoons firmly packed brown sugar
2 teaspoons FLEISCHMANN'S® Bread Machine Yeast

Add ingredients to bread machine pan in the order suggested by manufacturer. (If dough is too dry, stiff or soft, adjust dough consistency.) Recommended cycle: Basic/white bread cycle; medium/normal crust color setting.

Makes 1 (2-pound) loaf

The Original Kellogg's® All-Bran Muffin™

1¼ cups all-purpose flour
½ cup sugar
1 tablespoon baking powder
¼ teaspoon salt
2 cups KELLOGG'S® ALL-BRAN® cereal
1¼ cups milk
1 egg
¼ cup vegetable oil

1. Stir together flour, sugar, baking powder and salt. Set aside.

2. In large mixing bowl, combine Kellogg's® All-Bran® cereal and milk. Let stand about 5 minutes or until cereal softens. Add egg and oil. Beat well. Add flour mixture, stirring only until combined. Portion batter evenly into twelve 2½-inch muffin pan cups coated with cooking spray.

3. Bake at 400°F for 20 minutes or until lightly browned. Serve warm.

Makes 12 muffins

For muffins with reduced calories, fat and cholesterol: Use 2 tablespoons sugar, 2 tablespoons oil, replace milk with 1¼ cups skim milk, and substitute 2 egg whites for 1 egg. Prepare and bake as directed.

Peanut Butter & Chocolate Pull-Apart Rolls

Dough
- ½ cup milk
- ⅓ cup water (70 to 80°F)
- ¼ cup creamy peanut butter, at room temperature
- ½ teaspoon salt
- 2¼ cups bread flour
- ¼ cup sugar
- 1½ teaspoons FLEISCHMANN'S® Bread Machine Yeast

Filling
- ½ cup (3 ounces) semisweet chocolate pieces
- 2 tablespoons creamy peanut butter

Icing
- ½ cup sifted powdered sugar
- 1 tablespoon creamy peanut butter or cocoa powder
- 2 to 4 teaspoons milk

To make dough, add dough ingredients to bread machine pan in the order suggested by manufacturer. Select dough/manual cycle.

To make filling, combine filling ingredients in small bowl; blend well. To shape and fill, when cycle is complete, remove dough to floured surface. If necessary, knead in additional flour to make dough easy to handle.

Roll dough into 14-inch circle. Cut into 6 wedges; place filling, dividing evenly, at wide end of each wedge. Beginning at wide end, roll up tightly; curve to form crescent. Arrange crescents, seam side down, in spoke fashion on greased large baking sheet. Pinch ends at center to seal. Cover and let rise in warm, draft-free place until doubled in size, about 30 to 45 minutes. Bake at 375°F for 15 to 20 minutes or until done. Remove from pan; cool on wire rack.

To make icing, combine icing ingredients in small bowl; stir until smooth. Drizzle on rolls.

Makes 6 rolls

Note: Dough can be prepared in all size bread machines.

Peanut Butter & Chocolate Pull-Apart Rolls

Nutty Cinnamon Sticky Buns

Preparation Time: 10 minutes
Cook Time: 25 minutes
Total Time: 35 minutes

- ⅓ cup margarine or butter
- ½ cup packed brown sugar
- ½ cup PLANTERS® Pecans, chopped
- 1 teaspoon ground cinnamon
- 1 (17.3-ounce) package refrigerated biscuits (8 large biscuits)

1. Melt margarine or butter in 9-inch round baking pan in 350°F oven.

2. Mix brown sugar, pecans and cinnamon in small bowl; sprinkle over melted margarine or butter in pan. Arrange biscuits in pan with sides touching (biscuits will fit tightly in pan).

3. Bake at 350°F for 25 to 30 minutes or until biscuits are golden brown and center biscuit is fully cooked. Invert pan immediately onto serving plate. Spread any remaining topping from pan on buns. Serve warm.

Makes 8 buns

Raisin Scones

Prep Time: 25 minutes
Bake Time: 15 minutes

- 2¼ cups all-purpose flour
- ⅓ cup sugar
- 1 tablespoon grated orange peel
- 2¼ teaspoons baking powder
- ½ teaspoon baking soda
- ¼ teaspoon salt
- ½ cup margarine
- 1 cup DOLE® Seedless Raisins
- ½ cup nonfat milk or plain yogurt
- 1 teaspoon vanilla extract

• Combine flour, sugar, orange peel, baking powder, baking soda and salt.

• Cut in margarine, using two knives or pastry blender, until mixture resembles coarse crumbs.

• Stir in raisins. Combine milk and vanilla. Stir into mixture.

• Form dough into two balls. Pat one ball, on floured board, into 6-inch circle (½-inch thick). Cut into 6 wedges. Repeat with remaining dough. Place on baking sheet sprayed with cooking spray. Bake at 400°F 15 minutes. Cool on rack.

Makes 12 servings

Chocolate Chunk Banana Bread

Prep: 15 minutes
Bake: 55 minutes

    2 eggs, lightly beaten
    1 cup mashed ripe bananas
    ⅓ cup oil
    ¼ cup milk
    2 cups flour
    1 cup sugar
    2 teaspoons CALUMET®
        Baking Powder
    ¼ teaspoon salt
    1 package (4 ounces)
        BAKER'S® GERMAN'S®
        Sweet Baking Chocolate,
        coarsely chopped
    ½ cup chopped nuts

HEAT oven to 350°F.

STIR eggs, bananas, oil and milk until well blended. Add flour, sugar, baking powder and salt; stir until just moistened. Stir in chocolate and nuts. Pour into greased 9×5-inch loaf pan.

BAKE for 55 minutes or until toothpick inserted into center comes out clean. Cool in pan 10 minutes. Remove from pan; cool completely on wire rack.

Makes 18 (½-inch) servings

Note: For easier slicing, wrap bread and store overnight.

Cheese Pull-Apart Bread

    3 packages frozen bread dough
        dinner rolls, thawed to
        room temperature
    ⅓ cup butter, melted
    1 cup freshly grated
        BELGIOIOSO® Parmesan
        Cheese
    1 cup shredded BELGIOIOSO®
        Provolone Cheese

Roll each dinner roll in butter, and then roll in BelGioioso Parmesan Cheese to coat. Arrange half of rolls in well-greased fluted tube pan. Sprinkle with BelGioioso Provolone Cheese. Top with remaining half of coated rolls. Sprinkle with any remaining Parmesan. Let rise until doubled in size, about 1 hour. Bake in preheated 375°F oven 35 to 45 minutes or until golden brown. Use table knife to loosen edge of bread; remove from pan. Serve warm.   *Makes 12 servings*

Chocolate Chunk Banana Bread

Parker House Rolls

4¾ to 5¼ cups all-purpose flour
⅓ cup sugar
2 envelopes FLEISCHMANN'S®
    RapidRise™ Yeast
1½ teaspoons salt
¾ cup milk
¾ cup water
¼ cup butter or margarine
1 large egg
¼ cup butter or margarine,
    melted

In large bowl, combine 2 cups flour, sugar, undissolved yeast and salt. Heat milk, water and ¼ cup butter until very warm (120° to 130°F). Stir into dry ingredients. Beat 2 minutes at medium speed of electric mixer, scraping bowl occasionally. Add egg and ½ cup flour; beat 2 minutes at high speed. Stir in enough remaining flour to make a soft dough. Knead on lightly floured surface until smooth and elastic, about 8 to 10 minutes. Cover;* let rest 10 minutes.

Divide dough in half; roll each half to 12-inch square, about ¼-inch thick. Cut each into 6 (2×12-inch) strips. Cut each strip into 3 (4×2-inch) rectangles. Brush each rectangle with melted butter. Crease rectangles slightly off center with dull edge of knife and fold at crease. Arrange in rows, slightly overlapping, on greased baking sheets, with shorter side of each roll facing down. Allow ¼-inch of space between each row.

Cover; let rise in warm, draft-free place until doubled in size, about 30 minutes.

Bake at 400°F for 13 to 15 minutes or until done. Remove from sheets; cool on wire rack. Brush with remaining melted butter.

Makes 36 rolls

If desired, allow dough to rise in refrigerator 12 to 24 hours.

Monkey Bread

½ pound butter, melted
2 teaspoons LAWRY'S® Garlic
    Powder with Parsley
4 packages (9.5 ounces each)
    refrigerated buttermilk
    biscuits

In medium bowl, combine butter and Garlic Powder with Parsley; mix well. Separate biscuits and dip each into butter to coat. In tube pan, place one layer of dipped biscuits in bottom, slightly overlapping each biscuit. Arrange remaining biscuits in zig-zag fashion, some towards center and some towards outside edge of pan. Use all biscuits in as many layers as needed. Pour half of remaining butter over biscuits. Bake, uncovered, in 375°F oven 15 to 20 minutes. Invert onto serving platter and pour remaining butter over bread. Serve warm.

Makes 10 to 12 servings

Parker House Rolls

COMFORTING SOUPS & CHILIS

*Bring back memories of steaming bowls
of hearty soups and chilis. Your family will savor
the aroma and delicious flavor of these nourishing
and soul-satisfying soups.*

Minestrone (page 60)

And this explains why you are able to get Del Monte Quality

When you serve DEL MONTE products on your table you are interested only in their quality — in their irresistible goodness — their convenience and economy.

Yet back of all that fresh natural flavor and delicacy that ministers to your daily enjoyment, there is a story of far lands — of sunny climes — of care and thoroughness and long years of experience — as far-reaching in influence and as interesting in details as many a popular romance.

DEL MONTE perfection begins with the soil and the climate. Wherever Nature grows her best, there are located the DEL MONTE orchards and gardens and kitchens. There the pedigreed fruits and vegetables are grown, harvested and canned the day they are picked, with all their natural freshness and sun-ripened flavor, by specialists who have spent their lives in the canning industry and whose sole aim is to live up to the DEL MONTE ideal of quality.

This explains why DEL MONTE quality is always highest quality — why the red DEL MONTE shield is your guarantee of finest flavor in a long line of canned fruits and vegetables, dried fruits, raisins, jellies, jams, preserves, olives, catsup, salmon, and many other varieties.

SEND FOR THIS BOOK — "DEL MONTE Recipes of Flavor." It contains hundreds of simple and economical recipes and suggestions for utilizing the ever-ready goodness of DEL MONTE products in adding delicious variety and appetizing flavor to the every-day menu. Sent free upon request.

CALIFORNIA PACKING CORPORATION
DEPARTMENT A
SAN FRANCISCO, CALIFORNIA

Just a few of the many delicious
DEL MONTE PRODUCTS

"There's a variety for every need"

Minestrone

Prep Time: 7 minutes
Cook Time: 28 minutes

   3 slices bacon, diced
   ½ cup chopped onion
   1 large clove garlic, minced
   2 cans (10½ ounces each) beef broth
  1½ cups water
   2 cans (15½ ounces each) Great Northern white beans, undrained
   1 can (6 ounces) CONTADINA® Tomato Paste
   1 teaspoon Italian herb seasoning
   ¼ teaspoon ground black pepper
   2 medium zucchini, sliced
   1 package (10 ounces) frozen mixed vegetables
   ½ cup elbow macaroni, uncooked
   ½ cup (2 ounces) grated Parmesan cheese (optional)

1. Sauté bacon until crisp in large saucepan. Add onion and garlic; sauté until onion is tender.

2. Add broth, water, beans and liquid, tomato paste, Italian seasoning and pepper.

3. Reduce heat to low; simmer, uncovered, for 10 minutes. Add zucchini, mixed vegetables and macaroni. Return to a boil over high heat, stirring to break up vegetables.

4. Reduce heat to low; simmer for 8 to 10 minutes or until vegetables and macaroni are tender. Sprinkle with Parmesan cheese just before serving, if desired.   *Makes 8 cups*

Manhattan Clam Chowder

   2 pieces bacon, diced
   1 large red bell pepper, diced
   1 large green bell pepper, diced
   1 stalk celery, chopped
   1 carrot, peeled and chopped
   1 small onion, chopped
   1 clove garlic, finely chopped
   2 cups bottled clam juice
   1 cup CLAMATO® Tomato Cocktail
   2 medium potatoes, peeled and diced
   1 large tomato, chopped
   1 teaspoon oregano
   ½ teaspoon black pepper
   2 cups fresh or canned clams, chopped (about 24 shucked clams)

In heavy 4-quart saucepan, sauté bacon, bell peppers, celery, carrot, onion and garlic over medium heat until tender, about 10 minutes. (Do not brown bacon.) Add clam juice, Clamato, potatoes, tomato, oregano and black pepper. Simmer 35 minutes or until potatoes are tender. Add clams; cook 5 minutes more.   *Makes 8 servings*

Manhattan Clam Chowder

Carrot Cream Soup

¼ **cup butter or margarine**
¼ **cup chopped onion**
¼ **teaspoon LAWRY'S®**
   Seasoned Salt
½ **teaspoon LAWRY'S® Garlic**
   Powder with Parsley
2 **cups chopped carrots**
½ **cup all-purpose flour**
4½ **cups chicken broth**
¼ **cup whipping cream**
   Chopped fresh parsley for
   garnish

In large saucepan, heat butter. Add onion and cook over medium-high heat until tender. Add Seasoned Salt, Garlic Powder with Parsley and carrots; cook additional 5 minutes. Stir in flour; mix well. Stirring constantly, add chicken broth; mix well. Bring to a boil over medium-high heat; reduce heat to low and cook, covered, 30 minutes, stirring occasionally. In blender or food processor, purée carrot mixture; return to pan. Stir in cream; heat thoroughly.   *Makes 4 servings*

Serving Suggestion: Serve warm soup topped with a sprinkling of parsley. Warm French bread or crackers are great accompaniments.

Savory Onion Soup

½ **cup (1 stick) plus**
   2 **tablespoons I CAN'T**
   BELIEVE IT'S NOT
   BUTTER!® Spread, divided
4 **large Spanish onions (about**
   4 **pounds), sliced**
1 **teaspoon salt**
¼ **teaspoon ground black**
   pepper
4 **cans (14.5 ounces each) beef**
   broth
¼ **cup Madeira wine or dry**
   sherry (optional)
10 **round slices (½ inch thick)**
   French or Italian bread
1 **cup shredded Gruyère or**
   Swiss cheese (about
   4 **ounces)**

In Dutch oven or 6-quart saucepot, melt ½ cup I Can't Believe It's Not Butter! Spread over medium heat and cook onions, salt and pepper, stirring occasionally, 35 minutes or until onions are very soft and golden. Add broth and wine. Bring to a boil over high heat. Reduce heat to low and simmer, stirring occasionally, 10 minutes.

Meanwhile, evenly spread bread slices with remaining 2 tablespoons I Can't Believe It's Not Butter! Spread, then top with cheese. Toast until cheese is melted. To serve, ladle soup into serving bowls, then top with cheese toasts.

Makes about 5 (2-cup) servings

Campbell's® Hearty Chicken Noodle Soup

Campbell's® Hearty Chicken Noodle Soup

Prep/Cook Time: 20 minutes

2 cans (10½ ounces each) CAMPBELL'S® Condensed Chicken Broth

1 cup water
Generous dash pepper

1 medium carrot, sliced (about ½ cup)

1 stalk celery, sliced (about ½ cup)

2 skinless, boneless chicken breast halves, cut up

½ cup *uncooked* medium egg noodles

1. In medium saucepan mix broth, water, pepper, carrot, celery and chicken. Over medium-high heat, heat to a boil.

2. Stir in noodles. Reduce heat to medium. Cook 10 minutes or until noodles are done, stirring often.

Makes 4 servings

Hint: Save time by using precut carrots and celery from your supermarket salad bar.

Split Pea Soup

1 package (16 ounces) dried green or yellow split peas
1 pound smoked pork hocks *or* 1 meaty ham bone
7 cups water
1 medium onion, chopped
2 medium carrots, chopped
¾ teaspoon salt
½ teaspoon dried basil leaves
¼ teaspoon dried oregano leaves
¼ teaspoon black pepper
Ham and carrot strips for garnish

Rinse peas thoroughly in colander under cold running water, picking out any debris or blemished peas. Place peas, pork hocks and water in 5-quart Dutch oven.

Add onion, carrots, salt, basil, oregano and pepper to Dutch oven. Bring to a boil over high heat. Reduce heat to medium-low; simmer, uncovered, 1 hour 15 minutes or until peas are tender, stirring occasionally. Stir frequently near end of cooking to keep soup from scorching.

Remove pork hocks; cool. Cut meat into bite-size pieces.

Carefully ladle 3 cups hot soup into food processor or blender; cover and process until mixture is smooth.

Return puréed soup and meat to Dutch oven. (If soup is too thick, add a little water until desired consistency is reached.) Heat through. Ladle into bowls. Garnish, if desired.   *Makes 6 servings*

"Creamy" Wild Rice Soup

6 tablespoons butter
⅓ cup minced onion
½ cup all-purpose flour
3 cups chicken broth
2 cups cooked wild rice
4 ounces sliced mushrooms
½ cup finely chopped ham
½ cup finely grated carrots
3 tablespoons slivered almonds
½ teaspoon salt
1 cup half-and-half
2 tablespoons dry sherry wine
Minced parsley or chives

Melt butter; cook and stir onion until tender. Blend in flour; gradually add broth. Cook, stirring constantly, until mixture comes to a boil. Boil 1 minute. Stir in wild rice, mushrooms, ham, carrots, almonds and salt; simmer about 5 minutes. Blend in half-and-half and sherry. Garnish with minced parsley or chives.   *Makes 6 servings*

Favorite recipe from **Minnesota Cultivated Wild Rice Council**

Split Pea Soup

Tomato French Onion Soup

Prep and Cook Time: 35 minutes

> 4 medium onions, chopped
> 2 tablespoons butter or
>   margarine
> 1 can (14½ ounces)
>   DEL MONTE® Diced
>   Tomatoes
> 1 can (10½ ounces) condensed
>   beef consommé
> ¼ cup dry sherry
> 4 French bread slices, toasted
> 1½ cups (6 ounces) shredded
>   Swiss cheese
> ¼ cup (1 ounce) grated
>   Parmesan cheese

1. Cook onions in butter in large saucepan about 10 minutes. Add undrained tomatoes, 2 cups water, consommé and sherry to saucepan. Bring to boil, skimming off foam.

2. Reduce heat to medium-low; simmer 10 minutes. Place soup in four broilerproof bowls; top with bread and cheeses. Broil until cheeses are melted and golden.

Makes 4 servings

Hint: If broilerproof bowls are not available, place soup in ovenproof bowls and bake at 350°F, 10 minutes.

Classic Texas Chili

> ¼ cup vegetable oil
> 3 pounds beef round or chuck,
>   cut into 1-inch cubes
> 4 to 6 tablespoons chili
>   powder
> 3 cloves garlic, minced
> 2 teaspoons salt
> 2 teaspoons dried oregano
>   leaves
> 2 teaspoons ground cumin
> 2 teaspoons TABASCO® brand
>   Pepper Sauce
> 1½ quarts water
> ⅓ cup white cornmeal
>   Chopped onion (optional)

Heat oil in large saucepan over medium high heat. Add beef and brown on all sides. Stir in chili powder, garlic, salt, oregano, cumin, TABASCO® Sauce and water; heat to boiling. Reduce heat; cover and simmer 1¼ hours, stirring occasionally. Add cornmeal and mix well. Simmer, uncovered, 30 minutes or until beef is tender. Garnish with chopped onion, if desired. Serve with rice and beans.

Makes 6 to 8 servings

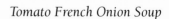
Tomato French Onion Soup

Shrimp Bisque

Prep Time: 15 minutes
Cook Time: 20 minutes

> **1 pound medium shrimp, peeled and deveined**
> **½ cup chopped onion**
> **½ cup chopped celery**
> **½ cup chopped carrot**
> **2 tablespoons butter or margarine**
> **2 cans (14 ounces each) chicken broth**
> **1 can (14½ ounces) DEL MONTE® Original Recipe Stewed Tomatoes, undrained**
> **¼ teaspoon dried thyme**
> **1 cup half-and-half**

1. Cut shrimp into small pieces; set aside. In large saucepan, cook onion, celery and carrot in butter until onion is tender.

2. Add shrimp; cook 1 minute. Add broth, tomatoes with juice and thyme; simmer 10 minutes. Ladle ⅓ of soup into blender container or food processor.

3. Cover and process until smooth. Repeat for remaining soup. Return to saucepan. Add half-and-half. Heat through. *Do not boil.*

Makes 6 servings
(approximately 1 cup each)

Variation: Substitute 2 cans (6 ounces each) of crab for shrimp.

Campbell's® Two-Bean Chili

Prep Time: 10 minutes
Cook Time: 15 minutes

> **1 pound ground beef**
> **1 large green pepper, chopped (about 1 cup)**
> **1 large onion, chopped (about 1 cup)**
> **2 tablespoons chili powder**
> **¼ teaspoon black pepper**
> **3 cups CAMPBELL'S® Tomato Juice**
> **1 can (about 15 ounces) kidney beans, rinsed and drained**
> **1 can (about 15 ounces) great Northern or white kidney (cannellini) beans, rinsed and drained**
> **Sour cream**
> **Sliced green onions**
> **Shredded Cheddar cheese**
> **Chopped tomato**

1. In medium skillet over medium-high heat, cook beef, green pepper, onion, chili powder and black pepper until beef is browned, stirring to separate meat. Pour off fat.

2. Add tomato juice and beans and heat through. Top each serving with sour cream, green onions, cheese and tomato. *Makes 6 servings*

Italian Rustico Soup

Italian Rustico Soup

1 cup BARILLA® Elbows
2 tablespoons olive or
 vegetable oil
1 pound fresh escarole or
 spinach, chopped
1 small onion, chopped
2 teaspoons minced garlic
4 cups water
2 cans (14½ ounces each)
 chicken broth
1 jar (26 ounces) BARILLA®
 Lasagna & Casserole
 Sauce or Marinara Pasta
 Sauce
1 can (15 ounces) white beans,
 drained
2 teaspoons balsamic or red
 wine vinegar
 Grated Parmesan cheese
 (optional)

1. Cook elbows according to package directions; drain.

2. Heat oil in 4-quart Dutch oven or large pot. Add escarole, onion and garlic; cook over medium heat, stirring occasionally, about 5 minutes or until onion is tender.

3. Stir in cooked elbows and remaining ingredients except cheese; heat to boiling. Reduce heat; cook, uncovered, 15 minutes, stirring occasionally. Serve with cheese, if desired.

Makes 12 servings

Shrimp & Sausage Gumbo

Prep Time: 20 minutes
Cook Time: 23 minutes

 1 tablespoon vegetable oil
 1 large onion, chopped
 2 ribs celery, chopped
 2 cloves garlic, minced
 ½ pound sweet Italian sausage,
  casings removed
 1 can (14½ ounces) tomatoes,
  cut up, undrained
 3 tablespoons *Frank's® RedHot®*
  Cayenne Pepper Sauce
 2 teaspoons minced fresh
  thyme *or* 1 teaspoon dried
  thyme leaves
 1 bay leaf
 1 package (10 ounces) frozen
  cut okra, thawed and
  drained
 ½ pound raw large shrimp,
  peeled and deveined
  Cooked white rice (optional)

1. Heat oil in large nonstick skillet over medium-high heat. Add onion, celery and garlic; cook until tender. Add sausage; cook until no longer pink, stirring to separate meat. Drain well.

2. Add tomatoes with liquid, *Frank's RedHot* Sauce, thyme and bay leaf. Bring to a boil. Reduce heat to low; cook, covered, 10 minutes.

3. Stir in okra and shrimp; cook, covered, 3 minutes or until okra is tender and shrimp turn pink. Remove and discard bay leaf. Serve over rice, if desired.

Makes 4 servings

Wisconsin Cheese 'n' Beer Soup

 2 tablespoons butter or
  margarine
 2 tablespoons all-purpose
  flour
 1 envelope LIPTON® RECIPE
  SECRETS® Golden Onion
  Soup Mix
 3 cups milk
 1 teaspoon Worcestershire
  sauce
 1 cup shredded Cheddar
  cheese (about 4 ounces)
 ½ cup beer
 1 teaspoon prepared mustard

In medium saucepan, melt butter and cook flour over medium heat, stirring constantly, 3 minutes or until bubbling. Stir in golden onion soup mix thoroughly blended with milk and Worcestershire sauce. Bring just to the boiling point, then simmer, stirring occasionally, 10 minutes. Stir in remaining ingredients and simmer, stirring constantly, 5 minutes or until cheese is melted. Garnish, if desired, with additional cheese, chopped red pepper and parsley.

Makes about 4 (1-cup) servings

Hearty Chicken and Rice Soup

Hearty Chicken and Rice Soup

10 cups chicken broth
1 medium onion, chopped
1 cup sliced celery
1 cup sliced carrots
¼ cup snipped parsley
½ teaspoon cracked black pepper
½ teaspoon dried thyme leaves
1 bay leaf
1½ cups chicken cubes (about ¾ pound)
2 cups cooked rice
2 tablespoons lime juice
Lime slices for garnish

Combine broth, onion, celery, carrots, parsley, pepper, thyme and bay leaf in Dutch oven. Bring to a boil; stir once or twice. Reduce heat; simmer, uncovered, 10 to 15 minutes. Add chicken; simmer, uncovered, 5 to 10 minutes or until chicken is no longer pink in center. Remove and discard bay leaf. Stir in rice and lime juice just before serving. Garnish with lime slices.

Makes 8 servings

*Favorite recipe from **USA Rice Federation***

Chicken Gumbo

Prep Time: 10 minutes
Cook Time: 1 hour

- 4 **TYSON® Fresh Skinless Chicken Thighs**
- 4 **TYSON® Fresh Skinless Chicken Drumsticks**
- ¼ **cup all-purpose flour**
- 2 **teaspoons Cajun or Creole seasoning blend**
- 2 **tablespoons vegetable oil**
- 1 **large onion, chopped**
- 1 **cup thinly sliced celery**
- 3 **cloves garlic, minced**
- 1 **can (14½ ounces) stewed tomatoes, undrained**
- 1 **can (14½ ounces) chicken broth**
- 1 **large green bell pepper, cut into ½-inch pieces**
- ½ **to 1 teaspoon hot pepper sauce or to taste**

PREP: CLEAN: Wash hands. Combine flour and Cajun seasonings in reclosable plastic bag. Add chicken, 2 pieces at a time; shake to coat. Reserve excess flour mixture. CLEAN: Wash hands.

COOK: In large saucepan, heat oil over medium heat. Add chicken and brown on all sides; remove and set aside. Sauté onion, celery and garlic 5 minutes. Add reserved flour mixture; cook 1 minute, stirring frequently. Add tomatoes, chicken broth, bell pepper and hot sauce. Bring to a boil. Return chicken to saucepan, cover and simmer over low heat, stirring occasionally, 30 minutes or until internal juices of chicken run clear.

(Or insert instant-read meat thermometer in thickest part of chicken. Temperature should read 180°F.)

SERVE: Serve in bowls, topped with hot cooked rice, if desired.

CHILL: Refrigerate leftovers immediately.

Makes 6 to 8 servings

Spam® & Potato Chowder

- 2 **tablespoons butter or margarine**
- ⅓ **cup shredded carrot**
- ¼ **cup finely chopped onion**
- 4 **cups milk**
- 3 **cups diced peeled potatoes**
- 2 **(10¾-ounce) cans cream of chicken soup**
- 1 **(12-ounce) can SPAM® Luncheon Meat, cubed**
- ½ **teaspoon dried thyme leaves**

In 4-quart saucepan, melt butter. Stir in carrot and onion. Cook, stirring occasionally, until onion is tender. Stir in remaining ingredients; mix well. Cook over medium-high heat, stirring occasionally, until mixture comes to a boil. Reduce heat to medium. Cover. Cook, stirring occasionally, until potatoes are tender. *Makes 6 servings*

Chicken Gumbo

Two-Bean Chili

1 pound sweet Italian sausage, casing removed
1 pound ground beef
2 medium onions, chopped
1 large green bell pepper, chopped
3 cloves garlic, minced
¼ cup all-purpose flour
3 tablespoons chili powder
2 teaspoons ground cumin
2 teaspoons dried basil leaves
2 teaspoons dried oregano leaves
1 teaspoon salt
2 (28-ounce) cans Italian-style tomatoes, undrained
3 tablespoons Worcestershire sauce
1¼ teaspoons TABASCO® brand Pepper Sauce
1 (20-ounce) can chick-peas, drained
1 (15½-ounce) can red kidney beans, drained
Sliced ripe olives, chopped onion, chopped green bell pepper, chopped tomato, shredded cheese and cooked rice (optional)

Cook sausage, beef, onions, bell pepper and garlic in large heavy saucepan or Dutch oven about 20 minutes or until meats are browned and vegetables are tender; drain fat. Stir in flour, chili powder, cumin, basil, oregano and salt; cook 1 minute. Add tomatoes; break up with fork. Stir in Worcestershire sauce and TABASCO® Sauce. Cover and simmer 1 hour, adding water if necessary; stir occasionally. Stir in chick-peas and kidney beans. Cook until heated through. Serve with olives, onion, bell pepper, tomato, cheese and rice, if desired.

Makes 8 servings

Calico Minestrone Soup

Prep Time: 5 minutes
Cook Time: 25 minutes

2 cans (14 ounces each) chicken broth
¼ cup uncooked small shell pasta
1 can (14½ ounces) DEL MONTE® Italian Recipe Stewed Tomatoes
1 can (8¾ ounces) *or* 1 cup kidney beans, drained
½ cup chopped cooked chicken or beef
1 carrot, diced
1 stalk celery, sliced
½ teaspoon dried basil, crushed

1. Bring broth to boil in large saucepan; stir in pasta and boil 5 minutes.

2. Add remaining ingredients.

3. Reduce heat; cover and simmer 20 minutes. Garnish with grated Parmesan cheese, if desired.

Makes approximately 6 servings (1 cup each)

Chile con Carne

- 2 tablespoons vegetable oil
- 2 pounds ground beef
- 2 cups (2 small) chopped onions
- 4 cloves garlic, finely chopped
- 3½ cups (two 15-ounce cans) kidney, pinto or black beans, drained
- 3½ cups (29-ounce can) crushed tomatoes
- 1¾ cups (16-ounce jar) ORTEGA® Salsa Prima-Thick & Chunky Mild
- ½ cup dry white wine
- ½ cup (4-ounce can) ORTEGA® Diced Green Chiles
- 3 tablespoons chili powder
- 1 to 2 tablespoons ORTEGA® Diced Jalapeños
- 1 tablespoon ground cumin
- 1 tablespoon dried oregano, crushed
- 2 teaspoons salt

HEAT vegetable oil in large saucepan over medium-high heat. Add beef, onions and garlic; cook for 4 to 5 minutes or until no longer pink; drain.

STIR in beans, crushed tomatoes, salsa, wine, chiles, chili powder, jalapeños, cumin, oregano and salt. Bring to a boil. Reduce heat to low; cover. Cook, stirring frequently, for 1 hour.   *Makes 10 to 12 servings*

Chile con Carne

Fix-It-Fast Chili

- ½ pound ground beef
- ¾ cup chopped onion
- ½ teaspoon finely chopped garlic
- 1 can (14½ ounces) whole peeled tomatoes, undrained and chopped
- 1 cup water
- 1 package LIPTON® Rice & Sauce—Spanish
- 2 teaspoons chili powder
- ½ teaspoon ground cumin (optional)
- 1 cup red kidney beans, rinsed and drained

In 12-inch skillet, cook ground beef, onion and garlic over medium-high heat, stirring occasionally, 5 minutes or until browned; drain. Stir in tomatoes, water, Rice & Sauce—Spanish, chili powder and cumin; bring to a boil. Reduce heat and simmer, stirring occasionally, 10 minutes or until rice is tender. Stir in beans and heat through.

Makes about 4 servings

Butternut Squash Soup

1 cup finely chopped onions
1 (3-pound) butternut squash, peeled and cubed
4 cups defatted* chicken broth
1½ cups MOTT'S® Natural Apple Sauce
½ teaspoon salt
¼ teaspoon ground white pepper
¼ teaspoon ground nutmeg
¼ teaspoon ground cloves
¼ teaspoon curry powder
¼ teaspoon ground coriander

*To defat chicken broth, chill canned broth thoroughly. Use can opener to punch two holes in top of can. Quickly pour out the contents of the can into bowl. Most of the fat will remain in the can and the remaining broth is "defatted."

1. Spray large saucepan or Dutch oven with nonstick cooking spray; heat over medium heat until hot. Add onions; cook and stir about 5 minutes or until transparent.

2. Add squash, chicken broth, apple sauce, salt, pepper, nutmeg, cloves, curry powder and coriander. Increase heat to high; bring mixture to a boil. Cover; reduce heat to low. Simmer 10 to 15 minutes or until squash is fork-tender, stirring occasionally.

3. In food processor or blender, process soup in small batches until smooth. Return soup to saucepan. Cook over low heat 5 minutes or until hot, stirring occasionally. Refrigerate leftovers.

Makes 8 servings

Microwave Directions: In large microwave-safe bowl, combine onions, squash, chicken broth, apple sauce, salt, pepper, nutmeg, cloves, curry powder and coriander. Cover; cook at HIGH (100% power) 15 minutes or until squash is fork-tender, stirring once. In food processor or blender, process soup in small batches until smooth. Return soup to bowl. Cover; cook at HIGH 3 minutes or until hot.

Chili Bean Del Monte®

Prep and Cook Time: 15 minutes

¾ cup sliced green onions, divided
1 can (15 ounces) pinto beans, drained
1 can (14½ ounces) DEL MONTE® Zesty Chili Style Chunky Tomatoes
1 can (8¾ ounces) *or* 1 cup kidney beans, drained
½ to 1 teaspoon minced jalapeño pepper
½ teaspoon ground cumin
¼ teaspoon garlic powder
¼ cup shredded sharp Cheddar cheese

1. Set aside ¼ cup green onions for garnish. In large skillet, combine remaining ½ cup green onions with remaining ingredients except cheese.

2. Bring to a boil; reduce heat to medium. Cook 5 minutes. Serve with cheese and reserved onions.

Makes 3 servings

Chilly Cucumber Soup

Chilly Cucumber Soup

**2 tablespoons margarine or
    butter**

**2 tablespoons all-purpose
    flour**

**4 large cucumbers, peeled,
    seeded and finely chopped
    (about 3½ cups)**

¼ cup finely chopped parsley

**¼ cup finely chopped celery
    leaves**

**1 envelope LIPTON® RECIPE
    SECRETS® Golden Onion
    Soup Mix**

2 cups water

**2 cups (1 pint) light cream or
    half-and-half**

In large saucepan, melt butter over medium heat; add flour and cook, stirring constantly, 3 minutes. Add cucumbers, parsley and celery leaves. Reduce heat to low and cook 8 minutes or until vegetables are tender. Stir in soup mix thoroughly blended with water. Bring to a boil over high heat. Reduce heat to low and simmer, covered, 15 minutes. Remove from heat, then cool.

In food processor or blender, purée soup mixture. Stir in cream; chill. Serve cold and garnish, if desired, with cucumber slices and lemon peel.

Makes about 6 (1 cup) servings

Cheddar Broccoli Soup

- **1 tablespoon BERTOLLI® Olive Oil**
- **1 rib celery, chopped (about ½ cup)**
- **1 carrot, chopped (about ½ cup)**
- **1 small onion, chopped (about ½ cup)**
- **½ teaspoon dried thyme leaves, crushed (optional)**
- **2 cans (13¾ ounces each) chicken broth**
- **1 jar (16 ounces) RAGÚ® Cheese Creations!® Double Cheddar Sauce**
- **1 box (10 ounces) frozen chopped broccoli, thawed and drained**

In 3-quart saucepan, heat oil over medium heat and cook celery, carrot, onion and thyme 3 minutes or until vegetables are almost tender. Add chicken broth and bring to a boil over high heat. Reduce heat to medium and simmer, uncovered, 10 minutes.

In food processor or blender, purée vegetable mixture until smooth; return to saucepan. Stir in Ragú Cheese Creations! Sauce and broccoli. Cook 10 minutes or until heated through.

Makes 6 (1-cup) servings

Hearty White Bean Soup

- **1 tablespoon BERTOLLI® Olive Oil**
- **1 medium onion, chopped**
- **2 medium carrots, sliced**
- **2 ribs celery, sliced**
- **2 cans (19 ounces each) cannelini or white kidney beans, rinsed and drained**
- **1 envelope LIPTON® RECIPE SECRETS® Savory Herb with Garlic Soup Mix**
- **2 cups water**
- **3 cups coarsely chopped escarole or spinach**
- **1 medium tomato, diced**
- **¼ cup crumbled feta cheese (optional)**

In 3-quart saucepan, heat oil over medium heat and cook onion, carrots and celery, stirring occasionally, 5 minutes or until tender. Stir in beans and soup mix blended with water. Bring to a boil over high heat. Reduce heat to low and simmer uncovered 15 minutes or until vegetables are tender. Stir in escarole and tomato and cook 2 minutes or until heated through. Top with cheese.

Makes about 6 cups soup

Cheddar Broccoli Soup

AMERICA'S FAVORITE SALADS

Get rave reviews with this collection of flavor-packed salads. Choose crispy garden, juicy fruit and creamy potato salads as the main attraction or perfect accompaniment to any meal.

Pineapple Boat with Citrus Creme (page 82)

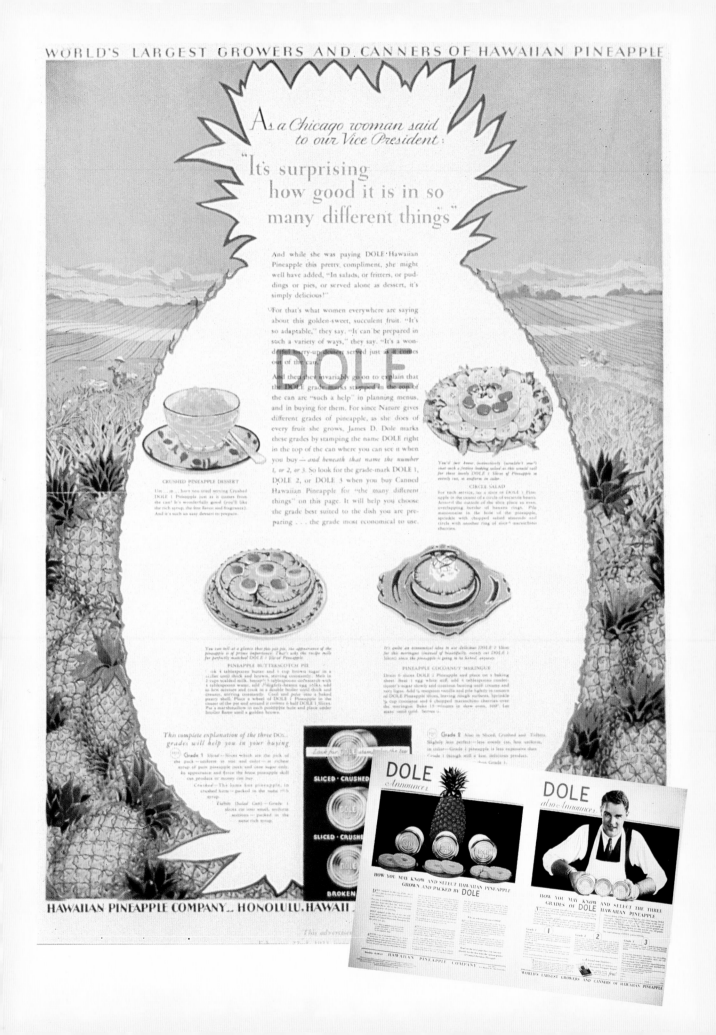

As a *Chicago woman said*
to our *Vice President*:

"It's surprising how good it is in so many different things"

And while she was paying DOLE Hawaiian Pineapple this pretty compliment, she might well have added, "In salads, or fritters, or puddings or pies, or served alone as dessert, it's simply delicious!"

For that's what women everywhere are saying about this golden-sweet, succulent fruit. "It's so adaptable," they say. "It can be prepared in such a variety of ways," they say. "It's a wonderful hurry-up dessert served just as it comes out of the can."

And then they invariably go on to explain that the DOLE grade-marks stamped in the top of the can are "such a help" in planning menus, and in buying for them. For since Nature gives different grades of pineapple, as she does of every fruit she grows, James D. Dole marks these grades by stamping the name DOLE right in the top of the can where you can see it when you buy — *and beneath that name the number 1, or 2, or 3.* So look for the grade-mark DOLE 1, DOLE 2, or DOLE 3 when you buy Canned Hawaiian Pineapple for "the many different things" on this page. It will help you choose the grade best suited to the dish you are preparing . . . the grade most economical to use.

CRUSHED PINEAPPLE DESSERT

Um . . . m . . . have you tried serving Crushed DOLE 3 Pineapple just as it comes from the can? It's wonderfully good (you'll like the rich syrup, the fine flavor and fragrance). And it's such an easy dessert to prepare.

You'd just know instinctively (wouldn't you?) that such a festive looking salad as this would call for those lovely DOLE 1 Slices of Pineapple so evenly cut, so uniform in color.

CIRCLE SALAD

For each service, lay a slice of DOLE 1 Pineapple in the center of a circle of escarole leaves. Around the outside of the slice place an even, overlapping border of banana rings. Pile mayonnaise in the hole of the pineapple, sprinkle with chopped salted almonds and circle with another ring of sliced maraschino cherries.

You can tell at a glance that this pie, the appearance of the pineapple is of prime importance. That's why the recipe calls for perfectly matched DOLE 1 Sliced Pineapple.

PINEAPPLE BUTTERSCOTCH PIE

Cook 4 tablespoons butter and 1 cup brown sugar in a skillet until thick and brown, stirring constantly. Melt in 3 cups scalded milk. Smooth 5 tablespoons cornstarch with 4 tablespoons water, add 2 slightly-beaten egg yolks; add to hot mixture and cook in a double boiler until thick and creamy, stirring constantly. Cool and pour into a baked pastry shell. Place a wheel of DOLE 1 Pineapple in the center of the pie and around it reserve 6 half DOLE 1 Slices. Put a meringue made from 2 egg whites over the top and place under broiler flame until a golden brown.

It's quite an economical idea to use delicious DOLE 2 Slices for this meringue (instead of beautifully, evenly cut DOLE 1 Slices) since the pineapple is going to be halved, anyway.

PINEAPPLE COCOANUT MERINGUE

Drain 6 slices DOLE 2 Pineapple and place on a baking sheet. Beat 1 egg white stiff, add 4 tablespoons confectioner's sugar slowly and continue beating until creamy and very light. Add ½ teaspoon vanilla and pile lightly in centers of DOLE Pineapple slices, leaving rough surfaces. Sprinkle ⅓ cup cocoanut and 4 chopped maraschino cherries over the meringue. Bake 15 minutes in slow oven, 300°. Let stand until gold. Serves 6.

This complete explanation of the three DOLE grades will help you in your buying

DOLE 1 **Grade 1** Sliced — Slices which are the pick of the pack — uniform in size and color — in richest syrup of pure pineapple juice and cane sugar only. As appearance and flavor the finest pineapple skill can produce or money can buy.

Crushed — The same fine pineapple, in crushed form — packed in that same rich syrup.

Tidbits (Diced Cuts) — Grade 1 slices cut into small, medium sections — packed in the same rich syrup.

DOLE 2 **Grade 2** Also in Sliced, Crushed and Tidbits. Slightly less perfect — less evenly cut, less uniform in color — Grade 2 pineapple is less expensive than Grade 1 through still a fine, delicious product. — from Grade 1.

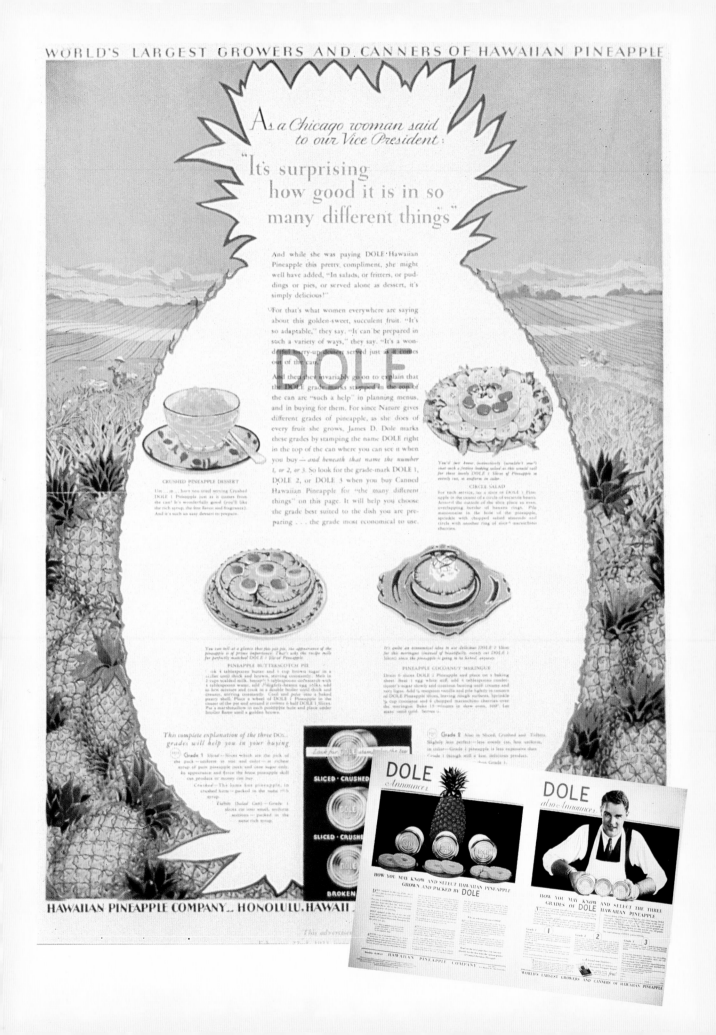

DOLE *Announces*

HOW YOU MAY KNOW AND SELECT HAWAIIAN PINEAPPLE GROWN AND PACKED BY DOLE

DOLE *also Announces*

HOW YOU MAY KNOW AND SELECT THE THREE GRADES OF DOLE HAWAIIAN PINEAPPLE

Grade 1	Grade 2	Grade 3
1	2	3

HAWAIIAN PINEAPPLE COMPANY

WORLD'S LARGEST GROWERS AND CANNERS OF HAWAIIAN PINEAPPLE

Pineapple Boats with Citrus Creme

Prep Time: 20 minutes

> 1 large DOLE® Fresh Pineapple
> 1 DOLE® Banana, peeled, sliced
> 1 orange, peeled, sliced
> 1 apple, cored, sliced
> 1 DOLE® Pear, cored, sliced
> 1 cup seedless DOLE® Grapes (red and green)

Citrus Creme:

> 1 cup plain nonfat yogurt
> 2 tablespoons brown sugar
> 1 tablespoon minced crystallized ginger (optional)
> 1 teaspoon *each* grated orange and lime peel

• Cut pineapple in half lengthwise through the crown. Cut fruit from shells, leaving shells intact. Core and chunk fruit.

• Combine pineapple chunks with remaining fruit. Spoon into pineapple boats.

• Combine all ingredients for Citrus Creme. Serve with pineapple boats.

Makes 8 servings

Antipasto Salad

Prep Time: 15 minutes plus refrigerating

> 1 cup MIRACLE WHIP® Salad Dressing
> ½ cup milk
> 2 packages GOOD SEASONS® Italian Salad Dressing Mix
> 1 package (16 ounces) uncooked mostaccioli, cooked, drained
> 1 package (8 ounces) OSCAR MAYER® Cotto Salami Slices, cut into strips
> 1 package (8 ounces) KRAFT® Low-Moisture Part-Skim Mozzarella Cheese, cubed
> ¾ cup *each* thin red bell pepper strips and thin zucchini strips
> ½ cup pitted ripe olives, drained, halved

• **MIX** salad dressing, milk and salad dressing mix in large bowl.

• **ADD** pasta; mix lightly.

• **ARRANGE** remaining ingredients over pasta mixture; cover. Refrigerate several hours or overnight until chilled.

Makes 10 to 12 servings

Antipasto Salad

Mexican Taco Salad

1 pound ground beef or turkey
1 cup (1 small) chopped onion
1 cup ORTEGA® Salsa Prima-Thick & Chunky Mild
¾ cup water
1 package (1¼ ounces) ORTEGA® Taco Seasoning Mix
1¾ cups (15-ounce can) kidney or pinto beans, rinsed and drained
½ cup (4-ounce can) ORTEGA® Diced Green Chiles
3 cups (3 ounces) tortilla chips *or* 6 tortilla shells
6 cups shredded lettuce, *divided*
Chopped tomatoes (optional)
¾ cup (3 ounces) shredded Nacho & Taco blend cheese, *divided*
Sour cream (optional)
Guacamole (optional)
ORTEGA® Thick & Smooth Taco Sauce

COOK beef and onion until beef is brown; drain. Stir in salsa, water and seasoning mix. Bring to a boil. Reduce heat to low; cook for 2 to 3 minutes. Stir in beans and chiles.

LAYER ingredients as follows on ½ cup chips: *1 cup* lettuce, *¾ cup* meat mixture, tomatoes, *2 tablespoons* cheese and sour cream. Serve with guacamole and taco sauce.

Makes 6 servings

Cobb Salad

Red leaf lettuce
8 cups mixed torn salad greens
1 cup prepared HIDDEN VALLEY® The Original Ranch® with Bacon Salad Dressing
1 can (16 ounces) thin asparagus spears
¼ pound cooked turkey, cut into strips
¼ pound cooked ham, cut into strips
¼ pound (about 4 slices) American cheese, cut into strips
4 hard-cooked eggs, sliced
4 radishes, thinly sliced
Freshly ground black pepper

Line 4 salad plates with lettuce leaves; divide salad greens among plates. Pour ¼ cup each salad dressing into individual containers. Place in center of each plate. Arrange asparagus, turkey, ham, cheese, eggs and radishes in spoke fashion around dressing. Sprinkle with pepper. *Makes 4 servings*

Mexican Taco Salad

Classic Potato Salad

1 cup HELLMANN'S® or BEST FOODS® Real or Light Mayonnaise or Low Fat Mayonnaise Dressing
2 tablespoons vinegar
1½ teaspoons salt
1 teaspoon sugar
¼ teaspoon freshly ground pepper
5 to 6 medium potatoes, peeled, cubed and cooked
1 cup sliced celery
½ cup chopped onion
2 hard-cooked eggs, diced

1. In large bowl, combine mayonnaise, vinegar, salt, sugar and pepper.

2. Add potatoes, celery, onion and eggs; toss to coat well.

3. Cover; chill to blend flavors.

Makes about 8 servings

Classic Potato Salad

3 Bean & Veggie Salad

Prep Time: 20 minutes
Chill Time: 1 hour

1 can (15¼ ounces) red kidney beans, drained and rinsed
1 can (15¼ ounces) garbanzo beans, drained and rinsed
1 package (9 ounces) frozen cut green beans, thawed and drained
½ cup thinly sliced carrots
½ cup thinly sliced celery
½ cup thinly sliced red onion
½ cup olive oil
¼ cup *French's*® Classic Yellow® Mustard
3 tablespoons chopped fresh dill *or* 2 teaspoons dried dill weed
2 tablespoons lemon juice
1 teaspoon sugar
¾ teaspoon salt
⅛ teaspoon black pepper

1. Combine beans, carrots, celery and onion in large bowl. Whisk oil, mustard, dill, lemon juice, sugar, salt and pepper in small bowl until well blended.

2. Pour dressing over beans and vegetables; toss well to coat evenly. Cover; chill in refrigerator 1 hour before serving.

Makes 6 (1-cup) servings

Fresh Greens with Hot Bacon Dressing

3 cups torn spinach leaves

3 cups torn romaine lettuce

2 small tomatoes, cut into wedges

1 cup sliced mushrooms

1 medium carrot, shredded

1 slice bacon, cut into small pieces

3 tablespoons red wine vinegar

1 tablespoon water

¼ teaspoon dried tarragon, crushed

⅛ teaspoon coarsely ground pepper

¼ teaspoon EQUAL® FOR RECIPES *or* 1 packet EQUAL® sweetener *or* 2 teaspoons EQUAL® SPOONFUL™

• Combine spinach, romaine, tomatoes, mushrooms and carrot in large bowl; set aside.

• Cook bacon in 12-inch skillet until crisp. Carefully stir in vinegar, water, tarragon and pepper. Heat to boiling; remove from heat. Stir in Equal®.

• Add spinach mixture to skillet. Toss 30 to 60 seconds or just until greens are wilted. Transfer to serving bowl. Serve immediately.

Makes 4 to 6 (1⅓-cup) servings

Fresh Greens with Hot Bacon Dressing

Caesar Salad

Prep Time: 15 minutes

12 cups torn romaine lettuce leaves

½ cup egg substitute

¼ cup olive oil*

¼ cup lemon juice

1 teaspoon GREY POUPON® Dijon Mustard

2 cloves garlic, minced

¼ teaspoon ground black pepper

Grated Parmesan cheese (optional)

Vegetable oil can be substituted.

Place lettuce in large bowl; set aside.

In small bowl, whisk together egg substitute, oil, lemon juice, mustard, garlic and pepper until well blended. To serve, pour dressing over lettuce, tossing until well coated. Serve with Parmesan cheese, if desired.   *Makes 8 servings*

Easy Greek Salad

Prep Time: 10 minutes

> 6 leaves Romaine lettuce, torn into 1½-inch pieces
> 1 cucumber, peeled and sliced
> 1 tomato, chopped
> ½ cup sliced red onion
> 1 ounce feta cheese, crumbled (about ⅓ cup)
> 2 tablespoons extra-virgin olive oil
> 2 tablespoons lemon juice
> 1 teaspoon dried oregano leaves
> ½ teaspoon salt

1. Combine lettuce, cucumber, tomato, onion and cheese in large serving bowl.

2. Whisk together oil, lemon juice, oregano and salt in small bowl. Pour over lettuce mixture; toss until coated. Serve immediately.

Makes 6 servings

German Potato Salad

> 4 cups sliced, peeled Colorado potatoes
> 4 slices bacon
> ¾ cup chopped onion
> ¼ cup sugar
> 3 tablespoons all-purpose flour
> 1½ teaspoons salt
> 1 teaspoon celery seeds
> ¼ teaspoon black pepper
> 1 cup water
> ¾ cup vinegar
> 2 hard-cooked eggs, chopped

Cook potatoes in boiling water until tender; drain. Meanwhile, cook bacon in medium skillet. Drain on paper towels; cool and crumble. Cook and stir onion in drippings until tender. Combine sugar, flour, salt, celery seeds and pepper; blend in water and vinegar. Stir into onion in skillet; heat until bubbly. Pour over combined potatoes, bacon and eggs; toss. Serve immediately.

Makes 6 servings

*Favorite recipe from **Colorado Potato Administrative Committee***

Easy Greek Salad

Classic Spinach Salad

½ pound fresh spinach leaves (about 10 cups)
1 cup sliced mushrooms
1 medium tomato, cut into wedges
⅓ cup seasoned croutons
¼ cup chopped red onion
4 slices bacon, crisp-cooked and crumbled
½ cup WISH-BONE® Olive Oil Vinaigrette Dressing
1 hard-cooked egg, sliced

In large salad bowl, combine spinach, mushrooms, tomato, croutons, red onion and bacon. Add olive oil vinaigrette dressing and toss gently. Garnish with egg.

Makes about 6 side-dish servings

Dilled Carrot Salad

Prep Time: 5 minutes

¼ teaspoon dill weed
1 can (8¼ ounces) DEL MONTE® Sliced Carrots, drained
5 cups torn romaine lettuce
Honey Dijon dressing

1. Sprinkle dill over carrots in large bowl.

2. Add lettuce; toss with dressing.

Makes 4 servings

Shell Salad with Peas and Bacon

1 package (16 ounces) BARILLA® Medium Shells
1 package (10 ounces) frozen peas
8 ounces (12 slices) bacon, cooked and crumbled
½ cup chopped red onion
1 cup mayonnaise
1 cup sour cream
½ cup (2 ounces) grated Parmesan cheese
1½ teaspoons salt
½ teaspoon pepper
½ teaspoon garlic powder

1. Cook pasta shells according to package directions; drain.

2. Combine pasta shells, peas, bacon and onion in serving bowl.

3. Combine mayonnaise, sour cream, cheese, salt, pepper and garlic powder in medium bowl; add to pasta mixture. Stir gently to combine. Cover and refrigerate at least one hour before serving.

Makes 10 servings

Watergate Salad (Pistachio Pineapple Delight)

Watergate Salad (Pistachio Pineapple Delight)

Preparation Time: 10 minutes
Refrigerating Time: 1 hour

   1 package (4-serving size)
       JELL-O® Pistachio Flavor
       Instant Pudding & Pie
       Filling
   1 can (20 ounces) crushed
       pineapple in juice,
       undrained
   1 cup miniature marshmallows
   ½ cup chopped nuts
   2 cups thawed COOL WHIP®
       Whipped Topping

STIR pudding mix, pineapple with juice, marshmallows and nuts in large bowl until well blended. Gently stir in whipped topping.

REFRIGERATE 1 hour or until ready to serve. Garnish as desired.
Makes 8 servings

Layered Pear Cream Cheese Mold

Preparation Time: 30 minutes
Refrigerating Time: 5 hours

- **1 can (16 ounces) pear halves, undrained**
- **1 package (8-serving size) or 2 packages (4-serving size) JELL-O® Brand Lime Flavor Gelatin Dessert**
- **1½ cups cold ginger ale or water**
- **2 tablespoons lemon juice**
- **1 package (8 ounces) PHILADELPHIA® Cream Cheese, softened**
- **¼ cup chopped pecans**

DRAIN pears, reserving liquid. Dice pears; set aside. Add water to liquid to make 1½ cups; bring to boil in small saucepan.

STIR boiling liquid into gelatin in large bowl at least 2 minutes until completely dissolved. Stir in cold ginger ale and lemon juice. Reserve 2½ cups gelatin at room temperature. Pour remaining gelatin into 5-cup mold. Refrigerate about 30 minutes or until thickened (spoon drawn through leaves definite impression). Arrange about ½ cup of the diced pears in thickened gelatin in mold.

STIR reserved 2½ cups gelatin gradually into cream cheese in large bowl with wire whisk until smooth. Refrigerate about 30 minutes or until slightly thickened (consistency of unbeaten egg whites). Stir in

remaining diced pears and pecans. Spoon over gelatin layer in mold.

REFRIGERATE 4 hours or until firm. Unmold. Garnish as desired.

Makes 10 servings

Beet and Pear Salad

Prep Time: 10 minutes

- **1 can (15¼ ounces) DEL MONTE® Bartlett Pear Halves**
- **1 can (14½ ounces) DEL MONTE® Sliced Beets, drained**
- **½ cup thinly sliced red onion, separated into rings**
- **2 tablespoons vegetable oil**
- **1 tablespoon white wine vinegar**
- **⅓ cup crumbled blue cheese Lettuce leaves (optional)**

1. Drain pears reserving 1 tablespoon syrup.

2. Cut pears in half lengthwise.

3. Place pears, beets and onion in medium bowl.

4. Whisk together oil, vinegar and reserved syrup. Pour over salad; toss gently.

5. Just before serving, add cheese and toss. Serve on bed of lettuce leaves, if desired.

Makes 4 to 6 servings

Layered Pear Cream Cheese Mold

Easy Niçoise Salad

Easy Niçoise Salad

Prep Time: 20 minutes

    Lettuce leaves
2 medium tomatoes, thinly sliced
1½ cups sliced cooked potatoes
1¼ cups cooked green beans
1 (7-ounce) pouch of STARKIST® Premium Albacore or Chunk Light Tuna
4 slices red or white onion, separated into rings
½ cup sliced pitted ripe olives
1 hard-cooked egg, sliced
4 whole anchovies (optional)

Vinegar 'n' Oil Dressing
    ½ cup white vinegar
    ⅓ cup vegetable oil
    1 tablespoon chopped parsley
    ½ teaspoon salt
    ¼ teaspoon pepper

On a large platter or 4 individual salad plates, arrange lettuce leaves. Arrange tomatoes, potatoes, beans, tuna, onion rings, olives and egg in a decorative design. Garnish with anchovies if desired.

For dressing, in a shaker jar combine dressing ingredients. Cover and shake until well blended. Drizzle some of the dressing over salad; serve remaining dressing on the side. *Makes 4 servings*

Classic Waldorf Salad

    ½ cup HELLMANN'S® or BEST FOODS® Mayonnaise
    1 tablespoon sugar
    1 tablespoon lemon juice
    ⅛ teaspoon salt
    3 medium-size red apples, cored and diced
    1 cup sliced celery
    ½ cup chopped walnuts

1. In medium bowl combine mayonnaise, sugar, lemon juice and salt.

2. Add apples and celery; toss to coat well. Cover; chill.

3. Just before serving, sprinkle with walnuts. *Makes about 8 servings*

Carrot Raisin Salad with Citrus Dressing

Carrot Raisin Salad with Citrus Dressing

¾ **cup reduced-fat sour cream**

¼ **cup nonfat milk**

1 **tablespoon honey**

1 **tablespoon orange juice concentrate**

1 **tablespoon lime juice**

Peel of 1 medium orange, grated

¼ **teaspoon salt**

8 **medium carrots, peeled and coarsely shredded (about 2 cups)**

¼ **cup raisins**

⅓ **cup chopped cashews**

Combine sour cream, milk, honey, orange juice concentrate, lime juice, orange peel and salt in small bowl. Blend well and set aside.

Combine carrots and raisins in large bowl. Pour dressing over; toss to coat. Cover and refrigerate 30 minutes. Toss again before serving. Top with cashews.

Makes 8 servings

Hoppin' John Salad

3 cups dried black-eyed peas, rinsed and drained
3 cups cooked white rice
¼ pound cooked Canadian bacon, finely chopped
1 small red onion, finely chopped
1 stalk celery, thinly sliced
2 tablespoons red wine vinegar
1 tablespoon vegetable oil
1 clove garlic, minced
1 teaspoon hot pepper sauce
½ teaspoon salt

1. Place 3 quarts water and black-eyed peas in large saucepan; bring to a boil over high heat. Cover; reduce heat to medium-low. Simmer 1 hour or until peas are tender. Rinse with cool water; drain. Cool.

2. Combine peas, rice, bacon, onion and celery in large bowl. Combine vinegar, oil, garlic, hot sauce and salt in small bowl until well blended. Drizzle over pea mixture; toss to coat. Cover; refrigerate 2 hours. Garnish as desired.

Makes 6 servings

Classic Italian Pasta Salad

8 ounces uncooked rotelle or spiral pasta
2½ cups assorted cut-up fresh vegetables (broccoli, carrots, tomatoes, bell peppers, cauliflower, onions and mushrooms)
½ cup cubed Cheddar or mozzarella cheese
⅓ cup sliced pitted ripe olives (optional)
1 cup WISH-BONE® Creamy Caesar Dressing*

*Also terrific with WISH-BONE® Italian, Robusto Italian, Fat Free Italian, Classic House Italian, Creamy Roasted Garlic, Fat Free Creamy Roasted Garlic, Ranch, Lite Ranch, Fat Free Ranch, Parmesan & Onion, Fat Free Parmesan & Onion, Red Wine Vinaigrette or Fat Free Red Wine Vinaigrette Dressing.

Cook pasta according to package directions; drain and rinse with cold water until completely cool.

In large bowl, combine all ingredients except creamy Caesar dressing. Add dressing; toss well. Serve chilled or at room temperature.

Makes 8 side-dish servings

Note: If preparing a day ahead, refrigerate, then stir in ¼ cup additional Wish-Bone® Dressing before serving.

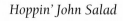
Hoppin' John Salad

Easy Pineapple Slaw

Prep Time: 5 minutes

> 1 can (15¼ ounces)
>   **DEL MONTE® Pineapple Tidbits In Its Own Juice**
> ⅓ cup mayonnaise
> 2 tablespoons vinegar
> 6 cups coleslaw mix or shredded cabbage

1. Drain pineapple, reserving 3 tablespoons juice.

2. Combine reserved juice, mayonnaise and vinegar; toss with pineapple and coleslaw mix. Season with salt and pepper to taste, if desired.   *Makes 4 to 6 servings*

Italian Pasta Salad

Prep Time: 15 minutes plus refrigerating

> 3 cups (8 ounces) tri-color rotini, cooked, drained
> 2 cups broccoli flowerets
> 1 (8-ounce) bottle KRAFT® Zesty Italian Dressing
> 1 cup KRAFT® 100% Grated Parmesan Cheese
> ½ cup *each* chopped red bell pepper, pitted ripe olives and sliced red onion

TOSS together all ingredients. Refrigerate until chilled.
      Makes 8 servings

Favorite Macaroni Salad

Prep Time: 20 minutes
Chill Time: 30 minutes

> 8 ounces uncooked medium shell pasta
> ⅓ cup reduced-fat sour cream
> ⅓ cup reduced-fat mayonnaise
> ⅓ cup *French's®* Hearty Deli Brown Mustard
> 1 tablespoon cider vinegar
> 3 cups bite-sized fresh vegetables, such as tomatoes, peppers, carrots and celery
> ¼ cup minced green onions

1. Cook pasta according to package directions using shortest cooking time; rinse with cold water and drain.

2. Combine sour cream, mayonnaise, mustard and vinegar in large bowl. Add pasta, vegetables and green onions. Toss gently to coat evenly. Season to taste with salt and pepper. Cover; chill in refrigerator 30 minutes. Stir before serving.
      Makes 6 (1-cup) servings

Note: Create German-style mustard by adding minced garlic to *French's®* Deli Brown Mustard.

Ginger Fruit Salad

Ginger Fruit Salad

⅓ cup HELLMANN'S® or BEST
    FOODS® Real or Light
    Mayonnaise or Low Fat
    Mayonnaise Dressing
2 tablespoons orange juice
⅛ teaspoon ground ginger
2 medium oranges, sectioned
1 kiwifruit, peeled and sliced
1 cup fresh raspberries
    Sliced star fruit for garnish
    (optional)
    Pomegranate seeds for
    garnish (optional)

1. In medium bowl combine mayonnaise, orange juice and ginger.

2. Arrange orange sections, kiwi slices and raspberries on 4 serving plates. Spoon dressing over fruit. Garnish with sliced star fruit and pomegranate seeds, if desired.

Makes 4 servings

SUPER SANDWICHES

Liven up lunchtime and casual meals with scrumptious sandwiches. You'll find all your favorites like heros, subs, burgers, grilled cheese, sloppy joes, chili dogs, tuna melts and BBQ. Super sandwiches are the every-popular, all-American portable meal.

Kielbasa & Kraut Hero (page 102)

1 Of Asiatic origin, mustard has been known to man since prehistoric times.

2 The Chinese used mustard thousands of years ago. The hot mustard served in Chinese restaurants is simply brown Oriental mustard powder and cold water stirred to a paste.

3 Pythagoras' theory is today basic to the study of geometry, but in his day Pythagoras was more famous for recommending mustard as an antidote for scorpion bites.

4 Hippocrates, the father of medicine, employed dry mustard extensively as a medicine, both internally and externally.

the history of

MUSTARD

18 Americans today consume over 30 million gallons of mustard every year, using it to perfect everything from Beef Wellington to Cheese Fondue. For some helpful hints, see opposite side of this chart.

5 Pliny the Elder, in Historica Naturalis wrote that mustard seeds initially brought from Egypt had become so established in Italy that they "grew wild ... without being planted."

17 Today, nearly all mustard is grown outside the United States in the prairie provinces of Canada. It needs only a short growing season and little moisture to thrive.

DIOCLETIAN

6 The Roman Emperor, Diocletian, included mustard in a price fixing edict, noting that in Eastern regions of his empire it was consumed as a food and a condiment.

16 In 1904 in Rochester, N.Y., George and Francis French pioneered the development of the first successfully prepared mustard in the U.S. It paralleled the "invention" of the hot dog at the St. Louis Exposition. The same year sales of the new product soared.

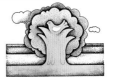

7 The Gospel according to Saint Matthew records a parable in which Christ likens the kingdom of heaven to a mustard seed ... which though it "is the least of all seeds ... becomes a tree, so that birds ... lodge in the branches."

15 For centuries mustard was used in Western countries as a stimulant, a diuretic, an emetic, and in mustard plasters to relieve chest colds, arthritis, and rheumatism.

8 In 800 A.D. mustard was grown on convent lands near Paris to provide a lucrative source of revenue for the Church.

mus • tard: genus Brassica of the family Cruciferae

14 The Spanish padres established the Mission Trail in California by scattering mustard seeds to mark the way as they went from mission to mission. Some of these fields still exist in the area of some missions.

THE R. T. FRENCH CO./ONE MUSTARD ST./ROCHESTER, N.Y. 14609

13 In 1720, Mrs. Clements of Durham, England, made a fortune by hulling, grinding and sifting mustard seeds to yield a pale yellow mustard flour ... Durham Mustard.

12 In Tewkesbury, England, mustard paste was sold in balls. In Henry IV, Shakespeare wrote: "His wit's as thick as Tewkesbury mustard ..."

11 Vasco da Gama provisions w first voyage in 1497.

Kielbasa & Kraut Heroes

Prep Time: 20 minutes
Cook Time: 20 minutes

    1 tablespoon vegetable oil
    2 large red onions, cut in half lengthwise and thinly sliced
    2 pounds kielbasa, thickly sliced
    2 pounds sauerkraut, rinsed and well drained
    1 can (12 ounces) beer or nonalcoholic malt beverage
    ½ cup *French's*® Hearty Deli Brown Mustard
    1 tablespoon caraway seeds
    8 hot dog or hero-style buns

1. Heat oil in large nonstick skillet over medium heat. Add onions; cook and stir 5 minutes or just until tender. Remove from skillet.

2. Add kielbasa to skillet; cook and stir 5 minutes or until lightly browned. Drain. Stir in sauerkraut, beer, mustard and caraway seeds. Cook over low heat 10 minutes or until liquid is almost absorbed. Serve in buns. *Makes 8 servings*

Velveeta® Ultimate Grilled Cheese

Prep Time: 5 minutes
Cook Time: 10 minutes

    2 slices bread
    2 ounces VELVEETA® Pasteurized Prepared Cheese Product, sliced
    2 teaspoons soft margarine

1. Top 1 bread slice with VELVEETA and second bread slice.

2. Spread outside of sandwich with margarine.

3. Cook in skillet on medium heat until lightly browned on both sides.
Makes 1 sandwich

❧ *tip* ☙

Kids love grilled cheese sandwiches. Cut sandwiches into quarters. Serve with mini carrot sticks and pieces of fruit for a tasty, nutritious, kid-sized meal.

Velveeta® Ultimate Grilled Cheese

French Dip Sandwiches

½ cup A.1.® Original or A.1.®
  BOLD & SPICY Steak
  Sauce, divided
1 tablespoon GREY POUPON®
  Dijon Mustard
4 steak rolls, split horizontally
8 ounces sliced cooked
  roast beef
1 (13¾-fluid ounce) can beef
  broth

Blend ¼ cup steak sauce and
mustard; spread mixture evenly on
cut sides of roll tops. Arrange
2 ounces beef on each roll bottom;
replace roll tops over beef. Slice
sandwiches in half crosswise if
desired.

Heat broth and remaining ¼ cup
steak sauce in small saucepan,
stirring occasionally. Serve as a
dipping sauce with sandwiches.
Garnish as desired.

Makes 4 servings

Sloppy Joes

Prep Time: 5 minutes
Cook Time: 10 minutes

1 pound ground beef or turkey
1 can (10¾ ounces) condensed
  tomato soup
2 tablespoons *French's®*
  Worcestershire Sauce
4 large rolls, split
  Garnish: shredded Cheddar
  cheese, sliced green
  onions, chopped tomatoes

1. Cook beef in large skillet until
browned; drain. Add soup, *¼ cup
water* and Worcestershire. Heat to
boiling. Simmer over low heat
5 minutes, stirring often.

2. Serve in rolls. Top with cheese,
onions and tomatoes.

Makes 4 servings

⋇ *tip* ⋇

*Spoon sloppy joe filling over shredded
lettuce and chopped tomatoes. Add
tortilla chips and toss for a quick,
taco-style salad.*

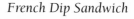

French Dip Sandwich

Monte Cristo Sandwiches

⅓ cup HELLMANN'S® or BEST FOODS® Real or Light Mayonnaise or Low Fat Mayonnaise Dressing
¼ teaspoon ground nutmeg
⅛ teaspoon freshly ground pepper
12 slices white bread, crusts removed
6 slices Swiss cheese
6 slices cooked ham
6 slices cooked chicken
2 eggs
½ cup milk

1. In small bowl, combine mayonnaise, nutmeg and pepper; spread on one side of each bread slice.

2. Layer cheese, ham and chicken on 6 bread slices; top with remaining bread, mayonnaise sides down. Cut sandwiches diagonally into quarters.

3. In small bowl, beat together eggs and milk; dip sandwich quarters into egg mixture.

4. Cook on preheated greased griddle or in skillet, turning once, 4 to 5 minutes or until browned and heated through.

Makes 24 mini sandwiches

Junior Joes

1 pound ground beef
1 can (10¾ ounces) condensed tomato soup
¼ cup water
1 tablespoon parsley flakes
1 teaspoon instant minced onion
½ teaspoon salt
½ teaspoon TABASCO® brand Pepper Sauce
 Processed American cheese slices
6 hamburger buns, split and toasted

Break up ground beef with fork in large skillet. Cook over medium heat, stirring frequently until meat loses pink color. Add undiluted tomato soup, water, parsley, onion, salt and TABASCO® Sauce. Cook over low heat, stirring occasionally, 15 to 20 minutes. Cut letters from cheese slices to make names or initials. Spoon hamburger mixture over bottom halves of toasted buns. Top with cheese names or initials. Serve with top halves of buns.

Makes 6 servings

Croque Monsieur

Croque Monsieur

Preparation Time: 8 minutes
Cooking Time: 6 minutes

> 8 slices firm white sandwich
>   bread
> 2 tablespoons butter, softened
> 8 slices SARGENTO® Deli Style
>   Sliced Swiss Cheese
> 2 tablespoons honey mustard
> 4 slices CURE 81® ham
> 4 slices cooked turkey breast

1. Spread one side of each slice of bread with butter; place butter side down on waxed paper. Top 4 slices of bread with 4 slices of cheese. Spread mustard over cheese; top with ham, turkey and remaining cheese. Close sandwiches with remaining bread, butter side out.

2. Heat a large skillet or griddle over medium heat until hot. Cook sandwiches in batches in skillet or on the griddle until golden brown, about 3 minutes per side.

Makes 4 servings

Muffuletta

1 (9¾-ounce) jar green olive
    salad, drained and
    chopped
¼ cup pitted black olives,
    chopped
1 large stalk celery, finely
    chopped
1½ teaspoons TABASCO® brand
    Pepper Sauce, divided
1 (8-inch) round loaf crusty
    French or sourdough bread
3 tablespoons olive oil
4 ounces sliced salami
4 ounces sliced baked ham
4 ounces sliced provolone
    cheese

Combine green olive salad, black
olives, celery and 1 teaspoon
TABASCO® Sauce in medium bowl.
Cut bread crosswise in half; remove
some of soft inside from each half.
Combine oil and remaining
½ teaspoon TABASCO® Sauce in
small bowl. Brush mixture on inside
of bread. Fill bottom with olive
mixture. Top with salami, ham and
provolone slices. Top with remaining
bread half. Cut loaf into quarters.

Makes 4 to 6 servings

Note: To heat Muffuletta, preheat
oven to 350°F. Before cutting, place
sandwich on rack in oven and heat
10 minutes or until cheese is
melted.

Cowboy Burgers

1 pound ground beef
½ teaspoon LAWRY'S®
    Seasoned Salt
½ teaspoon LAWRY'S®
    Seasoned Pepper
2 tablespoons plus
    2 teaspoons butter or
    margarine
1 large onion, thinly sliced
1 package (1.0 ounces)
    LAWRY'S® Taco Spices &
    Seasonings
4 slices Cheddar cheese
4 Kaiser rolls
  Lettuce leaves
  Tomato slices

In medium bowl, combine ground
beef, Seasoned Salt and Seasoned
Pepper; shape into four patties. Grill
or broil to desired doneness (about
5 to 6 minutes on each side for
medium). Meanwhile, in medium
skillet, heat butter. Add onion and
Taco Spices & Seasonings and cook
over medium-high heat until onion
is soft and transparent. Top each
patty with onions and cheese.
Return to grill or broiler until
cheese is melted. Place each patty on
roll; top with lettuce and tomato.

Makes 4 servings

Philadelphia Cheese Steak Sandwiches

2 cups sliced red or green bell peppers (about 2 medium)
1 small onion, thinly sliced
1 tablespoon vegetable oil
½ cup A.1.® Original or A.1.® BOLD & SPICY Steak Sauce
1 teaspoon prepared horseradish
8 ounces thinly sliced beef sandwich steaks
4 ounces thinly sliced mozzarella cheese
4 long sandwich rolls, split

Sauté peppers and onion in oil in medium saucepan over medium heat until tender. Stir in steak sauce and horseradish; keep warm.

Cook sandwich steaks in lightly greased medium skillet over medium-high heat until done. Portion beef, pepper mixture and cheese on roll bottoms.

Broil sandwich bottoms 4 inches from heat source for 3 to 5 minutes or until cheese melts; replace tops. Serve immediately.

Makes 4 sandwiches

Philadelphia Cheese Steak Sandwich

Lipton® Onion Burgers

Prep Time: 10 minutes
Cook Time: 12 minutes

1 envelope LIPTON® RECIPE SECRETS® Onion Soup Mix*
2 pounds ground beef
½ cup water

*Also terrific with LIPTON® RECIPE SECRETS® Beefy Onion, Onion Mushroom, Beefy Mushroom, Savory Herb with Garlic or Ranch Soup Mix.

1. In large bowl, combine all ingredients; shape into 8 patties.

2. Grill or broil until done.

Makes about 8 servings

America's Favorite Cheddar Beef Burgers

- **1 pound ground beef**
- **⅓ cup A.1.® Steak Sauce, divided**
- **1 medium onion, cut into strips**
- **1 medium green or red bell pepper, cut into strips**
- **1 tablespoon margarine or butter**
- **4 ounces Cheddar cheese, sliced**
- **4 hamburger rolls**
- **4 tomato slices**

Mix ground beef and 3 tablespoons steak sauce; shape mixture into 4 burgers. Set aside.

Cook and stir onion and pepper in margarine or butter in medium skillet until tender. Stir in remaining steak sauce; keep warm.

Grill burgers over medium heat for 4 minutes on each side or until done. When almost done, top with cheese; grill until cheese melts. Spoon 2 tablespoons onion mixture onto each roll bottom; top each with burger, tomato slice, some of remaining onion mixture and roll top. Serve immediately.

Makes 4 servings

Gourmet Deli Hero

Prep Time: 15 minutes
Chill Time: 30 minutes

- **1 loaf French or Italian bread (18 inches)**
- **⅓ cup reduced-fat mayonnaise**
- **⅓ cup *French's*® Hearty Deli Brown Mustard**
- **2 tablespoons minced red onion**
- **2 tablespoons horseradish**
- **½ pound *each* sliced ham and smoked turkey**
- **1 jar (7 ounces) roasted red peppers, well drained**
- **¼ pound sliced mozzarella cheese**
- **Lettuce leaves**

1. Slice bread in half lengthwise. Scoop out soft bread center; discard.

2. Combine mayonnaise, mustard, onion and horseradish in medium bowl. Spread mixture on both cut sides of bread. Layer remaining ingredients on bottom half of bread. Cover with top half of bread, pressing gently. Wrap in plastic wrap; chill in refrigerator 30 minutes or until ready to serve. Cut into thick slices to serve.

Makes 6 servings

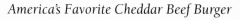

America's Favorite Cheddar Beef Burger

Grilled Reuben Sandwiches

Preparation Time: 10 minutes
Cooking Time: 10 minutes

- ¼ cup light or regular mayonnaise
- 2 tablespoons chili sauce or ketchup
- 1 teaspoon prepared horseradish
- 8 slices rye or pumpernickel bread
- 2 tablespoons butter or margarine, softened
- 8 slices SARGENTO® Deli Style Sliced Swiss Cheese
- 1 pound thinly sliced deli corned beef or turkey pastrami
- ¾ cup well drained sauerkraut

1. In small bowl, combine mayonnaise, chili sauce and horseradish; mix well.

2. Spread one side of each slice of bread with butter. Place cheese slices over unbuttered sides of bread. Arrange corned beef over half of bread slices, top with mayonnaise mixture and sauerkraut. Close sandwiches with remaining half of bread, cheese side down and butter side up.

3. Cook on a preheated large griddle (or cook two sandwiches at a time in a large skillet) over medium-low heat 4 to 5 minutes per side or until bread is toasted and cheese is melted. *Makes 4 servings*

Steak and Onion Subs

- 1 small flank steak (about 1 pound)
- 1 tablespoon olive oil
- 1 large onion, cut in half and sliced
- 1½ teaspoons TABASCO® brand Pepper Sauce
- ½ teaspoon sugar
- ¼ teaspoon salt
- 4 (6-inch) French rolls
  Lettuce leaves
- 1 large tomato, sliced

Preheat broiler. Place flank steak on rack in broiler pan. Broil 3 inches from heat source until desired doneness is reached, turning once.

Meanwhile, heat oil in 12-inch skillet over medium heat. Add onion; cook about 5 minutes. Stir in TABASCO® Sauce, sugar and salt; cook 5 minutes or until onions are tender, stirring occasionally.

To serve, cut flank steak into thin slices. Cut rolls in half crosswise. Arrange lettuce leaves on bottom halves of rolls; top with tomato slices, flank steak, onion mixture and remaining roll halves.

Makes 4 servings

Grilled Reuben Sandwich

Favorite Grilled Cheese Sandwiches

Prep Time: 10 minutes
Cook Time: 5 minutes

> *French's*® Mustard (any flavor)
> **Thick sliced bread**
> **Sliced cheese, such as American, Swiss, Muenster, provolone or mozzarella**
> **Luncheon meats, such as ham, pastrami, turkey, corned beef, salami or cooked bacon**
> **Sliced tomatoes (optional)**
> **Melted butter or margarine**

Generously spread mustard on each slice of bread. Arrange your favorite sliced cheese, luncheon meat and tomatoes on mustard sides of half the bread slices. Top with second slice of bread, mustard side down. Secure sandwiches with toothpicks.*

Brush outside surfaces of bread with melted butter. Place sandwiches on grid. Grill over medium-low coals until cheese melts, turning once. Remove toothpicks before serving.

Makes desired number of servings

*Soak toothpicks in water 20 minutes to prevent burning.

Roast Beef Po' Boy

> **6 tablespoons butter or margarine**
> **6 tablespoons flour**
> **1½ cups sliced onion (1 large)**
> **1 small green bell pepper, sliced (1 cup)**
> **2 cups beef broth**
> **1 teaspoon Worcestershire sauce**
> **1 teaspoon TABASCO® brand Pepper Sauce**
> **½ teaspoon dried thyme leaves**
> **4 (6-inch) French or round rolls**
> **1 pound thinly sliced cooked beef**

Melt butter in medium saucepan over medium heat; stir in flour. Cook about 4 minutes or until flour browns, stirring constantly. Add onion and green bell pepper; cook and stir about 5 minutes. Gradually stir in broth. Add Worcestershire sauce, TABASCO® Sauce and thyme; cook and stir until mixture boils and thickens.

Cut thin slice from top of each roll. Scoop out soft insides; fill with beef. Spoon gravy over beef. Replace tops on rolls. *Makes 4 sandwiches*

Best Ever Beef Hero

Best Ever Beef Heroes

Preparation Time: 10 minutes

    3 tablespoons mayonnaise
    1 tablespoon Dijon mustard
    **2 teaspoons prepared
       horseradish**
    **4 submarine or hoagie rolls,
       split**
    **4 red leaf or romaine lettuce
       leaves**
    1 pound sliced deli roast beef
    **1 thin slice red onion,
       separated into rings**
    **8 slices SARGENTO® Deli Style
       Sliced Swiss Cheese**

1. Combine mayonnaise, mustard and horseradish; mix well. Spread on cut sides of rolls.

2. Fill rolls with lettuce, roast beef, onion rings and cheese. Close sandwiches; cut in half.

Makes 4 servings

New York Deli-Style Tuna

Prep Time: 10 minutes

- 1 (3-ounce) pouch STARKIST® Premium Albacore Tuna
- 1 hard-cooked egg, minced
- 3 tablespoons minced celery
- 1 tablespoon chopped ripe olives
- 3 to 4 tablespoons mayonnaise
- 2 teaspoons mustard (optional)
- 1 tablespoon drained capers (optional)
- 3 New York-style bagels, split
- 3 ounces cream cheese, softened
  Baby kosher dill pickles, thinly sliced lengthwise
  Thinly sliced red onion rings

In medium bowl, combine tuna, egg, celery, olives and mayonnaise. Stir in mustard and capers, if desired; blend well. Chill.

To serve, toast bagels; spread each half with ½ ounce cream cheese. Top each with 3 pickle slices, about 3 tablespoons tuna mixture and red onion rings; serve open face.

Makes 6 servings

Easy Beef Barbecue

Prep Time: 10 minutes
Cook Time: 20 minutes

- 1 package KNORR® Recipe Classics™ Tomato Beef (Oxtail) Soup, Dip and Recipe Mix
- 1½ cups water
- ½ cup ketchup
- 1 small onion, chopped
- 2 tablespoons cider vinegar
- 1 tablespoon firmly packed brown sugar
- 1 tablespoon vegetable oil
- 1 (1-pound) beef flank steak, thinly sliced or 1 pound lean ground beef
  Sandwich rolls

• In small bowl, blend recipe mix, water, ketchup, onion, vinegar and brown sugar; set aside.

• In large skillet, heat oil over medium-high heat and brown steak slices in two batches.

• Stir in recipe mixture and steak. Bring to a boil over high heat. Reduce heat to low and simmer covered 10 minutes or until steak is tender. Serve over rolls.

Makes 6 servings

New York Deli-Style Tuna

Dad's Turkey Dagwood

Mock Guacamole (recipe follows)
16 slices low-calorie whole wheat bread
2 tomatoes, sliced
8 cups shredded iceberg lettuce
2 packages (6 ounces) smoked turkey breast slices
8 slices (1 ounce each) reduced-fat Cheddar cheese
8 tablespoons sweet hot mustard

Prepare Mock Guacamole. Spread 3 tablespoons Mock Guacamole on each of 8 slices bread. Arrange 2 tomato slices, 1 cup lettuce, 2 slices turkey and 1 slice cheese over Mock Guacamole on each bread slice.

Spread 1 tablespoon mustard over each remaining slice of bread and place on top of each to form sandwich. Cut each sandwich in half.   *Makes 8 servings*

*Favorite recipe from **National Turkey Federation***

Mock Guacamole

2 large cloves garlic
2 cups frozen peas, cooked and drained
½ cup fresh cilantro leaves
¼ cup chopped onion
1 tablespoon lemon juice
¼ teaspoon black pepper
⅛ teaspoon hot pepper sauce

Drop garlic cloves through feed tube of food processor fitted with metal blade while motor is running; process 10 seconds. Add peas, cilantro, onion, lemon juice, black pepper and hot pepper sauce; process until smooth. Refrigerate at least 1 hour.

*Favorite recipe from **National Turkey Federation***

Dad's Turkey Dagwood

Spicy Sausage Heroes

Prep Time: 10 minutes
Cook Time: 30 minutes

> 1 pound Italian sausage
> 1 onion, thinly sliced
> 1 green bell pepper, cut into strips
> 2 cloves garlic, chopped
> 1 can (14½ ounces) stewed tomatoes, undrained
> 2 tablespoons *French's*® Hearty Deli Brown Mustard
> 1 tablespoon *French's*® Worcestershire Sauce
> 4 crusty Italian-style rolls, split and toasted
> ½ cup (4 ounces) shredded mozzarella cheese

1. Cook sausage in large nonstick skillet over medium-high heat 20 minutes or until browned and cooked in center. Drain fat. Cut sausage into ½-inch pieces; set aside.

2. Heat *1 tablespoon oil* in same skillet until hot. Cook and stir onion, bell pepper and garlic 5 minutes or until tender. Add tomatoes, mustard and Worcestershire. Return sausage to skillet. Heat to boiling, stirring. Reduce heat to medium-low. Cook 5 minutes or until sauce thickens slightly.

3. Spoon sausage mixture into rolls, dividing evenly. Top with cheese.

Makes 4 servings

Italian Sausage Sandwich

> 1 pound Italian sausage, cut in 1-inch pieces
> 2 green bell peppers, seeded and sliced into lengthwise strips
> 2 cans (8 ounces each) tomato sauce
> ¼ cup dry red wine
> 1 package (1½ ounces) LAWRY'S® Original-Style Spaghetti Sauce Spices & Seasonings
> 1 loaf unsliced French or sourdough bread
> Grated Parmesan cheese

In large skillet, brown sausage. Add peppers when sausage is almost browned and cook over medium-high heat; drain fat. Add tomato sauce, wine and Original-Style Spaghetti Sauce Spices & Seasonings; mix well. Bring to a boil over medium-high heat; cover and simmer 30 minutes, stirring occasionally. To serve, slice bread in ¾-inch slices. Spoon sausage mixture over bread and sprinkle with Parmesan cheese.

Makes 8 servings

Serving Suggestion: For party service, serve sauce in chafing dish with sliced bread and Parmesan cheese in a basket and bowl respectively.

HOMESTYLE MEATS

You'll always be ready for dinner with these family-favorite entrées. Start with your favorite meat and prepare down-home dishes that your family will ask for again and again.

Italian-Style Meat Loaf (page 122)

Three sizes-one quality

Thanks to DEL MONTE, you can now buy canned fruits in sizes of cans to fit your needs and purse—large, medium or small—fruit graded in sizes to fit the container, but all of the same DEL MONTE quality.

In each size can there is a sufficient number of pieces to make a practical, economical service — you to choose the size as economy or occasion dictates.

All have the same splendid flavor, for all are DEL MONTE. Only tree-ripened fruit of highest quality goes under the DEL MONTE label — varying in dimension, but alike in flavor and quality — all packed in the same heavy syrup.

Insist on DEL MONTE—a size to fit your needs. (The cans reproduced here are actual size.)

CALIFORNIA PACKING CORPORATION
San Francisco, California

Number 2½ can—fancy, selected large fruit—ample for the average family even when guests drop in.

Del Monte
BRAND
QUALITY
REG. U.S.   PAT. OFF.
SELECTED LARGE SIZE
CANNED
PACKED IN

Del Monte
BRAND
QUALITY
PAT. OFF.
ECTED MEDIUM SIZE
NNED FRUITS
KED IN HEAVY SYRUP

Del Monte
BRAND
QUALITY
REG. U.S.   PAT. OFF.
SELECTED SMALL SIZE
CANNED FRUITS
PACKED IN HEAVY SYRUP

r 1 can—fancy, se-
ruit, smaller in size,
L MONTE quality—
e thing for small
s.

ND FOR THIS BOOK
Del Monte Recipes
f Flavor" contains
ver 500 simple and
onomical ways to
rve canned fruits
d vegetables Write
r a free copy to
ept. E, California
acking Corporation,
an Francisco, Calif.

Number 2 can—fancy, selected medium-size fruit, same DEL MONTE quality—an economical size for most occasions.

The DEL MONTE shield on canned foods stands for highest quality and finest flavor, insured by a rigid and scientific inspection made possible only through long experience and ceaseless devotion to the DEL MONTE ideal of perfection.

Saturday Evening Post February 5th, 1921.

Italian-Style Meat Loaf

Prep Time: 10 minutes
Cook Time: 75 minutes
Standing Time: 10 minutes

   1 egg
1½ pounds lean ground beef or turkey
   8 ounces hot or mild Italian sausage, casings removed
   1 cup CONTADINA® Seasoned Bread Crumbs
   1 can (8 ounces) CONTADINA® Tomato Sauce, divided
   1 cup finely chopped onion
  ½ cup finely chopped green bell pepper

1. Beat egg lightly in large bowl. Add beef, sausage, bread crumbs, ¾ cup tomato sauce, onion and bell pepper; mix well.

2. Press into *ungreased* 9×5-inch loaf pan. Bake, uncovered, in preheated 350°F oven for 60 minutes.

3. Spoon remaining tomato sauce over meat loaf. Bake 15 minutes longer or until no longer pink in center; drain. Let stand for 10 minutes before serving.

Makes 8 servings

French Beef Stew

Prep Time: 10 minutes
Cook Time: 1 hour

1½ pounds stew beef, cut into 1-inch cubes
  ¼ cup all-purpose flour
   2 tablespoons vegetable oil
   2 cans (14½ ounces each) DEL MONTE® Diced Tomatoes with Garlic & Onion
   1 can (14 ounces) beef broth
   4 medium carrots, peeled and cut into 1-inch chunks
   2 medium potatoes, peeled and cut into 1-inch chunks
  ¾ teaspoon dried thyme, crushed
   2 tablespoons Dijon mustard (optional)

1. Combine meat and flour in large plastic food storage bag; toss to coat evenly.

2. Brown meat in hot oil in 6-quart saucepan. Season with salt and pepper, if desired.

3. Add all remaining ingredients except mustard. Bring to a boil; reduce heat to medium-low. Cover; simmer 1 hour or until beef is tender.

4. Blend in mustard. Garnish and serve with warm crusty French bread, if desired.

Makes 6 to 8 servings

French Beef Stew

Apricot-Glazed Spareribs

6 pounds pork spareribs, cut into 2-rib portions
4 cloves garlic, crushed
Water
1 cup (12-ounce jar) SMUCKER'S® Apricot Preserves
¼ cup chopped onion
¼ cup ketchup
2 tablespoons firmly packed brown sugar
1 tablespoon oil
1 teaspoon ground ginger
1 teaspoon soy sauce
½ teaspoon salt

In very large saucepot or Dutch oven, combine pork spareribs and garlic; cover with water. Over high heat, heat to boiling. Reduce heat to low; cover and simmer 1 hour or until spareribs are fork-tender. Remove ribs to platter; cover and refrigerate.

Meanwhile, prepare apricot glaze. Combine preserves, onion, ketchup, brown sugar, oil, ginger, soy sauce and salt in small saucepan; mix well. Heat to boiling; boil 1 minute. Cover and refrigerate apricot glaze.

About 1 hour before serving, heat grill. When ready to barbecue, place cooked spareribs on grill over medium heat. Cook 12 to 15 minutes or until heated through, turning spareribs often. Brush occasionally with apricot glaze during last 10 minutes of cooking.

Makes 6 servings

Note: The precooked spareribs can be broiled in the oven. Place spareribs on broiler pan; brush with some apricot glaze. Broil about 7 to 9 inches from heat for 7 to 8 minutes, brushing with apricot glaze halfway through cooking time. Turn ribs, brush with apricot glaze and broil for 5 to 6 minutes, brushing with apricot glaze halfway through cooking time.

Citrus Glazed Ham Steak

Prep Time: 5 minutes
Cook Time: 10 minutes

2 fully cooked ham steaks, cut ½ inch thick (about 2 pounds)
⅓ cup *French's*® Hearty Deli Brown Mustard
¼ cup honey or molasses
½ teaspoon grated orange peel

Remove fat from edges of ham steaks with sharp knife. Combine mustard, honey and orange peel in small bowl. Brush on ham. Place ham on grid. Grill over medium-high coals until steaks are glazed and heated through, basting often with mustard mixture. Serve warm.

Makes 4 servings

Campbell's® Beefy Macaroni Skillet

Campbell's® Beefy Macaroni Skillet

Prep Time: 10 minutes
Cook Time: 15 minutes

> 1 pound ground beef
> 1 medium onion, chopped (about ½ cup)
> 1 can (10¾ ounces) CAMPBELL'S® Condensed Tomato Soup
> ¼ cup water
> 1 tablespoon Worcestershire sauce
> ½ cup shredded Cheddar cheese (2 ounces)
> 2 cups cooked corkscrew macaroni (about 1½ cups uncooked)

1. In medium skillet over medium-high heat, cook beef and onion until beef is browned, stirring to separate meat. Pour off fat.

2. Add soup, water, Worcestershire, cheese and macaroni. Reduce heat to low and heat through.

Makes 4 servings

Variation: Substitute 2 cups cooked elbow macaroni (about 1 cup uncooked) for corkscrew macaroni.

Sausages in Beer

> 8 ounces Italian sweet sausage
> 8 ounces Italian hot sausage
> 8 ounces kielbasa
> 8 ounces bockwurst (veal sausage)
> 5 green onions, minced
> 1 cup beer
> 1 tablespoon finely chopped fresh parsley *or* 1 teaspoon dried parsley (optional)
> ½ teaspoon TABASCO® brand Pepper Sauce

Cut sausages into ½-inch pieces with sharp knife. Cook Italian sausages in deep skillet over medium-high heat 3 to 5 minutes or until lightly browned. Drain.

Add remaining sausages and green onions to skillet; cook 5 minutes. Reduce heat to low; add beer, parsley, if desired, and TABASCO® Sauce. Simmer 8 to 10 minutes, stirring every 2 to 3 minutes. Remove from heat and pour into chafing dish. (Sausages may be frozen for future use.)

Makes 8 to 10 servings

Fruited Winter Pork Chops

Prep Time: 25 minutes.
Cook Time: 20 minutes.

> 4 (1-inch-thick) pork chops, trimmed
> ½ cup DOLE® Chopped Dates, divided
> 1 teaspoon vegetable oil
> ⅓ cup finely chopped onion
> ½ cup frozen DOLE® Pineapple Juice concentrate, thawed
> ¼ cup water
> 2 tablespoons white wine vinegar
> 1 tablespoon grated orange peel
> 1 teaspoon dried basil leaves, crushed
> 1 teaspoon chili powder
> 1 teaspoon cornstarch
> 2 large cloves garlic, finely chopped
> 2 cups Fresh DOLE® Pineapple, cut into chunks
> 1 orange, peeled and sliced

• Cut slit in side of each pork chop. Stuff each with 1 tablespoon dates.

• Brown chops in hot oil in large nonstick skillet oil. Stir in remaining dates and onion. Cover, reduce heat to low, cook 10 minutes or until pork is no longer pink in center.

• Stir together frozen concentrate, water, vinegar, orange peel, basil, chili, cornstarch and garlic in small bowl until blended. Stir into skillet. Cook, stirring, until sauce boils and thickens. Add pineapple and orange. Heat through.   *Makes 4 servings*

Campbell's® Shortcut Stroganoff

Prep Time: 5 minutes
Cook Time: 30 minutes

> 1 pound boneless beef sirloin steak, ¾ inch thick
> 1 tablespoon vegetable oil
> 1 can (10¾ ounces) CAMPBELL'S® Condensed Cream of Mushroom Soup *or* 98% Fat Free Cream of Mushroom Soup
> 1 can (10½ ounces) CAMPBELL'S® Condensed Beef Broth
> 1 cup water
> 2 teaspoons Worcestershire sauce
> 3 cups *uncooked* corkscrew pasta
> ½ cup sour cream

1. Slice beef into very thin strips.

2. In medium skillet over medium-high heat, heat oil. Add beef and cook until beef is browned and juices evaporate, stirring often.

3. Add soup, broth, water and Worcestershire. Heat to a boil. Stir in pasta. Reduce heat to medium. Cook 15 minutes or until pasta is done, stirring often. Stir in sour cream. Heat through.
Makes 4 servings

Ham and Cheese Frittata

Preparation Time: 15 minutes
Total Time: 45 minutes

> 3 tablespoons CRISCO® Oil*
> 2 cups frozen shredded potatoes *or* 2 Idaho or Russet potatoes, peeled and shredded
> ¾ teaspoon salt, divided
> ¼ teaspoon freshly ground black pepper
> ½ pound baked ham, cut into ½-inch dice
> 6 eggs
> 3 tablespoons milk
> ¼ teaspoon Italian seasoning
> 1 cup (4 ounces) shredded Cheddar, Swiss or Monterey Jack cheese
> ¾ cup chunky spaghetti sauce, heated

*Use your favorite Crisco Oil product.

1. Heat oven to 350°F.

2. Heat oil in 10- or 12-inch oven-proof skillet on medium heat. Add potatoes. Sprinkle with ½ teaspoon salt and pepper. Cook 8 minutes or until almost brown. Add ham. Cook 2 to 3 minutes more, turning occasionally with spatula.

3. Blend eggs with milk, Italian seasoning and remaining ¼ teaspoon salt while potatoes are cooking. Stir eggs into potatoes.

4. Bake covered at 350°F for 10 minutes. Remove from oven. Stir gently. Smooth top. Sprinkle with cheese. Return to oven. Bake 10 minutes, or until cheese is melted and eggs are set. Cut into 4 wedges. Top with spaghetti sauce.

Makes 4 servings

Carolina Barbecue

> 1 (5-pound) Boston butt roast
> 2 teaspoons vegetable oil
> 1½ cups water
> 1 can (8 ounces) tomato sauce
> ¼ cup packed brown sugar
> ¼ cup cider vinegar
> ¼ cup Worcestershire sauce
> Salt and black pepper to taste
> 1 teaspoon celery seeds
> 1 teaspoon chili powder
> Dash hot pepper sauce

Randomly pierce roast with sharp knife. In Dutch oven, brown roast on all sides in hot oil. In mixing bowl, combine remaining ingredients; mix well. Pour sauce over roast and bring to a boil. Reduce heat; cover and simmer 2 hours or until pork is fork-tender. Baste roast with sauce during cooking time. Slice or chop to serve.

Makes 20 servings

*Favorite recipe from **National Pork Board***

Barbecued Ribs

1 cup ketchup
½ cup GRANDMA'S® Molasses
¼ cup cider vinegar
¼ cup Dijon mustard
2 tablespoons Worcestershire sauce
1 teaspoon garlic powder
1 teaspoon hickory flavor liquid smoke (optional)
¼ teaspoon ground red pepper
¼ teaspoon hot pepper sauce
4 to 6 pounds baby back ribs

1. Prepare grill for direct cooking. While coals are heating, combine all ingredients except ribs in large bowl; mix well. Place ribs on grid over medium-hot coals. Cook ribs 40 to 45 minutes or until they begin to brown; turning occasionally.

2. Once ribs begin to brown, begin basting them with sauce. Continue to cook and baste ribs with sauce an additional 1 to 1½ hours or until tender and cooked through.*

Makes 4 to 6 servings

Do not baste during last 5 minutes of grilling.

tip

For a classic barbecue, serve ribs with lots of coleslaw and baked beans—and lots of napkins.

Family Baked Bean Dinner

1 can (20 ounces) DOLE® Pineapple Chunks
½ DOLE® Green Bell Pepper, julienne-cut
½ cup chopped onion
1 pound Polish sausage or frankfurters, cut into 1-inch chunks
⅓ cup packed brown sugar
1 teaspoon dry mustard
2 cans (16 ounces each) baked beans

Microwave Directions

• Drain pineapple; reserve juice for beverage. Add green pepper and onion to 13×9-inch microwavable dish.

• Cover; microwave on HIGH (100% power) 3 minutes. Add sausage, arranging around edges of dish. Cover; continue microwaving on HIGH 6 minutes.

• In bowl, combine brown sugar and mustard; stir in beans and pineapple. Add to sausage mixture. Stir to combine. Microwave, uncovered, on HIGH 8 to 10 minutes, stirring after 4 minutes.

Makes 6 servings

Barbecued Ribs

Beef Burgundy Stew

1 (1-pound) boneless beef sirloin steak, cut into 1½-inch cubes

3 tablespoons all-purpose flour

6 slices bacon, cut into 1-inch pieces (about ¼ pound)

1 large onion, cut into wedges (about 1½ cups)

3 carrots, peeled, cut into ½-inch pieces (about 1½ cups)

12 small fresh mushrooms

2 cloves garlic, minced

1 cup Burgundy or other dry red wine

½ cup A.1.® Original or A.1.® BOLD & SPICY Steak Sauce

Coat beef with flour, shaking off excess; set aside.

Cook bacon in 6-quart pot over medium heat until crisp; remove with slotted spoon. Set aside.

Brown beef in same pot, a few pieces at a time, in drippings. Return cooked beef and bacon to pot; stir in onion, carrots, mushrooms, garlic, wine and steak sauce. Cover; simmer 40 minutes or until carrots are tender, stirring occasionally. Serve immediately.

Makes 6 servings

Holiday Baked Ham

1 bone-in smoked ham (8½ pounds)

1 can (20 ounces) DOLE® Pineapple Slices

1 cup apricot preserves

1 teaspoon dry mustard

½ teaspoon ground allspice
  Whole cloves
  Maraschino cherries

• Preheat oven to 325°F. Remove rind from ham. Place ham on rack in open roasting pan, fat side up. Insert meat thermometer with bulb in thickest part away from fat or bone. Roast ham in oven about 3 hours.

• Drain pineapple; reserve syrup. In small saucepan, combine syrup, preserves, mustard and allspice. Bring to a boil; continue boiling, stirring occasionally, 10 minutes. Remove ham from oven, but keep oven hot. Stud ham with cloves; brush with glaze. Using wooden picks, secure pineapple and cherries to ham. Brush again with glaze. Return ham to oven. Roast 30 minutes longer or until thermometer registers 160°F (about 25 minutes per pound total cooking time). Brush with glaze 15 minutes before done. Let ham stand 20 minutes before slicing.

Makes 8 to 10 servings

Glazed Pork Chops & Apples

Prep Time: 5 minutes
Cook Time: 13 minutes

4 boneless pork chops, ½ inch thick
½ cup apple juice
¼ cup packed brown sugar
¼ cup *French's*® Hearty Deli Mustard
1 green or red apple, cut into small chunks

1. Heat *1 tablespoon oil* in nonstick skillet over medium-high heat. Cook pork chops for 5 minutes or until browned on both sides.

2. Add remaining ingredients. Bring to a full boil. Reduce heat to medium. Simmer, uncovered, for 8 to 10 minutes or until pork is no longer pink in center and sauce thickens slightly, stirring occasionally.

3. Serve with noodles, if desired.

Makes 4 servings

Glazed Pork Chop & Apples

Crown Roast of Pork with Peach Stuffing

Preparation Time: 45 minutes
Cook Time: 2 hours and 30 minutes
Total Time: 3 hours and 15 minutes

> 1 (7- to 8-pound) crown roast of pork (12 to 16 ribs)
> 1½ cups water
> 1 cup FLEISCHMANN'S® Original Margarine, divided
> 1 (15-ounce) package seasoned bread cubes
> 1 cup chopped celery
> 2 medium onions, chopped
> 1 (16-ounce) can sliced peaches, drained and chopped, liquid reserved
> ½ cup seedless raisins

1. Place crown roast, bone tips up, on rack in shallow roasting pan. Make a ball of foil and press into cavity to hold open. Wrap bone tips in foil. Roast at 325°F, uncovered, for 2 hours; baste with pan drippings occasionally.

2. Heat water and ¾ cup margarine to a boil in large heavy pot; remove from heat. Add bread cubes, tossing lightly with a fork; set aside.

3. Cook and stir celery and onions in remaining margarine in large skillet over medium-high heat until tender, about 5 minutes.

4. Add celery mixture, peaches with liquid and raisins to bread cube mixture, tossing to mix well.

5. Remove foil from center of roast. Spoon stuffing lightly into cavity. Roast 30 to 45 minutes more or until meat thermometer registers 155°F (internal temperature will rise to 160°F upon standing). Cover stuffing with foil, if necessary, to prevent overbrowning. Bake any remaining stuffing in greased, covered casserole during last 30 minutes of roasting.

Makes 12 to 16 servings

America's Favorite Pork Chops

> 4 top loin pork chops
> ¾ cup Italian dressing
> 1 teaspoon Worcestershire sauce

Place all ingredients in self-sealing bag; seal bag and place in refrigerator for at least 20 minutes (or as long as overnight). Remove chops from bag, discarding marinade, and grill over medium-hot heat, turning once, until just done, about 8 to 15 minutes total cooking time (depending upon thickness of chops).

Makes 4 servings

Favorite recipe from **National Pork Board**

Crown Roast of Pork with Peach Stuffing

Rouladen

1 (1½-pound) beef top round
    steak, about 1 inch thick,
    butterflied
1 cup chopped onion
¼ pound sliced OSCAR
    MAYER® Bacon, cooked,
    drained, crumbled
¼ cup all-purpose flour,
    divided
2 tablespoons margarine or
    butter
1 cup beef broth
½ cup A.1.® Original or A.1.®
    BOLD & SPICY Steak
    Sauce
1 cup sliced fresh mushrooms
2 tablespoons water
   Hot cooked egg noodles

1. Open butterflied steak like a book
on a smooth surface and pound to
¼-inch thickness. Slice steak into
4 rectangular pieces of equal size.
Arrange onion and bacon over half
of each piece.

2. Roll up steak pieces from short
edges; secure with wooden
toothpicks or tie with string if
necessary. Coat steak rolls with
3 tablespoons flour, shaking off
excess.

3. Brown steak rolls in margarine in
large skillet, over medium heat. Add
broth and steak sauce. Heat to a
boil; reduce heat. Cover; simmer
40 minutes or until steak is tender,
turning occasionally. Stir in
mushrooms during last 5 minutes.
Remove steak rolls from skillet;
remove toothpicks. Keep warm.

4. Dissolve remaining 1 tablespoon
flour in water; stir into liquid in
skillet. Cook and stir until mixture
thickens and begins to boil. Serve
sauce over steak rolls and noodles.

Makes 4 servings

Campbell's® Autumn Pork Chops

Prep Time: 5 minutes
Cook Time: 25 minutes

1 tablespoon vegetable oil
4 pork chops, ¾ inch thick
    (about 1½ pounds)
1 can (10¾ ounces)
    CAMPBELL'S® Condensed
    Cream of Celery Soup *or*
    98% Fat Free Cream of
    Celery Soup
½ cup apple juice *or* water
2 tablespoons spicy brown
    mustard
1 tablespoon honey
   Generous dash pepper

1. In medium skillet over medium-
high heat, heat oil. Add chops and
cook 10 minutes or until browned.
Set chops aside. Pour off fat.

2. Add soup, apple juice, mustard,
honey and pepper. Heat to a boil.
Return chops to pan. Reduce heat to
low. Cover and cook 10 minutes or
until chops are no longer pink.

Makes 4 servings

Peach-Glazed Virginia Ham

Glazed Ham
- 1 (8-pound) smoked Virginia ham (shank end)
- ½ cup peach preserves
- 1 tablespoon coarse-grained mustard
- ¾ teaspoon TABASCO® brand Pepper Sauce
- ⅛ teaspoon ground cloves

Peach-Corn Piccalilli
- 3 large ripe peaches
- 1 tablespoon vegetable oil
- 1 medium red bell pepper, seeded and diced
- ¼ cup sliced green onions
- 1 (17-ounce) can corn, drained
- 2 tablespoons brown sugar
- 2 tablespoons cider vinegar
- 1 teaspoon TABASCO® brand Pepper Sauce
- ¼ teaspoon salt

Heat oven to 325°F. Remove skin from ham; trim off any excess fat. Score fat ¼ inch deep in 1-inch diamonds. Place ham, fat side up, in roasting pan. Insert meat thermometer into thickest part of ham, not touching the bone. Bake 1½ hours until thermometer reaches 135°F.

Meanwhile, prepare glaze. Mix peach preserves, mustard, TABASCO® Sauce and cloves in small bowl. Remove ham from oven, maintaining oven temperature; brush with peach glaze. Bake 20 minutes longer or until the temperature reaches 160°F.

Meanwhile, prepare Peach-Corn Piccalilli. Cut peaches in half; peel and remove pits. Chop two of the peach halves; set aside. Heat oil in 2-quart saucepan over medium heat. Add red pepper and green onions. Cook 3 minutes, stirring frequently. Add corn, brown sugar, vinegar, TABASCO® Sauce and salt. Heat to boiling; stir in chopped peaches. Reduce heat to low; cover and simmer 5 minutes or until peaches are just tender.

To serve, arrange ham on large platter. Fill remaining peach halves with Peach-Corn Piccalilli and arrange around ham on platter.
Makes 8 to 12 servings

tip

Double the recipe for Peach-Corn Piccalilli and serve with other pork dishes such as grilled pork chops or roasted pork tenderloin.

Contadina® Classic Lasagne

Prep Time: 35 minutes
Cook Time: 30 minutes
Standing Time: 10 minutes

> 1 pound dry lasagne noodles, cooked
> 1 tablespoon olive or vegetable oil
> 1 cup chopped onion
> ½ cup chopped green bell pepper
> 2 cloves garlic, minced
> 1½ pounds lean ground beef
> 2 cans (14.5 ounces each) CONTADINA® Recipe Ready Diced Tomatoes, undrained
> 1 can (8 ounces) CONTADINA® Tomato Sauce
> 1 can (6 ounces) CONTADINA® Tomato Paste
> ½ cup dry red wine or beef broth
> 1½ teaspoons salt
> 1 teaspoon dried oregano leaves
> 1 teaspoon dried basil leaves
> ½ teaspoon ground black pepper
> 1 egg
> 1 cup (8 ounces) ricotta cheese
> 2 cups (8 ounces) shredded mozzarella cheese, divided

1. Cook pasta according to package directions; drain.

2. Meanwhile, heat oil in large skillet. Add onion, bell pepper and garlic; sauté 3 minutes or until vegetables are tender.

3. Add beef; cook 5 to 6 minutes or until evenly browned.

4. Add tomatoes and juice, tomato sauce, tomato paste, wine, salt, oregano, basil and black pepper; bring to a boil. Reduce heat to low; simmer, uncovered, 20 minutes, stirring occasionally.

5. Beat egg slightly in medium bowl. Stir in ricotta cheese and 1 cup mozzarella cheese.

6. Layer noodles, half of meat sauce, noodles, all of ricotta cheese mixture, noodles and remaining meat sauce in *ungreased* 13×9-inch baking dish. Sprinkle with remaining mozzarella cheese.

7. Bake in preheated 350°F oven 25 to 30 minutes or until heated through. Let stand 10 minutes before cutting to serve.

Makes 10 servings

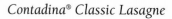

Contadina® Classic Lasagne

Old-Fashioned Beef Stew

1 tablespoon CRISCO® Oil*
1¼ pounds boneless beef round steak, trimmed and cut into 1-inch cubes
2¾ cups water, divided
1 teaspoon Worcestershire sauce
2 bay leaves
1 clove garlic, minced
½ teaspoon paprika
¼ teaspoon black pepper
8 medium carrots, quartered
8 small potatoes, peeled and quartered
4 small onions, quartered
1 package (9 ounces) frozen cut green beans
1 tablespoon cornstarch
Salt (optional)

*Use your favorite Crisco Oil product.

1. Heat oil in Dutch oven on medium-high heat. Add beef. Cook and stir until browned. Add 1½ cups water, Worcestershire sauce, bay leaves, garlic, paprika and pepper. Bring to a boil. Reduce heat to low. Cover. Simmer 1 hour 15 minutes, stirring occasionally. Remove and discard bay leaves.

2. Add carrots, potatoes and onions. Cover. Simmer 30 to 45 minutes or until vegetables are almost tender. Add beans. Simmer 5 minutes or until tender. Remove from heat. Add 1 cup water to Dutch oven.

3. Combine remaining ¼ cup water and cornstarch in small bowl. Stir well. Stir into ingredients in Dutch oven. Return to low heat. Cook and stir until thickened. Season with salt, if desired. *Makes 8 servings*

Campbell's® Savory Pot Roast

Prep Time: 10 minutes
Cook Time: 8 to 9 hours

1 can (10¾ ounces) CAMPBELL'S® Condensed Cream of Mushroom Soup *or* 98% Fat Free Cream of Mushroom Soup
1 pouch CAMPBELL'S® Dry Onion Soup and Recipe Mix
6 medium potatoes, cut into 1-inch pieces (about 6 cups)
6 medium carrots, thickly sliced (about 3 cups)
1 (3½- to 4-pound) boneless chuck pot roast, trimmed

Slow Cooker Directions
In slow cooker, mix soup, soup mix, potatoes and carrots. Add roast and turn to coat. Cover and cook on **low** 8 to 9 hours or until roast and vegetables are done.
Makes 7 to 8 servings

Old-Fashioned Beef Stew

Country Meat Loaf

1 tablespoon vegetable oil
2 stalks celery, minced
1 medium onion, minced
1 large clove garlic, crushed
**1 jar (16 ounces) TABASCO®
    7 Spice Chili Recipe**
1 pound lean ground beef
1 pound ground turkey
1 large egg
½ cup fresh bread crumbs
**1 tablespoon TABASCO® brand
    Pepper Sauce**
1½ teaspoons salt
1½ teaspoons dried thyme leaves
1 teaspoon ground cumin

In 10-inch skillet over medium heat in hot oil, cook celery, onion and garlic until tender, about 5 minutes, stirring occasionally.

Set aside ½ cup TABASCO® 7 Spice Chili Recipe. In large bowl combine remaining chili recipe, ground beef, ground turkey, egg, bread crumbs, TABASCO® Sauce, salt, thyme, cumin and cooked celery mixture until well mixed.

Preheat oven to 350°F. In 12×8-inch baking dish shape mixture into 10×4-inch oval loaf. Brush top with reserved ½ cup TABASCO® 7 Spice Chili Recipe. Bake 1 hour.

Makes 8 servings

Serving Suggestion: Serve meat loaf with roasted new potatoes and vegetables, such as baby carrots, broccoli, cauliflower and green beans.

Country Ham Slices with Golden Sauce

**1 can (20 ounces) DOLE®
    Pineapple Slices**
½ cup packed brown sugar
⅓ cup prepared yellow mustard
2 teaspoons cornstarch
¼ teaspoon ground cloves
**5 slices country ham (½ inch
    thick)**
2 teaspoons margarine

• Drain pineapple slices; reserve juice. Combine reserved juice, brown sugar, mustard, cornstarch and cloves in medium saucepan; stir until blended. Cook, stirring constantly, until sauce boils and thickens. Add pineapple. Heat through.

• Cook ham in margarine. Serve with sauce.   *Makes 5 servings*

Asian Variation: Add 3 tablespoons soy sauce and 1 teaspoon toasted sesame seeds.

Indian Variation: Add 1 teaspoon curry powder.

Southwestern Variation: Add 1 tablespoon chili powder.

Spaghetti Sauce

Spaghetti Sauce

Prep Time: 8 minutes
Cook Time: 35 minutes

    1 pound dry pasta
    1 pound mild Italian sausage, casing removed
    1 cup chopped onion
    1 clove garlic, minced
    ½ cup sliced fresh mushrooms
    1 can (28 ounces) CONTADINA® Recipe Ready Crushed Tomatoes
    1 can (15 ounces) CONTADINA® Tomato Sauce
    ½ teaspoon dried oregano leaves, crushed
    ¼ teaspoon dried basil leaves, crushed

1. Cook pasta according to package directions; drain and keep warm.

2. Meanwhile, brown sausage with onion and garlic in large skillet, stirring to break up sausage. Stir in mushrooms, crushed tomatoes, tomato sauce, oregano and basil.

3. Bring to a boil. Reduce heat to low; simmer, uncovered, for 30 minutes, stirring occasionally. Serve over pasta.

Makes 8 servings

Grilled Bratwurst German Potato Salad

4 medium baking potatoes
1 package BOB EVANS® Bratwurst (approximately 5 links)
1 cup red wine vinegar
½ cup vegetable oil
1 small yellow onion, chopped
2 tablespoons chopped fresh chives
2 teaspoons Dijon mustard
1 clove garlic, minced
½ teaspoon salt
¼ teaspoon freshly cracked black pepper
4 to 5 dashes hot pepper sauce
1 small cucumber, thinly sliced

Prepare grill for medium coals. Cook unpeeled potatoes in 4 quarts boiling water just until tender. Drain, peel and cut into ⅛-inch slices. Place in large bowl. Precook sausage 10 minutes in 2 quarts gently boiling water. Meanwhile, combine vinegar, oil, onion, chives, mustard, garlic, salt, black pepper and hot pepper sauce in small bowl; mix well. Remove bratwurst from water; grill until well browned. Cut bratwurst diagonally into ½-inch slices and add to bowl with potatoes. Pour vinegar mixture over potatoes and bratwurst. Add cucumber; toss gently to mix. Serve warm or cold. Refrigerate leftovers.

Makes 6 to 8 servings

Pork Chops with Apples and Bourbon

4 boneless pork loin chops, cut 1 inch thick, fat trimmed
1 clove garlic, halved lengthwise
Pinch dried sage
2 tablespoons margarine *or* butter
½ teaspoon TABASCO® brand Pepper Sauce
1 teaspoon fresh lemon juice
½ cup chopped onion
1 medium apple (preferably Granny Smith), peeled, cored and diced
⅓ cup bourbon *or* apple cider

Pat pork chops dry with paper towel. Rub both sides of chops with cut sides of garlic. Sprinkle with sage. Combine margarine and TABASCO® Sauce in large skillet over medium-high heat; heat until mixture sizzles. Add chops; cook 12 to 14 minutes, turning once, or until chops are golden brown on both sides and cooked through. Remove from pan; sprinkle with lemon juice and keep warm.

Add onion to skillet; cook and stir over medium heat 1 minute. Stir in apple; cook 1 minute longer. Add bourbon; cook, stirring, 1 minute. Spoon sauce over chops; serve immediately.   *Makes 4 servings*

Grilled Bratwurst German Potato Salad

Stuffed Cabbage Rolls

Prep Time: 15 minutes
Cook Time: 30 minutes

- ¾ **pound lean ground beef**
- ½ **cup chopped onion**
- 1 **cup cooked long grain white rice**
- ¼ **teaspoon ground cinnamon**
  Salt-free herb seasoning (optional)
- 1 **egg white**
- 6 **large cabbage leaves**
- 1 **can (14½ ounces) DEL MONTE® Stewed Tomatoes Original Recipe, No Salt Added**
- 1 **can (15 ounces) DEL MONTE® Tomato Sauce (No Salt Added)**

1. Brown meat and onion in large skillet over medium-high heat; drain. Add rice and cinnamon. Season with salt-free herb seasoning, if desired.

2. Remove from heat; stir in egg white. Pre-cook cabbage leaves 3 minutes in small amount of boiling water; drain. Divide meat mixture among cabbage leaves. Roll cabbage leaves loosely around meat mixture, allowing room for rice to swell. Secure with toothpicks.

3. Combine undrained tomatoes and tomato sauce in 4-quart saucepan; bring to boil. Reduce heat; add cabbage rolls. Simmer, uncovered, 30 minutes.

Makes 6 servings

Holiday Pork Roast

- 1 **tablespoon minced fresh ginger**
- 2 **cloves garlic, minced**
- 1 **teaspoon dried sage leaves, crushed**
- ¼ **teaspoon salt**
- 1 **(5- to 7-pound) pork loin roast**
- ⅓ **cup apple jelly**
- ½ **teaspoon TABASCO® brand Pepper Sauce**
- 2 **medium carrots, sliced**
- 2 **medium onions, sliced**
- 1¾ **cups water, divided**
- 1 **teaspoon browning and seasoning sauce**

Preheat oven to 325°F. Combine ginger, garlic, sage and salt; rub over pork. Place in shallow roasting pan. Roast pork 1½ hours. Remove from oven; score meat in diamond pattern.

Combine jelly and TABASCO® Sauce; spread generously over roast. Arrange carrots and onions around meat; add 1 cup water. Roast 1 hour until meat thermometer registers 170°F. Remove roast to serving platter; keep warm.

Skim fat from drippings in pan; discard fat. Place vegetables and drippings in food processor or blender; process until puréed. Return purée to roasting pan. Stir in remaining ¾ cup water and browning sauce; heat. Serve sauce with roast.   *Makes 6 to 8 servings*

Veal Parmesan

Prep Time: 25 minutes
Cook Time: 12 minutes

- ½ cup CONTADINA® Seasoned Bread Crumbs
- ¼ cup (1 ounce) grated Parmesan cheese
- 1 pound thin veal cutlets
- 1 egg, lightly beaten
- 3 tablespoons olive oil, divided
- 4 ounces mozzarella cheese, thinly sliced
- ¼ cup finely chopped onion
- 1 clove garlic, minced
- 1 can (8 ounces) CONTADINA® Tomato Sauce
- 1 tablespoon chopped fresh oregano *or* 1 teaspoon dried oregano leaves, crushed
- Additional grated Parmesan cheese (optional)

1. Combine bread crumbs and ¼ cup Parmesan cheese in shallow dish. Dip veal into egg; coat with crumb mixture.

2. Heat 2 tablespoons oil in large skillet over medium-high heat. Add veal; cook until golden brown on both sides. Drain on paper towels. Place veal on ovenproof platter; top with mozzarella cheese.

3. Bake in preheated 350°F oven for 5 to 10 minutes or until cheese is melted.

4. Meanwhile, heat remaining oil in medium saucepan. Add onion and garlic; sauté until tender.

5. Stir in tomato sauce and oregano. Bring to a boil. Reduce heat to low; simmer, uncovered, for 5 to 10 minutes or until heated through. Serve sauce over veal. Sprinkle with additional Parmesan cheese, if desired.   *Makes 4 servings*

Barbecued Leg of Lamb

- ⅓ cup A.1.® Steak Sauce
- 2 tablespoons red wine vinegar
- 2 tablespoons vegetable oil
- 1 teaspoon chili powder
- 1 teaspoon dried oregano leaves
- ½ teaspoon coarsely ground black pepper
- ½ teaspoon ground cinnamon
- 2 cloves garlic, crushed
- 1 (5- to 6-pound) leg of lamb, boned, butterflied and trimmed of fat (about 3 pounds after boning)

In small bowl, combine steak sauce, vinegar, oil, chili powder, oregano, pepper, cinnamon and garlic. Place lamb in nonmetal dish; coat with steak sauce mixture. Cover; refrigerate 1 hour, turning occasionally.

Remove lamb from marinade. Grill over medium heat for 25 to 35 minutes or until done, turning often. Cut lamb into thin slices; serve hot.   *Makes 12 servings*

Velveeta® Salsa Mac

Prep Time: 10 minutes
Cook Time: 15 minutes

> 1 pound ground beef
> 1 jar (16 ounces) TACO BELL®
> HOME ORIGINALS®*
> Thick 'N Chunky Salsa
> 1¾ cups water
> 2 cups (8 ounces) elbow
> macaroni, uncooked
> ¾ pound (12 ounces)
> VELVEETA® Pasteurized
> Prepared Cheese Product,
> cut up

TACO BELL and HOME ORIGINALS are registered trademarks owned and licensed by Taco Bell Corp.

1. Brown meat in large skillet; drain.

2. Stir in salsa and water. Bring to boil. Stir in macaroni. Reduce heat to medium-low; cover. Simmer 8 to 10 minutes or until macaroni is tender.

3. Add VELVEETA; stir until melted.
Makes 4 to 6 servings

Variation: For an extra spicy kick in Salsa Mac, try making it with VELVEETA Mild or Hot Mexican Pasteurized Process Cheese Spread with Jalapeño Peppers.

Ham Loaf

Prep Time: 10 minutes
Cook Time: 90 minutes

> 1 pound ground pork
> ½ pound ham, ground
> ¾ cup milk
> ½ cup fresh bread crumbs
> 1 egg
> 1 tablespoon instant tapioca
> ½ teaspoon prepared
> horseradish
> 3 to 4 drops red food color
> (optional)

Sauce
> ½ cup ketchup
> 2 tablespoons packed brown
> sugar
> 1 tablespoon Worcestershire
> sauce

In large bowl, mix together pork, ham, milk, crumbs, egg, tapioca, horseradish and food color until well blended. Place mixture in loaf pan and bake at 325°F for 1 hour. Stir together Sauce ingredients. Pour Sauce over Ham Loaf and bake for another 30 minutes, basting occasionally with Sauce. Remove from oven; let stand 10 minutes before removing from pan. Slice to serve.   *Makes 6 servings*

*Favorite recipe from **National Pork Board***

Velveeta® Salsa Mac

Classic Pepperoni Pizza

1 cup (½ of 15 ounce can) CONTADINA® Original Pizza Sauce
1 (12-inch) prepared, pre-baked pizza crust
1½ cups (6 ounces) shredded mozzarella cheese, divided
1½ ounces sliced pepperoni
1 tablespoon chopped fresh parsley

1. Spread pizza sauce onto crust to within 1 inch of edge.

2. Sprinkle with 1 cup cheese, pepperoni and remaining cheese.

3. Bake according to pizza crust package directions or until crust is crisp and cheese is melted. Sprinkle with parsley.   *Makes 8 servings*

tip

For a crisper crust, bake pizza on a pizza pan that is perforated with small holes or on a pan with a dark surface.

Steak Au Poivre with Dijon Sauce

Prep Time: 10 minutes
Cook Time: 15 minutes

4 beef tenderloin steaks, cut 1½ inches thick (about 1½ pounds)
1 tablespoon *French's®* Worcestershire Sauce
Crushed black peppercorns
⅓ cup *French's®* Dijon Mustard
⅓ cup mayonnaise
3 tablespoons dry red wine
2 tablespoons finely chopped red or green onion
2 tablespoons minced fresh parsley
1 clove garlic, minced

Brush steaks with Worcestershire and sprinkle with pepper to taste; set aside. To prepare Dijon Sauce, combine mustard, mayonnaise, wine, onion, parsley and garlic; mix well.

Place steaks on grid. Grill over hot coals 15 minutes for medium-rare or to desired doneness, turning often. Serve with Dijon Sauce.
      Makes 4 servings

Note: Dijon Sauce is also great with grilled salmon and swordfish. To serve with fish, substitute white wine for the red wine and minced fresh dill for the parsley.

Classic Pepperoni Pizza

Family Swiss Steak and Potatoes

½ cup all-purpose flour
1½ teaspoons salt
½ teaspoon pepper
2½ pounds beef round steak, about 1½ inches thick
2 tablespoons CRISCO® Oil*
2 cups sliced onion
1 can (14½ ounces) whole tomatoes, undrained and cut up
½ cup water
½ teaspoon dried thyme leaves
1 bay leaf
8 medium potatoes, peeled, cut in halves

Use your favorite Crisco Oil product.

1. Combine flour, salt and pepper in shallow dish. Add meat. Coat both sides with flour mixture. Pound flour into meat.

2. Heat oil in large deep skillet or Dutch oven on medium heat. Add meat. Brown on both sides, adding onion during last 2 to 3 minutes.

3. Add tomatoes, water, thyme and bay leaf. Bring to a boil. Reduce heat to low. Cover. Simmer 1 hour 15 minutes. Turn meat over. Add potatoes. Simmer until meat and potatoes are tender.

4. Arrange meat and potatoes on platter. Remove bay leaf from sauce. Pour sauce over meat and potatoes.

Makes 8 servings

Mustard-Glazed Ribs

¾ cup beer
½ cup firmly packed dark brown sugar
½ cup spicy brown mustard
3 tablespoons soy sauce
1 tablespoon catsup
¾ teaspoon TABASCO® brand Pepper Sauce
½ teaspoon ground cloves
4 pounds pork spareribs *or* beef back ribs

Combine beer, sugar, mustard, soy sauce, catsup, TABASCO® Sauce and cloves in medium bowl; mix well. Position grill rack as far from coals as possible. Place ribs on grill over low heat. For pork ribs, grill 45 minutes; turn occasionally. Brush with mustard glaze. Grill 30 minutes longer or until meat is cooked through; turn and baste ribs often with mustard glaze. (For beef back ribs, grill 15 minutes. Brush with mustard glaze. Grill 30 minutes longer or until meat is cooked to desired doneness; turn and baste ribs often with mustard glaze.) Heat any remaining glaze to a boil; serve with ribs.   *Makes 4 servings*

Campbell's® Homestyle Beef Stew

Prep Time: 10 minutes
Cook Time: 2 hours 15 minutes

- **2 tablespoons all-purpose flour**
- **⅛ teaspoon pepper**
- **1 pound beef for stew, cut into 1-inch cubes**
- **1 tablespoon vegetable oil**
- **1 can (10½ ounces) CAMPBELL'S® Condensed Beef Broth**
- **½ cup water**
- **½ teaspoon dried thyme leaves, crushed**
- **1 bay leaf**
- **3 medium carrots (about ½ pound), cut into 1-inch pieces**
- **2 medium potatoes (about ½ pound), cut into quarters**

1. Mix flour and pepper. Coat beef with flour mixture.

2. In Dutch oven over medium-high heat, heat oil. Add beef and cook until browned, stirring often. Set beef aside. Pour off fat.

3. Add broth, water, thyme and bay leaf. Heat to a boil. Return beef to pan. Reduce heat to low. Cover and cook 1½ hours.

4. Add carrots and potatoes. Cover and cook 30 minutes or until beef is fork-tender, stirring occasionally. Discard bay leaf.

Makes 4 servings

Campbell's® Homestyle Beef Stew

Country Ham Omelets

- **2 tablespoons butter or margarine**
- **3 slices HILLSHIRE FARM® Ham, chopped**
- **½ cup finely chopped potato**
- **¼ cup chopped green bell pepper**
- **¼ cup chopped onion**
- **½ cup sliced fresh mushrooms**
- **8 to 12 eggs, beaten**
- **½ cup (2 ounces) shredded sharp Cheddar cheese**

Melt butter in medium skillet over medium heat; sauté Ham, potato, pepper and onion 3 to 4 minutes. Add mushrooms; stir and heat through.

Prepare four 2 or 3 egg omelets. Fill each with 2 tablespoons cheese and ¼ cup ham mixture. Use remaining ham mixture as omelet topping.

Makes 4 to 6 servings

Campbell's® Best Ever Meatloaf

Prep Time: 10 minutes
Cook Time: 1 hour 20 minutes

> 1 can (10¾ ounces)
>   CAMPBELL'S® Condensed
>   Tomato Soup
> 2 pounds ground beef
> 1 pouch CAMPBELL'S®
>   Dry Onion Soup and
>   Recipe Mix
> ½ cup dry bread crumbs
> 1 egg, beaten
> ¼ cup water

1. Mix ½ *cup* tomato soup, beef, onion soup mix, bread crumbs and egg *thoroughly*. In baking pan shape *firmly* into 8×4-inch loaf.

2. Bake at 350°F. for 1¼ hours or until meatloaf is no longer pink (160°F.).

3. In small saucepan mix **2 tablespoons** drippings, remaining tomato soup and water. Heat through. Serve with meatloaf.

Makes 8 servings

Salisbury Steak with Mushroom & Onion Topping

Prep Time: 15 minutes
Cook Time: 25 minutes

> 2 pounds ground beef
> 2⅔ cups *French's*® French Fried
>   Onions, divided
> 1 teaspoon garlic salt
> ½ teaspoon ground black
>   pepper
> 1 tablespoon butter or
>   margarine
> 8 ounces mushrooms, wiped
>   clean and sliced (3 cups)
> 1 jar (12 ounces) brown gravy
> ¼ cup water
> 1 tablespoon *French's*®
>   Worcestershire Sauce

Combine ground beef, 1⅓ cups French Fried Onions, garlic salt and pepper in large bowl. Shape into 6 oval patties.

Heat large nonstick skillet over medium-high heat. Add patties; cook about 20 minutes or until browned on both sides and juices run clear. Transfer to platter; keep warm. Pour off drippings from pan; discard.

Melt butter in same skillet over high heat. Add mushrooms; cook and stir until browned. Stir in gravy, water and Worcestershire. Return patties to skillet. Bring to a boil. Cook until heated through. Sprinkle with remaining 1⅓ cups onions.

Makes 6 servings

Campbell's® Best Ever Meatloaf

Short Ribs Contadina®

Prep Time: 5 minutes
Cook Time: 2 hours 12 minutes

> 2 tablespoons olive or vegetable oil
> 4 pounds beef short ribs
> 1 onion, coarsely chopped
> 1 can (12 ounces) CONTADINA® Italian Paste with Italian Seasonings
> 2⅔ cups water
> ½ teaspoon salt
> ¼ teaspoon ground black pepper
> 2 carrots, peeled, cut into 2-inch pieces

1. Heat oil in large saucepan over medium heat. Add ribs; cook until browned on both sides. Add onion; cook for 1 minute.

2. Combine tomato paste, water, salt and pepper in small bowl. Pour over ribs; cover.

3. Simmer for 1½ hours. Add carrots; simmer, covered, for additional 30 minutes or until ribs are tender.   *Makes 6 servings*

Easy Chili Con Carne

Prep Time: 8 minutes
Microwave Cook Time: 12 minutes

> ½ medium onion, chopped
> 1 stalk celery, sliced
> 1 teaspoon chili powder
> 1 can (15 ounces) kidney beans, drained
> 1 can (14½ ounces) DEL MONTE® Zesty Chili Style Chunky Tomatoes
> 1 cup cooked cubed beef

Microwave Directions

1. Combine onion, celery and chili powder in 2-quart microwavable dish. Add 1 tablespoon water.

2. Cover; microwave on HIGH 3 to 4 minutes. Add beans, tomatoes and beef. Cover; microwave on HIGH 6 to 8 minutes or until heated, stirring halfway through cooking time. For a spicier chili, serve with hot pepper sauce.

Makes 4 servings

Short Rib Contadina®

PRIZED POULTRY

❧

The perfect choice for family and guests, this blue-ribbon selection of chicken and turkey favorites is sure to please. Choose from an endless variety of time-honored classics and elegant roasted specials—they're ideal for any occasion.

Campbell's® Easy Chicken & Biscuits (page 158)

To make a
long story short!

Ten million words
  Boiled down to three,
Brimful of meaning—
  "Campbell's for me."

Soup-making at home has always been a long, long story. But Campbell's have made it a *short* story for you. For almost while dinner is being announced, your soup is ready, and with so little trouble that it's really no trouble at all.

Regardless of the number at your table, the soup appears like magic. Three plates or a dozen, it's just as easy. The greater the number, the greater the convenience. (And Campbell's is so good, so homelike in flavor, that it will be praised as your own.)

Campbell's Soups are twenty-one long stories made short for you. One of them is Campbell's Vegetable Soup. Fifteen garden vegetables, picked at their very best. Rich beef broth—*double* rich—simmered ever so slowly for finest flavor and greatest nourishment. A delicious, hearty soup that's almost a meal in itself.

Serve Campbell's Vegetable Soup tomorrow. See what an appeal it makes the instant it appears. Hear the praises as it *dis*appears. An appetizing soup that would take hours and hours if you had to make it yourself—yet ready in almost a twinkling. So convenient — simply add water, heat for a few minutes, and there you are!

21 kinds to choose from . . Asparagus, Bean, Beef, Bouillon, Celery, Chicken, Chicken-Gumbo, Clam Chowder, Consommé, Julienne, Mock Turtle, Mulligatawny, Mushroom (Cream of), Mutton, Noodle with chicken, Ox Tail, Pea, Pepper Pot, Printanier, Tomato, Vegetable, Vegetable-Beef

Tune in
"HOLLYWOOD HOTEL"
starring
DICK POWELL
Fridays, 9 to 10 P. M. (E.S.T.)
Columbia Network
Coast-to-Coast

Campbell's Vegetable Soup
CONTAINING RICH BEEF BROTH PLUS 15 GARDEN VEGETABLES

Campbell's® Easy Chicken & Biscuits

Prep Time: 15 minutes
Cook Time: 30 minutes

- 1 can (10¾ ounces) CAMPBELL'S® Condensed Cream of Celery Soup *or* 98% Fat Free Cream of Celery Soup
- 1 can (10¾ ounces) CAMPBELL'S® Condensed Cream of Potato Soup
- 1 cup milk
- ¼ teaspoon dried thyme leaves, crushed
- ¼ teaspoon pepper
- 4 cups cooked cut-up vegetables*
- 2 cups cubed cooked chicken, turkey *or* ham
- 1 package (7½ or 10 ounces) refrigerated buttermilk biscuits (10 biscuits)

Use a combination of broccoli flowerets, cauliflower flowerets and sliced carrots or broccoli flowerets and sliced carrots or broccoli flowerets, sliced carrots and peas.

1. In 3-quart shallow baking dish mix soups, milk, thyme, pepper, vegetables and chicken.

2. Bake at 400°F. for 15 minutes or until hot. Stir.

3. Arrange biscuits over chicken mixture. Bake 15 minutes more or until biscuits are golden.

Makes 5 servings

Hint: To microwave vegetables, in 2-quart shallow microwave-safe baking dish arrange vegetables and ¼ cup water. Cover. Microwave on HIGH 10 minutes.

Chicken Salad

- 1 package (4 ounces) sliced almonds
- 2 cups cubed cooked chicken
- 1 package (10 ounces) frozen peas, thawed
- ¾ cup sliced celery
- 1 tablespoon minced onion
- 2 teaspoons lemon juice
- ¾ cup prepared HIDDEN VALLEY® The Original Ranch® Salad Dressing

Toast almonds in 350°F oven until fragrant and lightly browned, 8 to 10 minutes; cool. In large bowl, combine almonds, chicken, peas, celery and onion. Sprinkle with lemon juice. Add salad dressing and toss.   *Makes 4 to 6 servings*

Manhattan Turkey à la King

Manhattan Turkey à la King

Prep Time: 7 minutes
Cook Time: 20 minutes

> 8 ounces wide egg noodles
> 1 pound boneless turkey or chicken, cut into strips
> 1 tablespoon vegetable oil
> 1 can (14½ ounces) DEL MONTE® Diced Tomatoes with Garlic & Onions
> 1 can (10¾ ounces) condensed cream of celery soup
> 1 medium onion, chopped
> 2 stalks celery, sliced
> 1 cup sliced mushrooms

1. Cook noodles according to package directions; drain. In large skillet, brown turkey in oil over medium-high heat. Season with salt and pepper, if desired.

2. Add remaining ingredients, except noodles. Cover and cook over medium heat 5 minutes.

3. Remove cover; cook 5 minutes or until thickened, stirring occasionally. Serve over hot noodles. Garnish with chopped parsley, if desired.

Makes 6 servings

Hint: Cook pasta ahead; rinse and drain. Cover and refrigerate. Just before serving, heat in microwave or dip in boiling water.

Country Chicken Stew with Dumplings

1 tablespoon BERTOLLI® Olive Oil

1 chicken (3 to 3½ pounds), cut into serving pieces (with or without skin)

4 large carrots, cut into 2-inch pieces

3 ribs celery, cut into 1-inch pieces

1 large onion, cut into 1-inch wedges

1 envelope LIPTON® RECIPE SECRETS® Savory Herb with Garlic Soup Mix*

1½ cups water

½ cup apple juice

Parsley Dumplings (optional, recipe follows)

*Also terrific with Lipton® Recipe Secrets® Golden Onion Soup Mix.

In 6-quart Dutch oven or heavy saucepot, heat oil over medium-high heat and brown ½ of the chicken; remove and set aside. Repeat with remaining chicken. Return chicken to Dutch oven. Stir in carrots, celery, onion and savory herb with garlic soup mix blended with water and apple juice. Bring to a boil over high heat. Reduce heat to low and simmer covered 25 minutes or until chicken is done and vegetables are tender.

Meanwhile, prepare Parsley Dumplings. Drop 12 rounded tablespoonfuls of batter into simmering broth around chicken.

Continue simmering covered 10 minutes or until toothpick inserted in center of dumpling comes out clean. Season stew, if desired, with salt and pepper.

Makes about 6 servings

Parsley Dumplings: In medium bowl, combine 1⅓ cups all-purpose flour, 2 teaspoons baking powder, 1 tablespoon chopped fresh parsley and ½ teaspoon salt; set aside. In measuring cup, blend ⅔ cup milk, 2 tablespoons melted butter or margarine and 1 egg. Stir milk mixture into flour mixture just until blended.

Variation: Add 1 pound quartered red potatoes to stew with carrots; eliminate dumplings.

❧ *tip* ❧

For a quick, warm and comforting meal, make chicken stew ahead of time without the dumplings. Cool and refrigerate. When ready to serve, reheat stew and prepare dumplings as directed above.

Country Chicken Stew with Dumplings

Country Chicken and Biscuits

Country Chicken and Biscuits

1 can (10¾ ounces) condensed cream of celery soup

⅓ cup milk or water

4 boneless skinless chicken breast halves, cooked and cut into bite-sized pieces

1 can (14½ ounces) DEL MONTE® Cut Green Beans, drained

1 can (11 ounces) refrigerated biscuits

1. Preheat oven to 375°F.

2. Combine soup and milk in large bowl. Gently stir in chicken and green beans; season with pepper, if desired. Spoon into 11×7-inch microwavable dish.

3. Cover with plastic wrap; slit to vent. Microwave on HIGH 8 to 10 minutes or until heated through, rotating dish once. If using conventional oven, cover with foil and bake at 375°F, 20 to 25 minutes or until hot.

4. Separate biscuit dough into individual biscuits. Immediately arrange biscuits over hot mixture. Bake in conventional oven about 15 minutes or until biscuits are golden brown and baked through.

Makes 4 servings

Franco-American® Mom's Best Gravy

Prep Time: 5 minutes
Cook Time: 5 minutes

> 2 cans (10½ ounces *each*)
>   FRANCO-AMERICAN®
>   Turkey Gravy
> 6 tablespoons turkey pan
>   drippings
> ¼ teaspoon pepper
> ⅛ teaspoon sage
>   Hot mashed potatoes

In small saucepan mix gravy, drippings, pepper and sage. Over medium heat, heat through. Serve over mashed potatoes.

Makes 2½ cups

Mushroom-Herb Gravy: Heat 6 tablespoons turkey drippings in large saucepan. Add 1 cup sliced mushrooms and ¼ teaspoon dried thyme leaves, crushed, and cook until mushrooms are tender. Add 2 cans (10½ ounces *each*) FRANCO-AMERICAN® Turkey Gravy and heat through.

Sautéed Garlic & Onion Gravy: Heat 6 tablespoons turkey drippings in large saucepan. Add 1 cup chopped onion and 2 cloves garlic, minced, and cook until onion is tender. Add 2 cans (10½ ounces *each*) FRANCO-AMERICAN® Turkey Gravy and heat through.

Hint: Didn't roast a turkey? Just substitute 2 tablespoons vegetable oil for the turkey drippings.

Campbell's® Easy Chicken Pot Pie

Prep Time: 5 minutes
Cook Time: 30 minutes

> 1 can (10¾ ounces)
>   CAMPBELL'S® Condensed
>   Cream of Chicken with
>   Herbs Soup
> 1 package (about 9 ounces)
>   frozen mixed vegetables,
>   thawed
> 1 cup cubed cooked chicken *or*
>   turkey
> ½ cup milk
> 1 egg
> 1 cup all-purpose baking mix

1. Preheat oven to 400°F. In 9-inch pie plate mix soup, vegetables and chicken.

2. Mix milk, egg and baking mix. Pour over chicken mixture. Bake 30 minutes or until golden brown.

Makes 4 servings

Campbell's® No Guilt Chicken Pot Pie: Substitute 1 can CAMPBELL'S® Condensed 98% Fat Free Cream of Chicken Soup for Cream of Chicken with Herbs Soup and 1 cup reduced fat baking mix for all-purpose baking mix.

Hint: For 1 cup cubed cooked chicken: In medium saucepan over medium heat, in 3 to 4 cups simmering water, cook ½ pound skinless, boneless chicken breasts 5 minutes or until chicken is no longer pink (170°F).

Campbell's® Chicken & Noodles

Prep/Cook Time: 20 minutes

- 1 tablespoon vegetable oil
- 1 pound boneless chicken breasts, cut up
- 1 can (10¾ ounces) CAMPBELL'S® Cream of Chicken *or* 98% Fat Free Cream of Chicken Soup
- ½ cup milk
- ⅛ teaspoon pepper
- 3 cups cooked medium egg noodles
- ⅓ cup grated Parmesan cheese

HEAT oil in skillet. Add chicken and cook until browned, stirring often.

ADD soup, milk, pepper, noodles and cheese. Heat through.

Makes 4 servings

Barbecued Chicken

2½ to 3-pound broiler-fryer chicken, cut up

Barbecue Sauce
- 1 cup catsup
- ¼ cup GRANDMA'S® Molasses Unsulphured
- ¼ cup cider vinegar
- ¼ cup Dijon mustard
- 2 tablespoons Worcestershire sauce
- 1 teaspoon garlic powder
- 1 teaspoon hickory flavor liquid smoke
- ¼ teaspoon cayenne pepper
- ¼ teaspoon hot pepper sauce

In 12×8-inch (2-quart) microwave-safe baking dish, arrange chicken pieces with thickest portions to outside. In small bowl, combine all sauce ingredients, set aside.

Prepare barbecue grill. Cover chicken with waxed paper. Microwave on HIGH (100%) for 10 minutes. Immediately place chicken on grill over medium heat. Brush with sauce. Cook 20 to 25 minutes or until no longer pink, turning once and brushing frequently with sauce.

Makes 4 to 6 servings

Note: This Barbecue Sauce is equally delicious on ribs.

Campbell's® Chicken & Noodles

Coq au Vin

Prep and Cook Time: 45 minutes

- 4 thin slices bacon, cut into ½-inch pieces
- 6 chicken thighs, skinned
- ¾ teaspoon dried thyme leaves
- 1 large onion, coarsely chopped
- 4 cloves garlic, minced
- ½ pound small red potatoes, cut into quarters
- 10 mushrooms, cut into quarters
- 1 can (14½ ounces) DEL MONTE® Diced Tomatoes with Garlic & Onion
- 1½ cups dry red wine

1. Cook bacon in 4-quart heavy saucepan until just starting to brown. Sprinkle chicken with thyme; season with salt and pepper, if desired.

2. Add chicken to pan; brown over medium-high heat. Add onion and garlic. Cook 2 minutes; drain.

3. Add potatoes, mushrooms, undrained tomatoes and wine. Cook, uncovered, over medium-high heat about 25 minutes or until potatoes are tender and sauce thickens, stirring occasionally. Garnish with chopped parsley, if desired.   *Makes 4 to 6 servings*

Parmigiana Chicken

- 1 jar (26 ounces) BARILLA® Lasagna & Casserole Sauce or Marinara Pasta Sauce
- ¼ teaspoon red pepper flakes
- 8 frozen breaded chicken breast patties (2 packages, 10.5 ounces each), thawed
- 2 cups (8 ounces) shredded mozzarella cheese, divided
- ½ cup (2 ounces) grated Parmesan cheese

1. Preheat oven to 375°F. Spray 13×9×2-inch baking pan with nonstick cooking spray. Combine lasagna sauce and red pepper flakes.

2. Spread 1 cup lasagna sauce over bottom of pan. Arrange chicken patties in single layer over sauce. Top with ½ cup mozzarella, remaining lasagna sauce, Parmesan and remaining 1½ cups mozzarella.

3. Cover with foil and bake 15 minutes. Uncover and continue baking 20 to 30 minutes until chicken is hot and cheese is melted.
Makes 8 servings

Coq au Vin

Chicken Fajitas

4 boneless skinless chicken breast halves
2 teaspoons ground cumin
1½ teaspoons TABASCO® brand Pepper Sauce
1 teaspoon chili powder
½ teaspoon salt
Spicy Tomato Salsa (recipe follows)
Corn Relish (recipe follows)
8 flour tortillas
1 tablespoon vegetable oil
3 large green onions, cut into 2-inch pieces
½ cup shredded Cheddar cheese
½ cup guacamole or sliced avocado
½ cup sour cream

Cut chicken breasts into ½-inch strips. In large bowl toss chicken strips with cumin, TABASCO® Sauce, chili powder and salt; set aside. Prepare Spicy Tomato Salsa and Corn Relish. Wrap tortillas in foil; heat in preheated 350°F oven 10 minutes or until warm. Meanwhile, in large skillet, heat vegetable oil over medium-high heat. Add chicken mixture; cook 4 minutes, stirring frequently. Add green onions; cook 1 minute longer or until chicken is browned and tender.

To serve, arrange warmed tortillas with chicken, Spicy Tomato Salsa, Corn Relish, Cheddar cheese, guacamole and sour cream. To eat, place chicken in center of each tortilla; add Salsa, Relish, cheese, guacamole and sour cream. Fold bottom quarter and both sides of tortilla to cover filling.

Makes 4 servings

Spicy Tomato Salsa

1 large ripe tomato, diced
1 tablespoon chopped cilantro
1 tablespoon lime juice
¼ teaspoon TABASCO® brand Pepper Sauce
¼ teaspoon salt

In medium bowl toss tomato, cilantro, lime juice, TABASCO® Sauce and salt.

Corn Relish

1 can (11 ounces) corn, drained
½ cup diced green bell pepper
1 tablespoon lime juice
¼ teaspoon TABASCO® brand Pepper Sauce
¼ teaspoon salt

In medium bowl toss corn, green pepper, lime juice, TABASCO® Sauce and salt.

Chicken Rosemary

Prep Time: 10 minutes
Cook Time: 20 minutes

> 2 boneless skinless chicken breast halves
> 1 teaspoon margarine
> 1 teaspoon olive oil
>   Salt and pepper
> ½ small onion, sliced
> 1 large clove garlic, minced
> ½ teaspoon dried rosemary
> ⅛ teaspoon ground cinnamon
> ½ cup DOLE® Pineapple Juice
> 1 tablespoon orange marmalade
> 2 cups sliced DOLE® Carrots

Place chicken between 2 pieces of waxed paper or plastic wrap. Pound with flat side of meat mallet or rolling pin to ½-inch thickness. In medium skillet, brown chicken on both sides in margarine and oil. Sprinkle with salt and pepper. Stir in onion, garlic, rosemary and cinnamon. Cook and stir until onion is soft. Blend in juice and marmalade. Spoon over chicken. Cover; simmer 10 minutes. Stir in carrots. Cover; simmer 5 minutes or until carrots are tender-crisp and chicken is no longer pink in center. Garnish as desired.

Makes 2 servings

Chicken Chili

> 1 pound ground chicken
> 1 medium onion, chopped
> ½ cup chopped green bell pepper
> 1 clove garlic, minced
> 2 cans (14 ounces each) diced tomatoes with juice
> 1 can (16 ounces) kidney beans, undrained
> 1 cup water
> 1 can (6 ounces) tomato paste
> 4 teaspoons chili powder
> 1 teaspoon salt
> 1 teaspoon sugar
> 1 teaspoon ground cumin
> ¼ teaspoon ground red pepper

Spray nonstick Dutch oven with nonstick cooking spray; heat over medium-high heat. Add chicken, onion, bell pepper and garlic; cook, stirring, until meat is browned. Add tomatoes with juice, beans, water, tomato paste, chili powder, salt, sugar, cumin and red pepper; stir well. Reduce heat to low; simmer, uncovered, stirring occasionally, about 30 minutes.

Makes 6 servings

*Favorite recipe from **Delmarva Poultry Industry, Inc.***

follows: greens, mushrooms, drained tomatoes, chicken, onion, peas and cucumber.

2. Combine mayonnaise, reserved juice, seasoned salt, tarragon and pepper in small bowl; blend well.

3. Spread mayonnaise mixture over top of salad; cover with plastic wrap. Chill for several hours or overnight.

Makes 6 to 8 servings

Layered Chicken Salad

Layered Chicken Salad

Prep Time: 20 minutes
Chill Time: Several hours or overnight

> 2 cans (14.5 ounces each) CONTADINA® Recipe Ready Diced Tomatoes, undrained
> 4 cups torn salad greens
> 2 cups sliced fresh mushrooms
> 4 cups cubed cooked chicken
> 1 cup sliced red onion
> 1 package (16 ounces) frozen peas, thawed
> ½ cup sliced cucumber
> 1½ cups mayonnaise
> 1 teaspoon seasoned salt
> ¾ teaspoon dried tarragon leaves, crushed
> ⅛ teaspoon ground black pepper

1. Drain tomatoes, reserving 2 tablespoons juice. Layer ingredients in large salad bowl as

Divine Chicken Divan

> 1 package (10 ounces) PERDUE® SHORT CUTS® Fresh Original Roasted Carved Chicken Breast
> 1 can (10¾ ounces) roasted chicken and herb soup
> 1 teaspoon lemon juice
> ⅛ teaspoon ground red pepper or hot pepper sauce
> 2 packages (10 ounces each) frozen broccoli florets in Cheddar cheese sauce
> ½ cup shredded Cheddar cheese
> ¼ cup plain bread crumbs
> 1 tablespoon butter or margarine

Preheat oven to 350°F. In lightly greased 12×9-inch baking dish, combine chicken, soup, lemon juice and red pepper. Break up frozen broccoli mixture and place on top of chicken mixture. Sprinkle with shredded cheese and bread crumbs and dot with butter. Bake 40 to 45 minutes, until hot and bubbly.

Makes 4 to 6 servings

Chicken Parmesan

Chicken Parmesan

Prep and Cook Time: 30 minutes

> **4 boneless skinless chicken breast halves**
> **2 cans (14½ ounces each) DEL MONTE® Italian Recipe Stewed Tomatoes**
> **2 tablespoons cornstarch**
> **½ teaspoon dried oregano or basil, crushed**
> **¼ teaspoon hot pepper sauce (optional)**
> **¼ cup grated Parmesan cheese Hot cooked rice (optional)**

1. Preheat oven to 425°F. Slightly flatten each chicken breast; place in 11×7-inch baking dish.

2. Cover with foil; bake 20 minutes or until chicken is no longer pink. Remove foil; drain.

3. Meanwhile, in large saucepan, combine tomatoes, cornstarch, oregano and pepper sauce, if desired. Stir to dissolve cornstarch. Cook, stirring constantly, until thickened.

4. Pour sauce over chicken; top with cheese.

5. Return to oven; bake, uncovered, 5 minutes or until cheese is melted. Garnish with chopped parsley and serve with rice or pasta, if desired.

Makes 4 servings

Velveeta® Cheesy Chicken & Rice Skillet

Prep Time: 5 minutes
Cook Time: 15 minutes

  1 tablespoon oil
  4 small boneless skinless chicken breast halves (about 1 pound)
  1 can (10¾ ounces) condensed cream of chicken soup
  1 soup can (1⅓ cups) water
  2 cups MINUTE® White Rice, uncooked
  1 package (8 ounces) VELVEETA® Shredded Pasteurized Process Cheese Food, divided

1. Heat oil in large nonstick skillet on medium-high heat. Add chicken; cover. Cook 4 minutes on each side or until cooked through. Remove chicken from skillet.

2. Add soup and water to skillet; stir. Bring to boil.

3. Stir in rice and 1 cup of VELVEETA. Top with chicken. Sprinkle with remaining VELVEETA; cover. Cook on low heat 5 minutes.

Makes 4 servings

Note: Increase oil to 2 tablespoons if using regular skillet.

Quick Cacciatore

  1 package (about 1¾ pounds) PERDUE® Fresh Skinless Chicken Thighs
  Salt and black pepper
  2 tablespoons olive oil
  1 green bell pepper, cut into strips
  1 small onion, chopped
  1 clove garlic, minced
  1 can (14½ ounces) Italian-style stewed tomatoes, undrained
  1 tablespoon dried Italian herb seasoning

Sprinkle chicken lightly with salt and black pepper to taste. In large nonstick skillet over medium-high heat, heat oil. Add chicken; cook 3 to 4 minutes on each side or until browned; remove and set aside. Add bell pepper, onion and garlic. Sauté 2 to 3 minutes or until slightly softened. Stir in tomatoes and Italian seasoning. Return chicken to skillet; reduce heat to medium-low. Cover and simmer 30 to 40 minutes or until chicken is fork-tender and cooked through.

To serve, spoon bell pepper and tomatoes over chicken.

Makes 3 to 4 servings

Velveeta® Cheesy Chicken & Rice Skillet

Pepperidge Farm® Turkey & Stuffing Bake

Prep Time: 15 minutes
Cook Time: 30 minutes

> 1 can (14 ounces) SWANSON®
>   Chicken Broth (1¾ cups)
> Generous dash pepper
> 1 stalk celery, chopped (about
>   ½ cup)
> 1 small onion, coarsely
>   chopped (about ¼ cup)
> 4 cups PEPPERIDGE FARM®
>   Herb Seasoned Stuffing
> 4 servings sliced roasted *or*
>   deli turkey (about
>   12 ounces)
> 1 jar (12 ounces) FRANCO-
>   AMERICAN® Slow Roast™
>   Turkey Gravy

1. In medium saucepan mix broth, pepper, celery and onion. Over high heat, heat to a boil. Reduce heat to low. Cover and cook 5 minutes or until vegetables are tender. Add stuffing. Mix lightly.

2. Spoon into 2-quart shallow baking dish. Arrange turkey over stuffing. Pour gravy over turkey.

3. Bake at 350°F. for 30 minutes or until hot.   *Makes 4 servings*

Variation: Add ½ cup chopped nuts with the stuffing.

Grandma's Chicken Soup

> 8 chicken thighs, skinned, fat
>   trimmed
> 2 carrots, cut into ¼-inch
>   slices
> 2 ribs celery, cut into ¼-inch
>   slices
> 2 medium turnips, peeled and
>   cubed
> 1 large onion, chopped
> 8 cups water
> 1½ teaspoons salt
> ¼ teaspoon pepper
> ¼ teaspoon poultry seasoning
> ⅛ teaspoon dried thyme leaves
> 1 cup wide egg noodles,
>   uncooked

In large saucepan or Dutch oven, layer chicken, carrots, celery, turnips and onion. Add water, salt, pepper, poultry seasoning and thyme. Cook, covered, over medium heat until liquid boils. Reduce heat and simmer about 45 minutes or until chicken and vegetables are fork tender. Remove chicken; cool. Separate meat from bones; discard bones. Cut chicken into bite-size pieces. Heat soup mixture to boiling; stir in noodles. Cook, uncovered, about 5 to 7 minutes or until noodles are done. Stir in chicken.   *Makes 8 servings*

*Favorite recipe from **Delmarva Poultry Industry, Inc.***

*Pepperidge Farm® Turkey
& Stuffing Bake*

Sweet and Spicy Chicken Barbecue

1½ cups DOLE® Pineapple
    Orange Juice
1 cup orange marmalade
⅔ cup teriyaki sauce
½ cup packed brown sugar
½ teaspoon ground cloves
½ teaspoon ground ginger
4 broiler-fryer chickens, halved
    or quartered (about
    2 pounds each)
1 can (20 ounces) DOLE®
    Pineapple Slices, drained

• In saucepan, combine juice, marmalade, teriyaki sauce, brown sugar, cloves and ginger. Heat over medium heat until sugar dissolves; let cool. Sprinkle chicken with salt and pepper. Place chicken in glass baking dish. Pour juice mixture over chicken; turn to coat all sides. Marinate, covered, 2 hours in refrigerator, turning often.

• Preheat oven to 350°F. Drain chicken; reserve marinade. Bake chicken 20 minutes. Arrange chicken on lightly greased grill, 4 to 6 inches above glowing coals. Grill, turning and basting often with reserved marinade, 20 to 25 minutes or until meat near bone is no longer pink. Grill pineapple slices 3 minutes or until heated through. Serve chicken with pineapple.

Makes 8 servings

Greek Chicken

1 package (about 1¼ pounds)
    PERDUE® FIT 'N EASY®
    Fresh Skinless and
    Boneless OVEN STUFFER®
    Roaster Thighs
1½ teaspoons dried oregano
    leaves
Salt and ground pepper
1 tablespoon olive oil
2 cups fresh or frozen green
    beans
1 cup canned artichoke hearts
    packed in water, drained
1 cup frozen pearl onions,
    thawed
1 cup reduced-sodium chicken
    broth
½ cup white wine
1 large clove garlic, minced
1½ teaspoons grated lemon peel
2 cups hot cooked orzo or
    other small pasta

Remove excess fat from thighs. Flatten thighs and sprinkle with seasonings. In nonstick skillet over medium-high heat, heat oil. Add thighs and cook 8 to 10 minutes until browned on both sides, turning once. Stir in remaining ingredients, except orzo; reduce heat to medium-low. Cover and simmer 10 to 15 minutes until chicken is cooked and vegetables are tender-crisp. Serve over orzo.

Makes 5 servings

Campbell's® Chicken Broccoli Divan

Campbell's® Chicken Broccoli Divan

Prep Time: 15 minutes
Cook Time: 25 minutes

- **1 pound fresh broccoli, cut into spears, cooked and drained, *or* 1 package (about 10 ounces) frozen broccoli spears, cooked and drained**
- **1½ cups cubed cooked chicken *or* turkey**
- **1 can (10¾ ounces) CAMPBELL'S® Condensed Broccoli Cheese Soup *or* Cream of Chicken Soup**
- **⅓ cup milk**
- **½ cup shredded Cheddar cheese (2 ounces, optional)**
- **2 tablespoons dry bread crumbs**
- **1 tablespoon margarine *or* butter, melted**

1. In 9-inch pie plate or 2-quart shallow baking dish arrange broccoli and chicken. In small bowl mix soup and milk and pour over broccoli and chicken.

2. Sprinkle cheese over soup mixture. Mix bread crumbs with margarine and sprinkle over cheese.

3. Bake at 400°F. for 25 minutes or until hot. *Makes 4 servings*

❧ *tip* ❧

For a lighter version, substitute 1 can (10¾ ounces) CAMPBELL'S® 98% Fat Free Cream of Chicken Soup.

Velveeta® Grilled Chicken Fajitas

Prep Time: 10 minutes
Grill Time: 20 minutes

> 3 boneless skinless chicken breast halves (about ¾ pound)
> 1 clove garlic, halved
> 1 medium green or red bell pepper, quartered
> ½ red onion, sliced ¼-inch thick
> 1½ cups VELVEETA® Shredded Pasteurized Process Cheese Food
> 6 flour tortillas (6 inch), warmed
>   TACO BELL® HOME ORIGINALS®* Thick 'N Chunky Salsa

TACO BELL and HOME ORIGINALS are registered trademarks owned and licensed by Taco Bell Corp.

1. Rub both sides of chicken with garlic. Place chicken, green pepper and onion slices on greased grill over medium-hot coals.

2. Grill 20 minutes or until cooked through, turning occasionally. Cut chicken and green pepper into thin strips.

3. Spoon chicken mixture and ¼ cup VELVEETA in center of each tortilla; fold. Serve with salsa.

Makes 6 servings

Variation: Cut chicken into strips. Spray skillet with no stick cooking spray. Add chicken and 1 clove garlic, minced; cook and stir on medium-high heat 5 minutes.

Add green pepper, cut into strips, and onion; cook and stir 4 to 5 minutes or until chicken is cooked through and vegetables are tender-crisp. Continue as directed in step 3.

Skillet Roasted Chicken

> 1 PERDUE® Fresh Young Chicken (3½-4½ pounds)
> Salt and ground pepper to taste
> ½ teaspoon paprika
> 1 to 2 tablespoons butter or margarine, softened
> 1 can (10¾ ounces) low-sodium chicken broth
> Juice of ½ lemon (about 2 tablespoons)

Preheat oven to 375°F. Remove giblets from chicken and reserve for another use. Split chicken down backbone and press down on breast to flatten. Place chicken, breast-side up, in large ovenproof skillet or baking pan. Season with salt, pepper and paprika, and dot with butter. Roast, uncovered, 30 minutes, or until chicken begins to brown. Pour in chicken broth and lemon juice. Baste chicken and continue to roast 45 to 60 minutes longer, until skin is a rich, deep brown and juices run clear when thigh is pierced, basting occasionally. A meat thermometer inserted in thickest part of thigh should register 180°F.

Makes 4 servings

Velveeta® Grilled Chicken Fajitas

Spicy Fried Chicken

2 cups buttermilk
2 cloves garlic, crushed
1 tablespoon TABASCO® brand Pepper Sauce
2 (3½-pounds each) chickens, each cut into 8 pieces
2 cups vegetable oil
2 cups flour
2 tablespoons hot paprika
1 teaspoon dried basil
1 teaspoon dried thyme leaves
1 teaspoon black pepper
1 teaspoon salt
½ teaspoon garlic powder

Combine buttermilk, garlic and TABASCO® Sauce in large bowl. Add chicken and toss well to combine. Cover with plastic wrap and refrigerate at least 4 hours or overnight.

Preheat oven to 400°F. Heat oil in large, heavy skillet over medium-high heat until very hot but not smoking. Combine flour, paprika, basil, thyme, black pepper, salt and garlic powder in large paper bag. Remove one third of chicken pieces from marinade, shaking off any excess marinade.

Place chicken pieces in bag and shake to coat. Shake off excess flour and place in skillet. Cook, turning once, until browned, about 10 minutes. (Adjust heat so oil stays hot but not smoking.) Transfer cooked chicken to large baking sheet.

In two batches, repeat browning procedure with remaining chicken and transfer to baking sheet.

Bake chicken just until no longer pink when pierced near bone, 20 to 25 minutes. Transfer to baking sheet lined with paper towels to drain.

Makes 8 servings

Brandy-Orange Barbecued Hens

2 PERDUE® Fresh Cornish Hens (1½ pounds each)
1 tablespoon vegetable oil
2 tablespoons lemon juice, divided
½ teaspoon ground ginger, divided
Salt and pepper
¼ cup orange marmalade
1 tablespoon brandy

Prepare coals for grilling. Rinse hens and pat dry. With kitchen string, tie drumsticks together. Rub outside of hens with oil and 1 tablespoon lemon juice; sprinkle with ¼ teaspoon ginger. Season with salt and pepper.

Combine marmalade, brandy, remaining 1 tablespoon lemon juice and remaining ¼ teaspoon ginger in small bowl; set aside. Place hens, breast side up, on grill. Grill, covered, 5 to 6 inches over medium-hot coals 50 to 60 minutes. Brush hens with brandy-orange sauce after 40 minutes of grilling. Cook until juices run clear when thigh is pierced, basting additional 3 to 4 times. *Makes 2 to 4 servings*

Louisiana Jambalaya

1½ **pounds chicken tenders**
½ **teaspoon salt**
½ **teaspoon ground black pepper**
1 **tablespoon vegetable oil**
¾ **pound smoked turkey sausage, cut into ¼-inch slices**
2 **medium onions, chopped**
1 **large green bell pepper, chopped**
1 **cup chopped celery**
1 **clove garlic, minced**
2 **cups uncooked long grain white rice (not converted)**
¼ to ½ **teaspoon ground red pepper**
2½ **cups chicken broth**
1 **cup sliced green onions**
1 **medium tomato, chopped**
Celery leaves for garnish

Season chicken with salt and black pepper. Heat oil in large saucepan or Dutch oven over high heat until hot. Add chicken, stirring until brown on all sides. Add sausage; cook 2 to 3 minutes. Remove chicken and sausage from saucepan; set aside. Add chopped onions, green pepper, celery and garlic to same saucepan; cook and stir over medium-high heat until crisp-tender. Stir in rice, red pepper, broth and reserved chicken and sausage; bring to a boil. Reduce heat to low; cover and simmer 30 minutes. Stir in green onions and tomato. Garnish with celery leaves. Serve immediately.

Makes 8 servings

Microwave Directions: Season chicken with salt and black pepper. Place oil in deep 3-quart microwavable baking dish. Add chicken; cover with wax paper and cook on HIGH 3 minutes, stirring after 2 minutes. Add sausage; cover with wax paper and cook on HIGH 1 minute. Remove chicken and sausage with slotted spoon; set aside. Add chopped onions, green pepper, celery, and garlic to same dish. Cover and cook on HIGH 4 minutes, stirring after 2 minutes. Stir in rice, red pepper, broth, and reserved chicken and sausage; cover and cook on HIGH 8 minutes or until boiling. Reduce setting to MEDIUM (50% power); cover and cook 30 minutes, stirring after 15 minutes. Stir in green onions and tomato. Let stand 5 minutes before serving. Garnish with celery leaves.

Favorite recipe from **USA Rice Federation**

Louisiana Jambalaya

Campbell's® Turkey Stuffing Divan

Prep Time: 15 minutes
Cook Time: 30 minutes

1¼ cups boiling water
4 tablespoons margarine or butter, melted
4 cups PEPPERIDGE FARM® Herb Seasoned Stuffing
2 cups cooked broccoli cuts
2 cups cubed cooked turkey
1 can (10¾ ounces) CAMPBELL'S® Condensed Cream of Celery Soup *or* 98% Fat Free Cream of Celery Soup
½ cup milk
1 cup shredded Cheddar cheese (4 ounces), divided

1. Mix water and margarine. Add stuffing. Mix lightly.

2. Spoon into 2-quart shallow baking dish. Arrange broccoli and turkey over stuffing. In small bowl mix soup, milk and ½ *cup* cheese. Pour over broccoli and turkey. Sprinkle remaining cheese over soup mixture.

3. Bake at 350°F. for 30 minutes or until hot.   *Makes 6 servings*

Variation: Substitute 1 can (10¾ ounces) CAMPBELL'S® Condensed Cream of Chicken Soup *or* 98% Fat Free Cream of Chicken Soup for Cream of Celery Soup. Substitute 2 cups cubed cooked chicken for turkey.

Hint: For 2 cups cooked broccoli cuts use about 1 pound fresh broccoli, trimmed, cut into 1-inch pieces (about 2 cups) *or* 1 package (10 ounces) frozen broccoli cuts (2 cups).

Grilled Lemon Chicken

4 skinless boneless chicken breast halves (about 1 pound)
¼ cup HEINZ® Worcestershire Sauce
2 tablespoons lemon juice
1 tablespoon olive or vegetable oil
1 clove garlic, minced
½ teaspoon basil leaves
½ teaspoon grated lemon peel
½ teaspoon salt
¼ teaspoon pepper

Lightly flatten chicken breasts to uniform thickness. For marinade, combine Worcestershire sauce and remaining ingredients. Brush chicken generously with marinade. Grill or broil 4 minutes. Turn; brush with marinade. Grill an additional 3 to 4 minutes or until chicken is cooked.   *Makes 4 servings*

Campbell's® Turkey Stuffing Divan

FISH & SEAFOOD TRADITIONS

*Sample specialties of the sea and add
variety to weekly meals with these time-tested recipes.
Serve sensational seafood dishes—a delightful way to make
home-cooked suppers even more special.*

Campbell's® Tuna Noodle Casserole (page 186)

Good starting point for meal plans

Campbell's Tomato Soup is so well liked and so easily served that women call on it again and again.

Wise mothers know Campbell's Tomato Soup makes a bright part of any meal—that its inviting looks and aroma are sure to put an extra keen edge on appetites. They know, too, how everyone likes its delightful flavor—the flavor of specially-luscious tomatoes, enriched with butter, and perked up with delicate seasoning. And Campbell's Tomato Soup is a *healthful* dish, for people of all ages. It's light, and digestible, and soundly nourishing.

For these reasons, Campbell's Tomato Soup has become the most popular soup throughout the nation—the starting point of thousands of meal plans! Do *you* call on it frequently?

Campbell's Tomato Soup

LOOK FOR THE RED-AND-WHITE LABEL

Every weekday... Sunday, too! Campbell's Soups are _good_ for you!

Have _you_ had your soup today?

Campbell's® Tuna Noodle Casserole

Prep Time: 15 minutes
Cook Time: 25 minutes

- 1 can (10¾ ounces) CAMPBELL'S® Condensed Cream of Mushroom Soup *or* 98% Fat Free Cream of Mushroom Soup
- ½ cup milk
- 2 tablespoons chopped pimiento (optional)
- 1 cup cooked peas
- 2 cans (about 6 ounces *each*) tuna, drained and flaked
- 2 cups hot cooked medium egg noodles (about 1 cup uncooked)
- 2 tablespoons dry bread crumbs
- 1 tablespoon margarine *or* butter, melted

1. In 1½-quart casserole mix soup, milk, pimiento, peas, tuna and noodles. Bake at 400°F. for 20 minutes or until hot. Stir.

2. Mix bread crumbs with margarine and sprinkle over noodle mixture. Bake 5 minutes more.

Makes 4 servings

Hint: For a cheesy bread topping, mix ¼ cup shredded Cheddar cheese (about 1 ounce) with bread crumbs and margarine. For a change of taste, substitute 1 can (10¾ ounces) CAMPBELL'S® Condensed Cream of Celery Soup *or* 98% Fat Free Cream of Celery Soup for Cream of Mushroom Soup.

Lemon-Parsley Salmon Steaks

- ½ cup A.1.® Steak Sauce
- ½ cup parsley sprigs, finely chopped
- ¼ cup lemon juice
- ¼ cup finely chopped green onions
- 2 teaspoons sugar
- 2 cloves garlic, minced
- ½ teaspoon ground black pepper
- 4 (6- to 8-ounce) salmon steaks, about 1 inch thick

Blend steak sauce, parsley, lemon juice, onions, sugar, garlic and pepper. Place salmon steaks in glass dish; coat with ½ cup parsley mixture. Cover; refrigerate 1 hour, turning occasionally.

Remove steaks from marinade; discard marinade. Grill for 4 to 6 minutes on each side or until fish flakes easily when tested with fork, brushing often with reserved parsley mixture. *Makes 4 servings*

Lemon-Parsley Salmon Steak

Cioppino

Cioppino

Prep Time: 30 minutes
Cook Time: 35 minutes

  2 tablespoons olive or
      vegetable oil
1½ cups chopped onion
  1 cup chopped celery
  ½ cup chopped green bell
      pepper
  1 large clove garlic, minced
  1 can (28 ounces)
      CONTADINA® Recipe
      Ready Crushed Tomatoes
  1 can (6 ounces) CONTADINA®
      Tomato Paste
  1 teaspoon Italian herb
      seasoning
  1 teaspoon salt
  ½ teaspoon ground black
      pepper
  2 cups water
  1 cup dry red wine or chicken
      broth
  3 pounds white fish, shrimp,
      scallops, cooked crab,
      cooked lobster, clams
      and/or oysters (in any
      proportion)

1. Heat oil in large saucepan. Add onion, celery, bell pepper and garlic; sauté until vegetables are tender. Add tomatoes, tomato paste, Italian seasoning, salt, black pepper, water and wine.

2. Bring to a boil. Reduce heat to low; simmer, uncovered, for 15 minutes.

3. To prepare fish and seafood: scrub clams and oysters under running water. Place in ½-inch boiling water in separate large saucepan; cover. Bring to a boil. Reduce heat to low; simmer just until shells open, about 3 minutes. Set aside.

4. Cut crab, lobster, fish and scallops into bite-size pieces.

5. Shell and devein shrimp. Add fish to tomato mixture; simmer 5 minutes. Add scallops and shrimp; simmer 5 minutes.

6. Add crab, lobster and reserved clams; simmer until heated through.
Makes about 14 cups

✥ *tip* ✥

Cioppino is a tomato-based fish stew and a San Francisco Wharf-side specialty.

Tuna Pot Pie

1 (9-inch) Classic CRISCO® Single Crust (recipe page 294)
1 tablespoon CRISCO® Stick or 1 tablespoon CRISCO® all-vegetable shortening
¼ cup minced onion
3 tablespoons all-purpose flour
¼ teaspoon plus ⅛ teaspoon dried dill weed, divided
¼ teaspoon dried marjoram
¼ teaspoon salt
1½ cups skim milk
1 can (12½ to 13 ounces) solid white tuna in water, drained
1 (16-ounce) package frozen vegetable blend containing cauliflower, carrots, broccoli, green beans and lima beans
½ cup frozen peas
1 egg white, lightly beaten

1. Prepare crust; set aside.

2. In 3-quart saucepan over medium heat, melt shortening. Add onion; cook, stirring often, until tender. Combine flour, ¼ teaspoon dill, marjoram and salt; stir into onion mixture. Cook, stirring often, 1 minute. Stir in milk gradually; cook and stir until mixture thickens. Remove from heat. Break up tuna into bite-size pieces with fork; stir tuna, frozen vegetable blend and peas into mixture in saucepan.

3. Between lightly floured sheets of waxed paper, roll dough "pancake" into rectangle 1 inch larger than inverted 12×7½×1½-inch baking dish. Peel off top sheet.

4. Preheat oven to 400°F. Pour filling into baking dish. Moisten edge of dish with water. Flip crust onto filled dish. Remove waxed paper. Fold edge of pastry under. Flute. Cut slits or design in crust to allow steam to escape.

5. Brush egg white over crust. Sprinkle with ⅛ teaspoon dill. Bake pie 30 to 35 minutes or until crust is golden brown. *Do not overbake.*

Makes 8 servings

Seafood Cocktail Sauce

1 cup HEINZ® Chili Sauce
1 tablespoon prepared horseradish
1 teaspoon lemon juice*
Hot pepper sauce to taste

*One teaspoon HEINZ® Vinegar may be substituted.

Combine all ingredients. Serve with chilled shrimp, seafood, broiled fish or fish sticks.   *Makes about 1 cup*

Seafood Gumbo

1 bag SUCCESS® Rice

1 tablespoon reduced-calorie margarine

¼ cup chopped onion

¼ cup chopped green bell pepper

2 cloves garlic, minced

1 can (28 ounces) whole tomatoes, cut up, undrained

2 cups chicken broth

½ teaspoon ground red pepper

½ teaspoon dried thyme leaves, crushed

½ teaspoon dried basil leaves, crushed

¾ pound white fish, cut into 1-inch pieces

1 package (10 ounces) frozen cut okra, thawed and drained

½ pound shrimp, peeled and deveined

Prepare rice according to package directions. Melt margarine in large saucepan over medium-high heat. Add onion, green pepper and garlic; cook and stir until crisp-tender. Stir in tomatoes with juice, broth, red pepper, thyme and basil. Bring to a boil. Reduce heat to low; simmer, uncovered, until thoroughly heated, 10 to 15 minutes. Stir in fish, okra and shrimp; simmer until fish flakes easily with fork and shrimp curl and turn pink. Add rice; heat thoroughly, stirring occasionally, 5 to 8 minutes.   *Makes 4 servings*

Salmon Fillet with Leeks and Dill

½ cup chopped leeks

½ cup white wine

2 tablespoons chopped fresh dill

1 tablespoon TABASCO® brand Green Pepper Sauce

1 tablespoon lime juice

1 teaspoon salt

1 (2-pound) salmon fillet

Preheat oven to 375°F. Combine leeks, wine, dill, TABASCO® Green Pepper Sauce, lime juice and salt in small bowl.

Place salmon fillet on large piece heavy-duty foil, bringing up edges. Poke holes in salmon fillet with fork. Carefully pour wine mixture over salmon. Completely enclose salmon in foil, crimping foil to seal edges completely. Place in large baking pan; bake 20 to 25 minutes or until fish flakes easily when tested with fork.

Makes 4 to 6 servings

Seafood Gumbo

Biscuit-Topped Tuna Bake

Prep & Cook Time: 25 minutes

- **2 tablespoons vegetable oil**
- **½ cup chopped onion**
- **½ cup chopped celery**
- **1 (7-ounce) pouch of STARKIST® Premium Albacore or Chunk Light Tuna**
- **1 can (10¾ ounces) condensed cream of potato soup**
- **1 package (10 ounces) frozen peas and carrots, thawed**
- **¾ cup milk**
- **¼ teaspoon ground black pepper**
- **¼ teaspoon garlic powder**
- **1 can (7½ ounces) refrigerator flaky biscuits**

In large skillet, heat oil over medium-high heat; sauté onion and celery until onion is soft. Add remaining ingredients except biscuits; heat thoroughly. Transfer mixture to 1½-quart casserole. Arrange biscuits around top edge of dish; bake in 400°F oven 10 to 15 minutes or until biscuits are golden brown.

Makes 4 to 6 servings

Trout Almondine

- **2 tablespoons flour**
- **1½ teaspoons salt, divided**
- **¼ teaspoon pepper**
- **2 pounds trout or fish fillets**
- **6 tablespoons butter or margarine, divided**
- **¼ cup BLUE DIAMOND® Blanched Slivered Almonds**
- **3 tablespoons lemon juice***
- **1 tablespoon chopped parsley**

*If desired, reduce lemon juice to 1 teaspoon and add ¼ cup sherry or sauterne wine.

Mix flour, 1 teaspoon salt and pepper; sprinkle on fish. In skillet, over medium heat, fry fish in 4 tablespoons butter about 6 minutes or until lightly browned. Arrange fish on warmed platter. Add remaining butter to skillet and brown almonds lightly, stirring as needed. Stir in remaining salt, lemon juice and parsley; pour over fish. Serve immediately.

Makes 4 to 6 servings

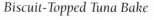

Biscuit-Topped Tuna Bake

Crispy Catfish

Preparation Time: 15 minutes
Total Time: 25 minutes

    4 catfish fillets (about 6 to 8 ounces each)
    ⅓ cup cornmeal
    ⅓ cup all-purpose flour
    1 teaspoon salt
    ½ teaspoon paprika
    ¼ teaspoon onion powder
    ⅛ teaspoon freshly ground black pepper
    1 egg, lightly beaten
    1 tablespoon water
    ½ cup CRISCO® Oil*
    Tartar sauce (optional)

*Use your favorite Crisco Oil product.

1. Rinse fish. Pat dry. Combine cornmeal, flour, salt, paprika, onion powder and pepper on sheet of plastic wrap or waxed paper.

2. Combine egg and water in shallow dish or pie plate. Dip fish in egg mixture. Coat with cornmeal mixture.

3. Heat oil to 365°F in electric skillet or on medium-high heat in large heavy skillet. Fry fish for 5 to 7 minutes on each side or until crisp and browned. Drain on paper towels. Serve with tartar sauce, if desired.   *Makes 4 servings*

Note: Any firm, white-fleshed fish fillet such as flounder, sole or cod can be cooked in the same way. The coating also works well on turkey cutlets or boneless, skinless chicken breasts.

Hint: To keep fried fish warm, place fish on baking sheet lined with paper towels in a 200°F oven.

Baked Fish

    1½ pounds firm-fleshed fish fillets (such as swordfish, tuna or seabass), cut into serving-sized pieces
    ½ cup SMUCKER'S® Plum Preserves
    1 tablespoon soy sauce
    1 teaspoon cornstarch
    ½ teaspoon ginger
    2 cloves garlic, finely minced
    Salt and pepper

Plum Sauce
    ½ cup SMUCKER'S® Plum Preserves
    1 clove garlic, finely minced
    2 teaspoons soy sauce
    ¼ teaspoon pepper

Rinse fish and pat dry. Place in 9-inch baking dish coated with nonstick cooking spray.

Combine preserves, soy sauce, cornstarch, ginger, garlic and salt and pepper. Mix well. Pour over fish. Bake, uncovered, at 350°F for 20 minutes or until the thickest pieces of fish flake with a fork. *Do not overbake.*

Meanwhile, in small saucepan, combine all ingredients for plum sauce and cook over low heat, stirring occasionally for 3 minutes. Serve with fish.   *Makes 4 servings*

Velveeta® Tuna Mac

Velveeta® Tuna Mac

Prep Time: 10 minutes
Cook Time: 15 minutes

   2 cups water
   2 cups (8 ounces) elbow
       macaroni, uncooked
   ¾ pound (12 ounces)
       VELVEETA® Pasteurized
       Prepared Cheese Product,
       cut up
   1 package (16 ounces) frozen
       vegetable blend, thawed,
       drained
   1 can (6 ounces) tuna,
       drained, flaked
   2 tablespoons milk

1. Bring water to boil in saucepan. Stir in macaroni. Reduce heat to medium-low; cover. Simmer 8 to 10 minutes or until macaroni is tender.

2. Add VELVEETA, vegetables, tuna and milk; stir until VELVEETA is melted.   *Makes 4 to 6 servings*

Crawfish (Seafood) Boil

1 gallon water
2 (3-ounce) packages crab boil
⅓ cup salt
¼ cup TABASCO® brand
   Pepper Sauce
1 large lemon, cut into
   quarters
8 medium white onions, peeled
4 artichokes, cut into halves
3 carrots, peeled and cut into
   2-inch pieces
1½ pounds small red potatoes
4 ears corn, cut into 3-inch
   pieces
3 pounds crawfish*
1 pound large shrimp,
   unpeeled
1 pound andouille sausage *or*
   kielbasa, cut into 2-inch
   pieces

Or, substitute other shellfish for crawfish. Cook blue crabs 20 minutes, lobsters 25 minutes per pound or Dungeness crabs 25 to 30 minutes.

Heat water, crab boil, salt, TABASCO® Sauce and lemon to boiling in very large pot with removable wire basket. Add onions, artichokes, carrots and potatoes; heat to boiling. Reduce heat to low; cover and simmer 20 minutes or until vegetables are tender. Remove vegetables from pot; keep warm.

Add corn, crawfish, shrimp and sausage to boiling mixture; bring to boil over high heat. Reduce heat to low; cover and simmer 5 to 8 minutes or until crawfish and shrimp are pink and corn is tender.

Carefully remove corn, seafood and sausage.

To serve, arrange vegetables, seafood and sausage on large platter or place on newspaper or brown paper. Serve with cold beer and French bread.
Makes 8 servings

Note: Crab boil, also called shrimp boil, is a blend of herbs and spices found in the spice section of supermarkets and specialty stores.

A.1.® Grilled Fish Steaks

1 pound salmon steaks or
   other fish steaks, about
   1 inch thick
¼ cup A.1.® Steak Sauce
1 tablespoon margarine or
   butter, melted
½ teaspoon garlic powder

Coat large sheet of aluminum foil with nonstick cooking spray; place fish steaks on foil. In small bowl, combine steak sauce, margarine and garlic powder; spoon over fish. Fold edges of foil together to seal; place seam side up on grill. Grill for about 10 minutes or until fish flakes easily when tested with fork. Carefully remove from grill. Serve immediately.   *Makes 4 servings*

Baked Stuffed Snapper

Baked Stuffed Snapper

1 red snapper (1½ pounds)
2 cups hot cooked rice
1 can (4 ounces) sliced mushrooms, drained
½ cup diced water chestnuts
¼ cup thinly sliced green onions
¼ cup diced pimiento
2 tablespoons chopped parsley
1 tablespoon finely shredded lemon peel
½ teaspoon salt
⅛ teaspoon black pepper
1 tablespoon margarine, melted

Preheat oven to 400°F. Clean and butterfly fish. Combine rice, mushrooms, water chestnuts, onions, pimiento, parsley, lemon peel, salt and pepper; toss lightly. Fill cavity of fish with rice mixture; close with wooden toothpicks soaked in water. Place fish in 13×9-inch baking dish coated with nonstick cooking spray; brush fish with margarine. Bake 18 to 20 minutes or until fish flakes easily when tested with fork. Wrap any remaining rice in foil and bake in oven with fish. *Makes 4 servings*

Favorite recipe from **USA Rice Federation**

Tuna and Broccoli Bake

Prep Time: 35 minutes

- 1 package (16 ounces) frozen broccoli cuts, thawed and well drained
- 2 slices bread, cut in ½-inch cubes
- 1 (7-ounce) pouch of STARKIST® Premium Albacore or Chunk Light Tuna
- 3 eggs
- 2 cups cottage cheese
- 1 cup shredded Cheddar cheese
- ¼ teaspoon ground black pepper

Place broccoli on bottom of 2-quart baking dish. Top with bread cubes and tuna. In medium bowl, combine eggs, cottage cheese, Cheddar cheese and pepper. Spread evenly over tuna mixture. Bake in 400°F oven 30 minutes or until golden brown and puffed.

Makes 4 servings

Shrimp with Pasta

- 1 package fresh angel hair pasta
- 2 tablespoons extra virgin olive oil
- 2 tablespoons chopped onion
- 1 teaspoon chopped garlic
- 12 medium shrimp, peeled and deveined
- 1 cup fish stock *or* bottled clam juice
- ½ cup dry white wine
- 2 tablespoons lemon juice
- 2 teaspoons chopped Italian parsley
- 1 teaspoon chopped fresh basil leaves
- 1 teaspoon Worcestershire sauce
- ½ teaspoon salt
- ½ teaspoon TABASCO® brand Pepper Sauce

Bring large pot of water to a boil and cook pasta according to package instructions. Meanwhile, heat olive oil in sauté pan until very hot. Sauté onion and garlic until lightly browned. Add shrimp and sauté until pink; remove and keep warm.

Add fish stock and white wine to pan. Bring to a boil; add lemon juice, parsley, basil, Worcestershire, salt and TABASCO® Sauce. Return shrimp to pan and simmer about 30 seconds on each side. Remove shrimp and arrange over pasta; pour sauce over shrimp.

Makes 2 servings

Tuna and Broccoli Bake

Salmon en Papillote

Prep Time: 30 minutes
Cook Time: 20 minutes

   ⅔ cup *French's®* Dijon Mustard
   ½ cup (1 stick) butter or
      margarine, melted
   3 cloves garlic, minced
   ¼ cup minced fresh dill weed
      or 1 tablespoon dried
      dill weed
   4 pieces (2 pounds) salmon
      fillet, cut into 4×3×1½-
      inch portions
    Salt
    Ground black pepper
    Vegetable cooking spray
   2 cups very thin vegetable
      strips, such as bell
      peppers, carrots, leek,
      celery or fennel bulb
   2 tablespoons capers, drained

Combine mustard, butter, garlic and dill weed in medium microwave-safe bowl. Cover loosely with vented plastic wrap. Microwave on HIGH 1 minute. Whisk sauce until smooth; set aside.

Sprinkle salmon with salt and black pepper. Cut four 12-inch circles of heavy-duty foil. Coat one side of foil with vegetable cooking spray. Place 1 piece salmon in center of each piece of foil. Spoon about 2 tablespoons mustard sauce over each piece of fish. Reserve remaining sauce. Top fish with vegetables and capers, dividing evenly. Fold foil in half over salmon and vegetables. Seal edges securely with tight double folds.

Place packets on grid. Cook over hot coals 15 to 20 minutes until fish flakes easily with a fork, opening foil packets carefully. Serve with reserved mustard sauce.

Makes 4 servings

Albacore Quiche

Prep Time: 60 minutes

   1 (9-inch) pie shell or
      1 refrigerated (½ of
      15-ounce package) pie
      crust
   1 (3-ounces) pouch of
      STARKIST® Solid White
      Tuna, drained and flaked
   ⅓ cup chopped green onions
   ¾ cup shredded Cheddar or
      Swiss cheese or a
      combination of cheeses
   3 large eggs
  1¼ cups half and half or milk
   ½ teaspoon dried basil or dill
      weed
   ¼ teaspoon ground black
      pepper

Line pie shell with foil; fill with pie weights, dry beans or rice. Bake in 375°F oven 10 minutes. Remove foil and pie weights; place tuna, onions and cheese in pie shell. In medium bowl, combine eggs, half and half and seasonings; pour over pie shell. Continue baking 40 to 50 more minutes or until quiche is set and knife inserted near center comes out clean. Cool slightly before serving.

Makes 6 servings

Barbecued Salmon

4 salmon steaks, ¾ to 1 inch
   thick
3 tablespoons lemon juice
2 tablespoons soy sauce
   Salt and black pepper
½ cup KC MASTERPIECE™
   Original Barbecue Sauce
   Fresh oregano sprigs
   Grilled mushrooms
   (optional)

Rinse salmon; pat dry with paper towels. Combine lemon juice and soy sauce in shallow glass dish. Add salmon; let stand at cool room temperature no more than 15 to 20 minutes, turning salmon several times. Remove salmon from marinade; discard marinade. Season lightly with salt and pepper.

Lightly oil hot grid to prevent sticking. Grill salmon on covered grill over medium KINGSFORD® Briquets 10 to 14 minutes. Halfway through cooking time brush salmon with barbecue sauce, then turn and continue grilling until fish flakes easily when tested with fork. Remove fish from grill; brush with barbecue sauce. Garnish with oregano sprigs and mushrooms.

Makes 4 servings

Bayou Shrimp

1 medium green pepper, cut
   into 1-inch chunks
1 clove garlic, minced
1 tablespoon vegetable oil
1 can (14½ ounces) stewed
   tomatoes
½ cup HEINZ® Chili Sauce
¼ to ½ teaspoon hot pepper
   sauce
1 pound medium-size raw
   shrimp, peeled and
   deveined
   Hot cooked rice (optional)

In large skillet, cook and stir green pepper and garlic in oil 1 minute. Stir in tomatoes, chili sauce and hot pepper sauce; simmer about 4 minutes or until slightly thickened, stirring occasionally. Stir in shrimp; simmer 3 to 4 minutes or until shrimp turn pink and opaque. Serve over rice. *Makes 4 servings*

Barbecued Salmon

Shrimp Scampi

2 tablespoons olive or
vegetable oil
½ cup diced onion
1 large clove garlic, minced
1 small green bell pepper, cut
into strips
1 small yellow bell pepper, cut
into strips
8 ounces medium shrimp,
peeled, deveined
1 can (14.5 ounces)
CONTADINA® Recipe
Ready Diced Tomatoes
with Italian Herbs,
undrained
2 tablespoons chopped fresh
parsley *or* 2 teaspoons
dried parsley flakes
1 tablespoon lemon juice
½ teaspoon salt
Hot cooked orzo pasta
(optional)

1. Heat oil in large skillet over
medium-high heat. Add onion and
garlic; sauté 1 minute.

2. Add bell peppers; sauté
2 minutes. Add shrimp; cook
2 minutes or until shrimp turn pink.

3. Add undrained tomatoes, parsley,
lemon juice and salt; cook 2 to
3 minutes or until heated through.
Serve over hot cooked orzo pasta, if
desired.   *Makes 4 servings*

Halibut with Red Pepper Sauce

1 cup LAWRY'S® Herb &
Garlic Marinade with
Lemon Juice
1 to 1½ pounds halibut fillets,
cut into 4 (1-inch) steaks
Red Pepper Sauce (recipe
follows)

In large resealable plastic food
storage bag, combine Herb & Garlic
Marinade and halibut; seal bag.
Marinate in refrigerator at least
30 minutes. Remove halibut from
marinade; discard used marinade.
Grill or broil halibut 10 minutes or
until fish flakes easily when tested
with fork, turning halfway through
grilling time. Serve with Red Pepper
Sauce.   *Makes 4 servings*

Red Pepper Sauce

2 red bell peppers, roasted,
peeled and seeded
¾ cup fresh bread crumbs
¼ cup fish or chicken broth
2 tablespoons olive oil
1 teaspoon LAWRY'S® Garlic
Powder with Parsley
1 teaspoon LAWRY'S®
Seasoned Salt
½ teaspoon LAWRY'S®
Seasoned Pepper

In blender or food processor,
combine all ingredients. Blend or
process until sauce is smooth.
                Makes about 2 cups

Shrimp Scampi

Homestyle Tuna Pot Pie

Prep & Cook Time: 55 to 60 minutes

> 1 package (15 ounces) refrigerated pie crusts
> 1 (7-ounce) pouch of STARKIST® Premium Albacore or Chunk Light Tuna
> 1 package (10 ounces) frozen peas and carrots, thawed and drained
> 1 can (10¾ ounces) condensed cream of potato or cream of mushroom soup
> ½ cup chopped onion
> ⅓ cup milk
> ½ teaspoon poultry seasoning or dried thyme leaves
> Salt and pepper to taste

Line 9-inch pie pan with one crust; set aside. Reserve second crust. In medium bowl, combine remaining ingredients; mix well. Pour tuna mixture into pie shell; top with second crust. Crimp edges to seal. Cut slits in top crust to vent. Bake in 375°F oven 45 to 50 minutes or until golden brown.

Makes 6 servings

Sole Almondine

> 1 package (6.5 ounces) RICE-A-RONI® Broccoli Au Gratin
> 1 medium zucchini
> 4 sole, scrod or orange roughy fillets
> 1 tablespoon lemon juice
> ¼ cup grated Parmesan cheese, divided
> Salt and pepper (optional)
> ¼ cup sliced almonds
> 2 tablespoons margarine or butter, melted

1. Prepare Rice-A-Roni® Mix as package directs.

2. While Rice-A-Roni® is simmering, cut zucchini lengthwise into 12 thin strips. Heat oven to 350°F.

3. In 11×7-inch glass baking dish, spread prepared rice evenly. Set aside. Sprinkle fish with lemon juice, 2 tablespoons cheese, salt and pepper, if desired. Place zucchini strips over fish; roll up. Place fish seam-side down on rice.

4. Combine almonds and margarine; sprinkle evenly over fish. Top with remaining 2 tablespoons cheese. Bake 20 to 25 minutes or until fish flakes easily with fork.

Makes 4 servings

Homestyle Tuna Pot Pie

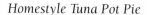

Fillets Stuffed with Crabmeat

- 1 envelope LIPTON® RECIPE SECRETS® Savory Herb with Garlic Soup Mix*
- ½ cup fresh bread crumbs
- 1 package (6 ounces) frozen crabmeat, thawed and well-drained
- ½ cup water
- 2 teaspoons lemon juice
- 4 fish fillets (about 1 pound)
- 1 tablespoon I CAN'T BELIEVE IT'S NOT BUTTER!® Spread, melted

Also terrific with LIPTON® RECIPE SECRETS® Golden Onion Soup Mix.

Preheat oven to 350°F.

In medium bowl, combine soup mix, bread crumbs, crabmeat, water and lemon juice.

Top fillets evenly with crabmeat mixture; roll up and secure with wooden toothpicks. Place in lightly greased 2-quart oblong baking dish. Brush fish with I CAN'T BELIEVE IT'S NOT BUTTER!® Spread and bake 25 minutes or until fish flakes. Remove toothpicks before serving.

Makes 4 servings

Elaine's Tuna Tetrazzini

Prep Time: 20 minutes

- 8 ounces fresh mushrooms, sliced
- 1 cup chopped onion
- 2 tablespoons vegetable oil
- 3 tablespoons all-purpose flour
- 1 cup chicken broth
- ½ cup low-fat milk
- ½ teaspoon paprika
- ½ teaspoon salt
- ¼ teaspoon pepper
- 1 (3-ounce) pouch of STARKIST® Premium Albacore or Chunk Light Tuna
- ¼ cup grated Parmesan or Romano cheese
- 2 tablespoons minced parsley
- 8 ounces thin spaghetti or linguine, broken into halves, hot cooked

In large skillet, sauté mushrooms and onion in oil for 3 minutes or until limp. Sprinkle flour over vegetables; stir until blended. Add chicken broth and milk all at once; cook and stir until mixture thickens and bubbles. Stir in paprika, salt and pepper; cook 2 minutes more. Stir in tuna, cheese and parsley; cook 1 to 2 minutes, or until heated through. Spoon over pasta.

Makes 4 servings

Velveeta®
Tuna & Noodles

Prep Time: 10 minutes
Cook Time: 15 minutes

   2¼ **cups water**
   3 **cups (6 ounces) medium egg noodles, uncooked**
   ¾ **pound (12 ounces) VELVEETA® Pasteurized Prepared Cheese Product, cut up**
   1 **package (16 ounces) frozen vegetable blend, thawed, drained**
   1 **can (6 ounces) tuna, drained, flaked**
   ¼ **teaspoon black pepper**

1. Bring water to boil in saucepan. Stir in noodles. Reduce heat to medium-low; cover. Simmer 8 minutes or until noodles are tender.

2. Add VELVEETA, vegetables, tuna and pepper; stir until VELVEETA is melted.   *Makes 4 to 6 servings*

Hint: When cooking pasta for Tuna & Noodles, you can double the amount you make and save half for a meal later in the week. Thoroughly drain the pasta you're not using, then put it in a bowl of ice water to stop the cooking. Drain thoroughly, then toss with 1 to 2 teaspoons of oil. Store in a zipper-style plastic bag in the refrigerator for up to 3 days.

Velveeta® Tuna & Noodles

Spicy Marinated Shrimp

   1 **green onion, finely chopped**
   2 **tablespoons olive oil**
   2 **tablespoons fresh lemon juice**
   2 **tablespoons prepared horseradish**
   2 **tablespoons ketchup**
   1 **tablespoon finely chopped chives**
   1 **teaspoon TABASCO® brand Pepper Sauce**
   1 **teaspoon Dijon mustard**
   1 **clove garlic, minced**
      Salt to taste
   2 **pounds medium shrimp, cooked, peeled and deveined**

Combine all ingredients except shrimp in large bowl. Add shrimp and toss to coat. Cover and refrigerate 4 to 6 hours or overnight. Transfer shrimp mixture to serving bowl and serve with toothpicks.

Makes 30 to 40 shrimp

SAVORY SIDES

❧

*No meal is complete without a wonderful
dish served on the side. Complement every meal
with tasty vegetables, creamy pastas or savory rice.
Your entrée deserves the very best!*

Country Skillet Hash (page 210)

Country Skillet Hash

Prep Time: 10 minutes
Cook Time: 15 minutes

>   **2 tablespoons butter or margarine**
>   **4 boneless pork chops (¾ inch thick), diced**
>   **¼ teaspoon black pepper**
>   **¼ teaspoon cayenne pepper (optional)**
>   **1 medium onion, chopped**
>   **2 cloves garlic, minced**
>   **1 can (14½ ounces) DEL MONTE® Whole New Potatoes, drained and diced**
>   **1 can (14½ ounces) DEL MONTE® Diced Tomatoes, undrained**
>   **1 medium green bell pepper, chopped**
>   **½ teaspoon thyme, crushed**

1. Melt butter in large skillet over medium heat. Add meat; cook, stirring occasionally, until no longer pink in center. Season with black pepper and cayenne pepper, if desired.

2. Add onion and garlic; cook until tender. Stir in potatoes, tomatoes, green pepper and thyme. Cook 5 minutes, stirring frequently. Season with salt, if desired.

Makes 4 servings

Hint: The hash may be topped with a poached or fried egg.

Vegetables in Garlic Cream Sauce

Prep Time: 10 minutes
Cook Time: 15 minutes

>   **1 cup water**
>   **4 cups cut-up vegetables such as DOLE® Asparagus, Bell Peppers, Broccoli, Carrots, Cauliflower or Sugar Peas**
>   **1 teaspoon olive or vegetable oil**
>   **4 cloves garlic, finely chopped**
>   **⅓ cup fat-free or reduced-fat mayonnaise**
>   **⅓ cup nonfat or low-fat milk**
>   **2 tablespoons chopped fresh parsley**

• Place water in large saucepan; bring to a boil. Add vegetables; reduce heat to low. Cook, uncovered, 9 to 12 minutes or until vegetables are tender-crisp; meanwhile, prepare sauce.

• Heat oil in small saucepan over medium heat. Add garlic; cook and stir garlic until golden brown. Remove from heat; stir in mayonnaise and milk.

• Drain vegetables; place in serving bowl. Pour in garlic sauce; toss to evenly coat. Sprinkle with parsley.

Makes 4 servings

Vegetables in Garlic Cream Sauce

Golden Corn Pudding

Prep Time: 10 minutes
Bake Time: 35 minutes

> 2 tablespoons butter or margarine
> 3 tablespoons all-purpose flour
> 1 can (14¾ ounces) DEL MONTE® Cream Style Golden Sweet Corn
> ¼ cup yellow cornmeal
> 2 eggs, separated
> 1 package (3 ounces) cream cheese, softened
> 1 can (8¾ ounces) DEL MONTE® Whole Kernel Golden Sweet Corn, drained

1. Preheat oven to 350°F.

2. Melt butter in medium saucepan. Add flour and stir until smooth. Blend in cream style corn and cornmeal. Bring to a boil over medium heat, stirring constantly.

3. Place egg yolks in small bowl; stir in ½ cup hot mixture. Pour mixture back into saucepan. Add cream cheese and whole kernel corn.

4. Place egg whites in clean narrow bowl and beat until stiff peaks form. With rubber spatula, gently fold egg whites into corn mixture.

5. Pour mixture into 1½-quart straight-sided baking dish. Bake 30 to 35 minutes or until lightly browned.   *Makes 4 to 6 servings*

Cheesy Mashed Potatoes and Turnips

> 2 pounds all-purpose potatoes, peeled
> 1 pound turnips, peeled
> ¼ cup milk
> ½ cup shredded Cheddar cheese
> ¼ cup butter *or* margarine
> 1 teaspoon TABASCO® brand Pepper Sauce
> ½ teaspoon salt

In large saucepan over high heat, combine potatoes and turnips with enough water to cover. Bring to a boil and reduce heat to low; cover and simmer 25 to 30 minutes or until vegetables are tender. Drain. Return vegetables to saucepan; heat over high heat for a few seconds to eliminate any excess moisture, shaking saucepan to prevent sticking.

In small saucepan over medium heat, bring milk to a simmer. In large bowl, mash vegetables. Stir in warmed milk, cheese, butter, TABASCO® Sauce and salt.

Makes 8 servings

Note: Potatoes may be made up to 2 days in advance and reheated in microwave or double boiler above simmering water.

Red Beans and Rice

Red Beans and Rice

Vegetable cooking spray
½ **cup chopped onion**
½ **cup chopped celery**
½ **cup chopped green bell
    pepper**
2 **cloves garlic, minced**
2 **cans (15 ounces each) red
    beans,* drained**
½ **pound fully-cooked low-fat
    turkey sausage, cut into
    ¼-inch slices**
1 **can (8 ounces) tomato sauce**
1 **teaspoon Worcestershire
    sauce**
¼ **teaspoon ground red pepper**
¼ **teaspoon hot pepper sauce**
3 **cups hot cooked rice**
    Hot pepper sauce (optional)

*Substitute your favorite bean for red beans.

Coat Dutch oven with cooking
spray and place over medium-high
heat until hot. Add onion, celery,
green pepper and garlic. Cook 2 to
3 minutes. Add beans, sausage,
tomato sauce, Worcestershire sauce,
red pepper and pepper sauce.
Reduce heat; cover and simmer
15 minutes. Serve beans with rice
and pepper sauce, if desired.

Makes 6 servings

Favorite recipe from **USA Rice Federation**

Lemon Rice

1 cup uncooked rice*
**1 teaspoon margarine
    (optional)**
1 clove garlic, minced
1 teaspoon grated lemon peel
⅛ to ¼ teaspoon black pepper
2 cups chicken broth
2 tablespoons snipped parsley

*Recipe based on regular-milled long grain white rice.

Combine rice, margarine, garlic, lemon peel, black pepper and broth in 2- to 3-quart saucepan. Bring to a boil; stir once or twice. Reduce heat; cover and simmer 15 minutes or until rice is tender and liquid is absorbed. Stir in parsley.

Makes 6 servings

Favorite recipe from **USA Rice Federation**

❧ *tip* ❧

Before serving, fluff rice with fork. Rice can be cooked up to 1 hour in advance. Remove cover of pan and drape a clean kitchen towel loosely over the pan.

Vegetable & Cheese Platter

Prep Time: 15 minutes
Cook Time: 15 minutes

1 cup water
**2 cups DOLE® Broccoli or
    Cauliflower, cut into
    florets**
**1½ cups DOLE® Peeled Mini
    Carrots**
**1 cup DOLE® Sugar Peas or
    green beans**
**2 medium DOLE® Red, Yellow
    or Green Bell Peppers, cut
    into 2-inch pieces**
**1 package (8 ounces)
    mushrooms, stems
    trimmed**
**3 cups hot cooked brown or
    white rice**
**1 cup (4 ounces) shredded
    low-fat Cheddar cheese**
⅓ cup crumbled feta cheese

• Pour water into large pot; bring to a boil. Add broccoli and carrots. Reduce heat to low; cover and cook 5 minutes. Add sugar peas, bell peppers and mushrooms; cook 5 minutes more or until vegetables are tender-crisp. Drain vegetables.

• Spoon hot rice onto large serving platter; top with vegetables. Sprinkle with cheeses.

• Cover with aluminum foil; let stand 3 minutes or until cheeses melt. *Makes 4 servings*

Lemon Rice

Campbell's® One-Dish Pasta & Vegetables

Prep Time: 15 minutes
Cook Time: 15 minutes

1½ cups *uncooked* corkscrew macaroni
2 medium carrots, sliced (about 1 cup)
1 cup broccoli flowerets
1 can (10¾ ounces) CAMPBELL'S® Condensed Cheddar Cheese Soup
½ cup milk
1 tablespoon prepared mustard

1. In large saucepan prepare macaroni according to package directions. Add carrots and broccoli for last 5 minutes of cooking time. Drain.

2. In same pan mix soup, milk, mustard and macaroni mixture. Over medium heat, heat through, stirring often.   *Makes 5 servings*

Pineapple Sausage Stuffing

Prep Time: 30 minutes
Bake Time: 40 minutes

1 package (12 ounces) pork sausage
1 cup margarine
1½ cups finely chopped celery
1 cup chopped onion
8 cups fresh white bread, torn into small pieces
1½ cups finely chopped DOLE® Fresh Pineapple
1¼ cups chopped pecans, toasted
1 cup dried cranberries
⅓ cup chopped fresh parsley
1 teaspoon dried oregano leaves
1 teaspoon ground sage

• Crumble sausage into large skillet; cook over medium high heat until sausage is completely browned. Drain sausage. Set aside.

• Melt margarine in another skillet. Stir in celery and onion; cook about 10 minutes or until vegetables are tender.

• Stir together bread, sausage, celery mixture, onion, pineapple, pecans, cranberries, parsley, oregano and sage in large bowl. Pour into lightly greased 3-quart casserole; cover.

• Bake at 350°F, 30 to 35 minutes or until heated through. Garnish with fresh sage, if desired. Serve with roasted turkey and peeled mini carrots.   *Makes 16 servings*

Campbell's® One-Dish Pasta & Vegetables

Down Home Macaroni & Cheese

Down Home Macaroni & Cheese

Prep Time: 10 minutes
Bake Time: 20 minutes

    2 tablespoons margarine,
        divided
    ¼ cup flour
    ¼ teaspoon salt
    2 cups fat-free milk
    ¼ pound (4 ounces) VELVEETA
        LIGHT® Pasteurized
        Prepared Cheese Product,
        cut up
    1 package (8 ounces) KRAFT
        FREE® Shredded Non Fat
        Cheddar Cheese, divided
    2 cups (8 ounces) elbow
        macaroni, cooked, drained
    2 tablespoons seasoned dry
        bread crumbs

1. Heat oven to 350°F.

2. Melt 1 tablespoon margarine in saucepan on low heat. Blend in flour and salt; cook and stir 1 minute. Gradually add milk; cook, stirring constantly, until thickened. Add VELVEETA and 1½ cups of the shredded cheese; stir until melted. Stir in macaroni.

3. Pour into 1½-quart casserole. Melt remaining 1 tablespoon margarine; toss with bread crumbs. Sprinkle casserole with remaining ½ cup shredded cheese and bread crumb mixture.

4. Bake 20 minutes or until thoroughly heated.

Makes 6 (1-cup) servings

Candied Pineapple Yams

Prep Time: 90 minutes

> **5 pounds yams or sweet potatoes, washed and pierced with fork**
> **½ cup DOLE® Pineapple Juice**
> **¼ cup margarine, melted**
> **½ teaspoon salt**
> **½ teaspoon pumpkin pie spice**
> **½ cup packed brown sugar**
> **1 container (16 ounces) DOLE® Fresh Pineapple, cut into slices**

• Place yams on foil-lined baking sheet. Bake at 350°F, 90 minutes or until yams are tender when pricked with fork.

• Spoon out baked yams from skins and place into large mixing bowl. Add pineapple juice, margarine, salt and pumpkin pie spice. Beat until fluffy.

• Spoon mixture into lightly greased 13×9-inch baking dish. Sprinkle with brown sugar. Arrange pineapple slices over yams. Continue baking at 350°F, 15 minutes or until hot. Garnish with fresh rosemary, if desired. Serve with roasted pork tenderloin and green peas. *Makes 10 servings*

Eggplant Parmesan

Prep Time: 20 minutes
Cook Time: 30 minutes

> **½ cup olive or vegetable oil**
> **1 medium eggplant (about 1½ pounds), peeled, sliced, divided**
> **1 carton (15 ounces) ricotta cheese, divided**
> **1 can (15 ounces) CONTADINA® Italian-Style Tomato Sauce**
> **1 clove garlic, minced**
> **½ teaspoon dried oregano leaves, crushed**
> **½ cup CONTADINA® Seasoned Bread Crumbs**
> **2 tablespoons grated Parmesan cheese**

1. Heat oil in large skillet. Add eggplant; cook for 2 to 3 minutes on each side or until tender. Remove from oil with slotted spoon. Drain on paper towels.

2. Place half of eggplant slices in greased 12×7½-inch baking dish. Spoon half of ricotta cheese over eggplant.

3. Combine tomato sauce, garlic and oregano in small bowl. Pour half of tomato sauce mixture over ricotta cheese.

4. Combine bread crumbs and Parmesan cheese in separate small bowl; sprinkle half over top of sauce mixture. Repeat layers.

5. Bake in preheated 350°F oven for 30 minutes or until sauce is bubbly. *Makes 6 servings*

Campbell's® Baked Macaroni & Cheese

Prep Time: 20 minutes
Cook Time: 20 minutes

>   1 can (10¾ ounces)
>   CAMPBELL'S® Condensed
>   Cheddar Cheese Soup
>   ½ soup can milk
>   ⅛ teaspoon pepper
>   2 cups hot cooked corkscrew
>   *or* medium shell macaroni
>   (about 1½ cups uncooked)
>   1 tablespoon dry bread crumbs
>   2 teaspoons margarine *or*
>   butter, melted

1. In 1-quart casserole mix soup, milk, pepper and macaroni.

2. Mix bread crumbs with margarine and sprinkle over macaroni mixture.

3. Bake at 400°F. for 20 minutes or until hot.   *Makes 4 servings*

To Double Recipe: Double all ingredients, except increase margarine to 1 tablespoon, use 2-quart casserole and increase baking time to 25 minutes.

Variation: Substitute 2 cups hot cooked elbow macaroni (about 1 cup uncooked) for corkscrew *or* shell macaroni.

Homestead Succotash

Prep & Cook Time for Stove Top: 13 minutes

>   ¼ pound bacon, diced
>   1 cup chopped onion
>   ½ teaspoon dried thyme leaves
>   1 can (15¼ ounces)
>   DEL MONTE® Whole
>   Kernel Golden Sweet Corn,
>   drained
>   1 can (15¼ ounces)
>   DEL MONTE® Green Lima
>   Beans, drained

1. Cook bacon in skillet until crisp; drain. Add onion and thyme; cook until onion is tender.

2. Stir in vegetables and heat through.   *Makes 6 to 8 servings*

Microwave Directions: In shallow 1-quart microwavable dish, cook bacon on HIGH 6 minutes or until crisp; drain. Add onion and thyme; cover and cook on HIGH 2 to 3 minutes or until onion is tender. Add vegetables. Cover and cook on HIGH 3 to 4 minutes or until heated through.

Campbell's® Baked Macaroni & Cheese

Velveeta® Easy Pasta Primavera

Velveeta® Easy Pasta Primavera

Prep Time: 15 minutes
Cook Time: 20 minutes

- **3 cups (8 ounces) rotini, uncooked**
- **2 cups water**
- **1 package (16 ounces) frozen vegetable blend**
- **¾ pound (12 ounces) VELVEETA LIGHT® Pasteurized Prepared Cheese Product, cut up**
- **2 tablespoons reduced fat milk**
- **¼ teaspoon *each* garlic powder and pepper**

1. Bring pasta and water to boil in saucepan; simmer 10 minutes or until pasta is tender.

2. Add vegetables, VELVEETA Light, milk and seasonings. Stir until VELVEETA Light is melted and mixture is thoroughly heated.
Makes 4 to 6 servings

Bayou Dirty Rice

Prep & Cook Time: 40 minutes

- **¼ pound spicy sausage, crumbled**
- **½ medium onion, chopped**
- **1 stalk celery, sliced**
- **1 package (6 ounces) wild and long grain rice seasoned mix**
- **1 can (14½ ounces) DEL MONTE® Original Recipe Stewed Tomatoes**
- **½ green bell pepper, chopped**
- **¼ cup chopped parsley**

1. Brown sausage and onion in large skillet over medium-high heat; drain. Add celery, rice and rice seasoning packet; cook and stir 2 minutes.

2. Drain tomatoes reserving liquid; pour liquid into measuring cup. Add water to measure 1⅓ cups; pour over rice. Add tomatoes; bring to boil. Cover and cook over low heat 20 minutes. Add bell pepper and parsley.

3. Cover and cook 5 minutes or until rice is tender. Serve with roasted chicken or Cornish game hens.   *Makes 4 to 6 servings*

Old-Fashioned Onion Rings

½ cup buttermilk
½ cup prepared Ranch dressing
2 large onions, sliced ½ inch thick and separated into rings
  WESSON® Vegetable or Canola Oil
2 cups self-rising flour
2 teaspoons garlic salt
2 teaspoons lemon pepper
½ teaspoon cayenne pepper
2 eggs, slightly beaten with 2 tablespoons water

In large bowl, combine buttermilk and Ranch dressing; blend well. Add onions and toss until well coated. Cover; refrigerate at least 1 hour or overnight. Fill large deep-fry pot or electric skillet to no more than half its depth with Wesson® Oil. Heat oil between 325°F to 350°F. In large bowl, combine flour, garlic salt, lemon pepper and cayenne pepper; blend well. Working in small batches, place onion rings in flour mixture; coat well. Remove; dip into egg mixture. Return rings to flour mixture; coat well. Lightly shake off excess flour; fry until golden brown. Drain on paper towels. Sprinkle with additional garlic salt, if desired.

Makes 4 servings

Pineapple Wild Rice

Prep Time: 75 minutes

1 cup uncooked brown rice
½ cup uncooked wild rice
¼ cup margarine
2 cups sliced fresh mushrooms
1 cup chopped onion
1 cup finely chopped DOLE® Fresh Pineapple
1 cup finely chopped dried apricots
½ cup toasted pine nuts
1 teaspoon chopped fresh thyme *or* ¼ teaspoon dried thyme leaves

• Cook brown rice and wild rice according to package directions, omitting oils.

• Melt margarine in large skillet. Stir in mushrooms and onion, cooking 10 minutes or until onion is tender.

• Stir pineapple, apricots, pine nuts and thyme into skillet. Stir in rices. Heat through. Serve hot or at room temperature. Garnish with fresh thyme sprig, if desired. Serve with lamb and green beans.

Makes 10 servings

Scalloped Garlic Potatoes

3 medium all-purpose
  potatoes, peeled and thinly
  sliced (about 1½ pounds)
1 envelope LIPTON® RECIPE
  SECRETS® Garlic
  Mushroom Soup Mix*
1 cup (½ pint) whipping or
  heavy cream
½ cup water

*Also terrific with LIPTON® RECIPE SECRETS®
Savory Herb with Garlic Soup Mix.*

1. Preheat oven to 375°F. In lightly
greased 2-quart shallow baking dish,
arrange potatoes. In medium bowl,
blend remaining ingredients; pour
over potatoes.

2. Bake, uncovered, 45 minutes or
until potatoes are tender.

Makes 4 servings

❧ *tip* ❧

*The surface of peeled potatoes
discolors quickly. Use immediately or
cover with water to prevent
discoloration.*

Spanish Rice

4 slices bacon, diced
1 medium green bell pepper,
  diced
1 small onion, chopped
1 large clove garlic, crushed
½ pound ground beef
2 cups canned stewed
  tomatoes, undrained
1 cup long grain rice,
  uncooked
1 cup water
1½ teaspoons TABASCO® brand
  Pepper Sauce
1 teaspoon salt

Cook bacon until crisp in 12-inch
skillet over medium-high heat,
stirring occasionally. With slotted
spoon, remove to paper towels; set
aside. Cook green pepper, onion and
garlic in drippings remaining in
skillet over medium heat until
tender-crisp, about 5 minutes.
Remove to bowl.

Cook ground beef in same skillet
over medium-high heat until well
browned on all sides, stirring
frequently. Drain. Add tomatoes
with their liquid, rice, water,
TABASCO® Sauce, salt and green
pepper mixture. Bring to boil over
high heat; reduce heat to low. Cover
and simmer 20 minutes or until rice
is tender, stirring occasionally.

To serve, sprinkle mixture with
cooked bacon.   *Makes 4 servings*

Scalloped Garlic Potatoes

Festive Green Beans

1 tablespoon olive oil
1 tablespoon butter *or* margarine
3 medium leeks, well rinsed and sliced
2 large red bell peppers, seeded and cut into thin strips
2 pounds green beans, trimmed
1 large clove garlic, minced
1½ teaspoons salt
1 teaspoon TABASCO® brand Pepper Sauce
1 teaspoon grated lemon peel
¼ cup sliced natural almonds, toasted

Heat oil and butter in 12-inch skillet over medium heat; add leeks. Cook 5 minutes, stirring occasionally. Add red peppers; cook 5 minutes longer or until vegetables are tender.

Meanwhile, steam green beans 5 minutes or until crisp-tender. Add beans, garlic, salt, TABASCO® Sauce and lemon peel to skillet; toss to mix well. Sprinkle with toasted almonds.   *Makes 8 servings*

Wild Rice and Dried Fruit Pilaf

2 cups chicken broth
1 cup uncooked California wild rice, rinsed
1 tablespoon butter
1 onion, sliced into thin wedges
2 teaspoons firmly packed brown sugar
¼ cup golden raisins
¼ cup dried cranberries or cherries
¼ cup chopped dried apricots
1 teaspoon grated orange zest
Juice from 1 orange
¼ teaspoon black pepper
2 tablespoons chopped parsley

Combine chicken broth and wild rice in medium saucepan; bring to a boil. Reduce heat, cover and simmer 40 minutes or until almost tender.

Melt butter in small saucepan over low heat; stir in onion and brown sugar. Cook 10 minutes, stirring occasionally, until onion is tender and lightly browned.

Add cooked onions, raisins, cranberries, apricots, orange zest, orange juice and pepper to rice mixture. Cover and simmer 10 minutes or until rice is tender and grains have puffed open. Stir in parsley.   *Makes 6 servings*

*Favorite recipe from **California Wild Rice Advisory Board***

Mallow Topped Sweet Potatoes

Mallow Topped Sweet Potatoes

Preparation Time: 10 minutes
Cook Time: 25 minutes
Total Time: 35 minutes

>   **3 (15-ounce) cans sweet
>   potatoes, drained**
>   **2 tablespoons margarine or
>   butter, melted**
>   **2 tablespoons orange juice**
>   **2 tablespoons packed brown
>   sugar**
>   **1 teaspoon ground cinnamon**
>   **¼ teaspoon ground nutmeg**
>   **3 cups JET-PUFFED®
>   Marshmallows (about 25)**

1. Place sweet potatoes into greased 9×9×2-inch baking pan.

2. Blend margarine, orange juice, brown sugar, cinnamon and nutmeg; pour over potatoes. Bake at 350°F for 15 minutes.

3. Top potatoes with marshmallows. Bake 10 minutes more or until marshmallows are golden brown.

Makes 8 servings

Hint: 10 miniature marshmallows equals 1 large marshmallow;
1 (10-ounce) package contains 40 large marshmallows;
1 (10½-ounce) package contains 5½ cups miniature marshmallows

Oriental Rice Pilaf

½ cup chopped onion
1 clove garlic, minced
1 tablespoon sesame oil
1¾ cups beef broth
1 cup uncooked long grain white rice
1 tablespoon reduced-sodium soy sauce
⅛ to ¼ teaspoon red pepper flakes
⅓ cup thinly sliced green onions
⅓ cup diced red bell pepper
2 tablespoons sesame seeds, toasted

Cook onion and garlic in oil in 2- to 3-quart saucepan over medium heat until onion is tender. Add broth, rice, soy sauce and pepper flakes. Bring to a boil; stir once or twice. Reduce heat; cover and simmer 15 minutes or until rice is tender and liquid is absorbed. Stir green onions, red bell pepper and sesame seeds into cooked rice; cover and let stand 5 minutes. Fluff with fork.

Makes 6 servings

Favorite recipe from **USA Rice Federation**

Italian Eggplant Parmigiana

Prep Time: 15 minutes
Cook Time: 30 minutes

1 large eggplant, sliced ¼ inch thick
2 eggs, beaten
½ cup dry bread crumbs
1 can (14½ ounces) DEL MONTE® Stewed Tomatoes Italian Recipe
1 can (15 ounces) DEL MONTE® Tomato Sauce
2 cloves garlic, minced
½ teaspoon dried basil
6 ounces mozzarella cheese, sliced

1. Dip eggplant slices into eggs, then bread crumbs; arrange in single layer on baking sheet. Broil 4 inches from heat until brown and tender, about 5 minutes per side.

2. *Reduce oven temperature to 350°F.* Place eggplant in 13×9-inch baking dish.

3. Combine tomatoes, tomato sauce, garlic and basil; pour over eggplant and top with cheese.

4. Cover and bake at 350°F, 30 minutes or until heated through. Sprinkle with grated Parmesan cheese, if desired.

Makes 4 servings

Oriental Rice Pilaf

Baked Squash

2 medium-sized acorn squash
2 tart red apples, diced
½ cup chopped nuts
½ cup SMUCKER'S® Apple Jelly
¼ cup butter or margarine, softened

Cut squash in half crosswise or lengthwise; scoop out centers. Place in baking pan. Combine apples, nuts, jelly and butter. Fill squash with mixture. Pour a small amount of boiling water in bottom of pan around squash. Cover pan with foil.

Bake at 400°F for 45 to 60 minutes or until fork-tender. Remove foil during last 5 minutes of baking.

Makes 4 servings

Campbell's® Cheesy Broccoli

Prep/Cook Time: 10 minutes

1 can (10¾ ounces) CAMPBELL'S® Condensed Cheddar Cheese Soup
¼ cup milk
4 cups frozen broccoli cuts

Microwave Directions

1. In 2-quart microwave-safe casserole mix soup and milk. Add broccoli.

2. Cover and microwave on HIGH 8 minutes or until broccoli is tender-crisp, stirring once during heating. *Makes 4 servings*

Pepperidge Farm® Vegetable Stuffing Bake

Prep Time: 15 minutes
Cook Time: 35 minutes

4 cups PEPPERIDGE FARM® Herb Seasoned Stuffing, divided
2 tablespoons margarine *or* butter, melted
1 can (10¾ ounces) CAMPBELL'S® Condensed Cream of Mushroom Soup *or* 98% Fat Free Cream of Mushroom Soup
½ cup sour cream
2 small zucchini, shredded (about 2 cups)
2 medium carrots, shredded (about 1 cup)
1 small onion, finely chopped (about ¼ cup)

1. Mix *1 cup* stuffing and margarine. Set aside.

2. Mix soup, sour cream, zucchini, carrots and onion. Add remaining stuffing. Mix lightly. Spoon into 1½-quart casserole. Sprinkle with reserved stuffing mixture.

3. Bake at 350°F. for 35 minutes or until hot. *Makes 6 servings*

Noodles Stroganoff

- 1 package (12 ounces) BARILLA® Wide or Extra Wide Egg Noodles
- 2 tablespoons butter or margarine
- 2 packages (8 ounces each) sliced mushrooms
- 1 medium onion, chopped
- 1 clove garlic, minced *or* ½ teaspoon bottled minced garlic
- 1½ teaspoons salt
- ½ teaspoon pepper
- 1 pound ground beef
- 1 jar (12 ounces) beef gravy
- 1 container (8 ounces) sour cream
- ⅛ teaspoon paprika

1. Cook noodles according to package directions; drain.

2. Meanwhile, melt butter in large skillet. Add mushrooms, onion, garlic, salt and pepper. Cook over medium heat, stirring occasionally, until mushrooms are lightly browned. Add ground beef and cook until no longer pink, stirring to break up meat.

3. Add gravy and heat to boiling. Remove from heat; stir in sour cream. Serve beef mixture over noodles; sprinkle with paprika.

Makes 8 to 10 servings

Velveeta® Ultimate Macaroni & Cheese

Prep Time: 5 minutes
Cook Time: 15 minutes

- 2 cups (8 ounces) elbow macaroni, uncooked
- 1 pound (16 ounces) VELVEETA® Pasteurized Prepared Cheese Product, cut up
- ½ cup milk
  Dash pepper

1. Cook macaroni as directed on package; drain well. Return to same pan.

2. Add VELVEETA, milk and pepper to same pan. Stir on low heat until VELVEETA is melted. Serve immediately.

Makes 4 to 6 servings

Velveeta® Ultimate Macaroni & Cheese

Velveeta® Twice Baked Ranch Potatoes

Prep Time: 20 minutes plus baking potatoes
Bake Time: 20 minutes

>   4 baking potatoes
> ½ cup KRAFT® Ranch Dressing
> ¼ cup BREAKSTONE'S® or KNUDSEN® Sour Cream
>   1 tablespoon OSCAR MAYER® Real Bacon Bits
> ¼ pound (4 ounces) VELVEETA® Pasteurized Prepared Cheese Product, cut up

1. Bake potatoes at 400°F for 1 hour. Slice off tops of potatoes; scoop out centers, leaving ⅛-inch shell.

2. Mash potatoes. Add dressing, sour cream and bacon bits; beat until fluffy. Stir VELVEETA into potato mixture. Spoon into shells.

3. Bake at 350°F for 20 minutes.

Makes 4 servings

How to Bake Potatoes: Russet potatoes are best for baking. Scrub potatoes well, blot dry and rub the skin with a little oil and salt. Prick the skin of the potatoes with a fork so steam can escape. Stand them on end in a muffin tin. Bake at 400°F for 60 minutes or until tender.

Campbell's® Green Bean Casserole

Prep Time: 10 minutes
Cook Time: 30 minutes

>   1 can (10¾ ounces) CAMPBELL'S® Condensed Cream of Mushroom Soup *or* 98% Fat Free Cream of Mushroom Soup
> ½ cup milk
>   1 teaspoon soy sauce
>   Dash pepper
>   4 cups cooked cut green beans*
>   1 can (2.8 ounces) *French's®* French Fried Onions (1⅓ cups)

*Use 1 bag (16 to 20 ounces) frozen green beans, 2 packages (9 ounces each) frozen green beans, 2 cans (about 16 ounces each) green beans or about 1½ pounds fresh green beans for this recipe.

1. In 1½-quart casserole mix soup, milk, soy sauce, pepper, beans and ½ *can* French Fried Onions.

2. Bake at 350°F. for 25 minutes or until hot.

3. Stir. Sprinkle remaining onions over bean mixture. Bake 5 minutes more or until onions are golden.

Makes 6 servings

Velveeta® Twice Baked Ranch Potatoes

BEST-LOVED CAKES

Kick off any celebration with one of these beloved cakes. Choose a scrumptious layer cake, an old-fashioned pound cake, a moist and delicious pudding cake or a fabulous chocolate cake—all overflow with memorable, made-from-scratch flavor.

German Chocolate Cake (page 236)

HERSHEY'S
Milk Chocolate

A Meal In Itself

MADE IN HERSHEY, PA., "THE CHOCOLATE AND COCOA TOWN"

German Chocolate Cake

¼ cup HERSHEY'S Cocoa
½ cup boiling water
1 cup plus 3 tablespoons
    butter or margarine,
    softened
2¼ cups sugar
1 teaspoon vanilla extract
4 eggs
2 cups all-purpose flour
1 teaspoon baking soda
½ teaspoon salt
1 cup buttermilk or sour milk*
    Coconut Pecan Frosting
    (recipe follows)
    Pecan halves (optional)

To sour milk: Use 1 tablespoon white vinegar plus milk to equal 1 cup.

1. Heat oven to 350°F. Grease and flour three 9-inch round cake pans. Combine cocoa and water in small bowl; stir until smooth. Set aside to cool.

2. Beat butter, sugar and vanilla in large bowl until fluffy. Add eggs, one at a time, beating well after each addition. Stir together flour, baking soda and salt; add alternately with chocolate mixture and buttermilk to butter mixture. Mix until smooth. Pour batter into prepared pans.

3. Bake 25 to 30 minutes or until top springs back when touched lightly. Cool 5 minutes; remove from pans. Cool completely on wire rack. Prepare Coconut Pecan Frosting; spread between layers and over top. Garnish with pecan halves, if desired.   *Makes 10 to 12 servings*

Coconut Pecan Frosting

1 can (14 ounces) sweetened
    condensed milk
3 egg yolks, slightly beaten
½ cup butter or margarine
1 teaspoon vanilla extract
1⅓ cups MOUNDS® Sweetened
    Coconut Flakes
1 cup chopped pecans

1. Place sweetened condensed milk, egg yolks and butter in medium saucepan. Cook over low heat, stirring constantly, until mixture is thickened and bubbly.

2. Remove from heat; stir in vanilla, coconut and pecans. Cool to room temperature.
   Makes about 2⅔ cups frosting

tip

To make sure that a cake rises properly, do not open the oven during the first half of the baking time. Cold air interferes with the rising of the cake.

Chocolate Icebox Cake

18 ladyfingers, split
1 envelope unflavored gelatin
2 tablespoons sugar, divided
¼ teaspoon salt
2 eggs, separated
1 cup milk
1 cup (12-ounce jar) SMUCKER'S® Chocolate Fudge Topping
½ teaspoon vanilla
1 cup heavy or whipping cream, whipped

Line 9×5-inch loaf pan with 2 crossed strips of waxed paper, extending paper beyond rim. Line bottom and sides with 18 ladyfinger halves, cut sides up; set aside.

In medium saucepan, mix gelatin, 1 tablespoon of the sugar and salt. Beat together egg yolks, milk and fudge topping; stir into gelatin mixture.

Cook over low heat, stirring constantly, until gelatin dissolves, about 6 to 8 minutes. Remove from heat; stir in vanilla. Chill, stirring occasionally, until mixture mounds slightly when dropped from a spoon.

Beat egg whites until stiff but not dry; add remaining 1 tablespoon sugar and beat until very stiff. Fold ¼ of egg whites into chocolate mixture, then gently fold in whipped cream and remaining egg whites. Pour half of mixture into prepared pan; add layer of 9 ladyfinger halves, then remaining chocolate mixture. Top with remaining 9 ladyfinger halves, cut side down. Chill until firm, at least 4 hours or overnight.

To serve, using waxed paper, lift cake from pan and transfer to serving plate; gently remove waxed paper. Garnish top with additional chocolate fudge topping, if desired.

Makes 8 to 10 servings

Variation: For Chocolate Fudge Pie, substitute one 9-inch baked pastry or crumb crust for ladyfingers. Pour chocolate mixture into prepared pie shell. Chill until firm. Garnish with additional whipped cream and chocolate fudge topping.

Choca-Cola Cake

Cake

  1¾ cups granulated sugar

  ¾ cup CRISCO® Stick or ¾ cup CRISCO® all-vegetable shortening

  2 eggs

  2 tablespoons cocoa

  1 tablespoon vanilla

  ¼ teaspoon salt

  ½ cup buttermilk or sour milk*

  1 teaspoon baking soda

  2½ cups all-purpose flour

  1 cup cola soft drink (not sugar-free)

Frosting

  1 box (1 pound) confectioners' sugar (3½ to 4 cups)

  6 tablespoons or more cola soft drink (not sugar-free)

  ¼ cup cocoa

  ¼ cup CRISCO® Stick or ¼ cup CRISCO® all-vegetable shortening

  1 cup chopped pecans, divided

To sour milk: Combine 1½ teaspoons white vinegar plus enough milk to equal ½ cup. Stir. Wait 5 minutes before using.

1. Heat oven to 350°F. Line bottom of 13×9×2-inch baking pan with waxed paper.

2. For cake, combine granulated sugar and shortening in large bowl. Beat at medium speed of electric mixer 1 minute. Add eggs. Beat until blended. Add 2 tablespoons cocoa, vanilla and salt. Beat until blended.

3. Combine buttermilk and baking soda in small bowl. Add to creamed mixture. Beat until blended. Reduce speed to low. Add flour alternately with 1 cup cola, beginning and ending with flour, beating at low speed after each addition until well blended. Pour into pan.

4. Bake at 350°F for 30 to 35 minutes or until cake begins to pull away from sides of pan. *Do not overbake.* Cool 10 minutes before removing from pan. Invert cake on wire rack. Remove waxed paper. Cool completely. Place cake on serving tray.

5. For frosting, combine confectioners' sugar, 6 tablespoons cola, ¼ cup cocoa and ¼ cup shortening in medium bowl. Beat at low, then medium speed until blended, adding more cola, if necessary, until desired spreading consistency is reached. Stir in ½ cup nuts. Frost top and sides of cake. Sprinkle remaining nuts over top of cake. Let stand at least 1 hour before serving.

Makes 1 (13×9×2-inch) cake
(12 to 16 Servings)

Note: Flavor of cake improves if made several hours or a day before serving.

Choca-Cola Cake

1. Heat oven to 350°F. Grease and flour 13×9-inch baking pan.**

2. Beat butter and sugar in large bowl; add eggs and vanilla, beating well. Stir together buttermilk and food color. Stir together flour, cocoa and salt; add alternately to butter mixture with buttermilk mixture, mixing well. Stir in baking soda and vinegar. Pour into prepared pan.

3. Bake 30 to 35 minutes or until wooden pick inserted into center comes out clean. Cool completely in pan on wire rack. Frost; garnish with chocolate chips, if desired.

Makes about 15 servings

**This recipe can be made in 2 (9-inch) cake pans. Bake at 350°F for 30 to 35 minutes.*

❧ *tip* ❧

A butter cake is done when it begins to pull away from the sides of the pan, the top springs back when lightly touched or a cake tester or wooden toothpick inserted into the center comes out clean and dry.

Hershey's Red Velvet Cake

Hershey's Red Velvet Cake

½ cup (1 stick) butter or margarine, softened
1½ cups sugar
2 eggs
1 teaspoon vanilla extract
1 cup buttermilk or sour milk*
2 tablespoons (1-ounce bottle) red food color
2 cups all-purpose flour
⅓ cup HERSHEY'S Cocoa
1 teaspoon salt
1½ teaspoons baking soda
1 tablespoon white vinegar
1 can (16 ounces) ready-to-spread vanilla frosting
HERSHEY'S MINI CHIPS™ Semi-Sweet Chocolate Chips or HERSHEY'S Milk Chocolate Chips (optional)

To sour milk: Use 1 tablespoon white vinegar plus milk to equal 1 cup.

Chocolate Mayonnaise Cake

2 cups all-purpose flour
⅔ cup unsweetened cocoa
1¼ teaspoons baking soda
¼ teaspoon baking powder
3 eggs
1⅔ cups sugar
1 teaspoon vanilla
1 cup HELLMANN'S® or BEST FOODS® Real or Light Mayonnaise
1⅓ cups water

1. Preheat oven to 350°F. Grease and flour bottoms of two 9×1½-inch round cake pans.

2. In medium bowl, combine flour, cocoa, baking soda and baking powder; set aside.

3. In large bowl with mixer at high speed, beat eggs, sugar and vanilla, scraping bowl occasionally, 3 minutes or until smooth and creamy. Reduce speed to low; beat in mayonnaise until blended. Add flour mixture in 4 additions alternately with water, beginning and ending with flour mixture. Pour into prepared pans.

4. Bake 30 to 35 minutes or until cake springs back when touched lightly in center. Cool in pans on wire racks 10 minutes. Remove from pans; cool completely on racks. Fill and frost as desired.

Makes 1 (9-inch) layer cake

Lemon Cake Top Pudding

4 eggs, separated
1 cup sugar, divided
3 tablespoons butter or margarine, softened
3 tablespoons all-purpose flour
¼ teaspoon salt
⅓ cup fresh squeezed SUNKIST® lemon juice
1 cup milk
Grated peel of ½ SUNKIST® lemon
¼ cup sliced natural almonds

In small bowl of electric mixer, beat egg whites until foamy; gradually add ¼ cup sugar, beating until soft peaks form. Set aside. In large bowl, using same beaters, beat egg yolks and butter well. Gradually add remaining ¾ cup sugar, beating until well blended (about 5 minutes). Add flour, salt and lemon juice; mix well. Blend in milk and lemon peel. Gently fold in beaten egg whites. Sprinkle almonds over bottom of buttered 1½ quart casserole; pour in batter. Set casserole in shallow baking pan filled with ½ inch hot water. Bake, uncovered, at 325°F 55 to 60 minutes or until lightly browned. Serve warm or chilled. Refrigerate leftovers.

Makes 6 servings

Citrus Poppy Seed Cake

Cake

> PAM® Cooking Spray
> 1⅓ cups orange juice
> ½ cup WESSON® Vegetable Oil
> 3 eggs
> 1 box (18.25 ounces) lemon cake mix
> 2 tablespoons poppy seeds
> Grated peel from 1 orange and 1 lemon

Icing

> 2 cups powdered sugar, sifted
> 2 to 3 tablespoons orange juice
> Dash salt
> ½ tablespoons poppy seeds (optional)
> Grated peel from 1 orange and 1 lemon

For cake, preheat oven to 350°F. Lightly spray Bundt pan with PAM Cooking Spray. Using electric mixer, beat orange juice, oil and eggs; mix well. Slowly add cake mix to batter; mix on low speed until just moistened. Beat on medium speed for 2 minutes. Fold in poppy seeds and orange and lemon peel. Pour batter into Bundt pan; bake for 40 to 45 minutes or until toothpick inserted into cake comes out clean. Cool on wire rack for 10 minutes. Invert cake onto cake plate; let cool completely. Spoon icing over cake and top with additional orange and lemon peel.

For icing, combine all icing ingredients; mix well. Icing should be moderately thick but not thin enough to run off cake. Add more sugar or juice to achieve desired consistency.   *Makes 12 servings*

Quick & Easy Chocolate Cake

> 4 bars (4 ounces) HERSHEY'S Unsweetened Baking Chocolate, broken into pieces
> ¼ cup (½ stick) butter or margarine
> 1⅔ cups boiling water
> 2⅓ cups all-purpose flour
> 2 cups sugar
> ½ cup dairy sour cream
> 2 eggs
> 2 teaspoons baking soda
> 1 teaspoon salt
> 1 teaspoon vanilla extract

1. Heat oven to 350°F. Grease and flour 13×9×2-inch baking pan.

2. Combine chocolate, butter and water in large bowl; with spoon, stir until chocolate is melted and mixture is smooth. Add flour, sugar, sour cream, eggs, baking soda, salt and vanilla; beat on low speed of mixer until smooth. Pour batter into prepared pan.

3. Bake 35 to 40 minutes or until wooden pick inserted into center comes out clean. Cool completely in pan on wire rack. Frost as desired.

Makes 12 to 15 servings

Christmas Rainbow Cake

Christmas Rainbow Cake

Prep Time: 30 minutes
Bake Time: 30 minutes

- 1 package (2-layer size) white cake mix
- 1 package (4-serving size) JELL-O® Brand Lime Flavor Gelatin
- 1 package (4-serving size) JELL-O® Brand Strawberry Flavor Gelatin
- 2 tubs (8 ounces each) COOL WHIP® Whipped Topping, thawed

HEAT oven to 350°F.

PREPARE cake mix as directed on package. Divide batter equally between 2 bowls. Add lime gelatin to one bowl and strawberry gelatin to the other bowl. Stir until well blended. Pour each color batter into separate greased and floured 9-inch round cake pans.

BAKE 25 to 30 minutes or until toothpick inserted into centers comes out clean. Cool 10 minutes; remove from pans. Cool to room temperature on wire racks.

SLICE each cooled cake layer in half horizontally. Place 1 lime-flavored cake layer on serving plate; frost with whipped topping. Top with 1 strawberry-flavored cake layer; frost with whipped topping. Repeat layers. Frost top and side of cake with remaining whipped topping.
Makes 10 to 12 servings

Classic Boston Cream Pie

⅓ cup shortening
1 cup sugar
2 eggs
1 teaspoon vanilla extract
1¼ cups all-purpose flour
1½ teaspoons baking powder
¼ teaspoon salt
¾ cup milk
   Rich Filling (recipe follows)
   Dark Cocoa Glaze (recipe follows)

1. Heat oven to 350°F. Grease and flour 9-inch round baking pan.

2. Beat shortening, sugar, eggs and vanilla in large bowl until fluffy. Stir together flour, baking powder and salt; add alternately with milk to shortening mixture, beating well after each addition. Pour batter into prepared pan.

3. Bake 30 to 35 minutes or until wooden pick inserted into center comes out clean. Cool 10 minutes; remove from pan to wire rack. Cool completely.

4. Prepare Rich Filling. With long serrated knife, cut cake in half horizontally. Place one layer, cut side up, on serving plate; spread with prepared filling. Top with remaining layer, cut side down. Prepare Dark Cocoa Glaze; spread over cake, allowing glaze to run down sides. Refrigerate several hours or until cold. Garnish as desired. Refrigerate leftover pie.

Makes 8 to 10 servings

Rich Filling

⅓ cup sugar
2 tablespoons cornstarch
1½ cups milk
2 egg yolks, slightly beaten
1 tablespoon butter or margarine
1 teaspoon vanilla extract

Stir together sugar and cornstarch in medium saucepan; gradually add milk and egg yolks, stirring until blended. Cook over medium heat, stirring constantly, until mixture comes to a boil. Boil 1 minute, stirring constantly. Remove from heat; stir in butter and vanilla. Cover; refrigerate several hours or until cold.

Dark Cocoa Glaze

3 tablespoons water
2 tablespoons butter or margarine
3 tablespoons HERSHEY'S Cocoa
1 cup powdered sugar
½ teaspoon vanilla extract

Heat water and butter in small saucepan over medium heat until mixture comes to a boil; remove from heat. Immediately stir in cocoa. Gradually add powdered sugar and vanilla, beating with whisk until smooth and of desired consistency; cool slightly.

Makes about ¾ cup glaze

Classic Boston Cream Pie

1. Preheat oven to 350°F.

2. For topping, melt butter over low heat in 12-inch cast-iron skillet or skillet with oven-proof handle. Remove from heat. Stir in brown sugar. Spread to cover bottom of skillet. Arrange pineapple slices, maraschino cherries and walnut halves in skillet. Set aside.

3. For cake, combine cake mix, pudding mix, eggs, water and oil in large mixing bowl. Beat at medium speed with electric mixer for 2 minutes. Pour batter over fruit in skillet. Bake at 350°F for 1 hour or until toothpick inserted into center comes out clean. Invert onto plate.
Makes 16 to 20 servings

Variation: Cake can be made in a 13×9-inch pan. Bake at 350°F for 45 to 55 minutes or until toothpick inserted into center comes out clean. Cake is also delicious using Duncan Hines® Moist Deluxe Yellow Cake Mix.

Pineapple Upside Down Cake

Pineapple Upside Down Cake

Topping
½ cup butter or margarine
1 cup firmly packed brown sugar
1 can (20 ounces) pineapple slices, well drained
Maraschino cherries, halved and drained
Walnut halves

Cake
1 package DUNCAN HINES® Moist Deluxe® Pineapple Supreme Cake Mix
1 package (4-serving size) vanilla instant pudding and pie filling mix
4 eggs
1 cup water
½ cup oil

Flourless Chocolate Torte

1¼ cups (2½ sticks) butter
¾ cup HERSHEY'S Cocoa
2 cups sugar, divided
6 eggs, separated
¼ cup water
1 teaspoon vanilla extract
1 cup blanched sliced almonds, toasted and ground*
½ cup plain dry bread crumbs
Mocha Cream (recipe follows)

To toast almonds: Heat oven to 350°F. Place almonds in single layer in shallow baking pan. Bake 7 to 8 minutes, stirring occasionally, until light brown. Cool completely.

1. Heat oven to 350°F. Grease and flour 9-inch springform pan.

2. Melt butter in saucepan over low heat. Add cocoa and 1½ cups sugar; stir until smooth. Cool to room temperature.

3. Beat egg yolks in large bowl until thick. Gradually beat in chocolate mixture; stir in water and vanilla. Combine ground almonds and bread crumbs; stir into chocolate mixture. Beat egg whites until foamy; gradually add remaining ½ cup sugar, beating until soft peaks form. Fold about one-third of egg whites into chocolate. Fold chocolate into remaining egg whites. Pour into prepared pan.

4. Bake 50 to 60 minutes or until wooden pick inserted into center comes out clean. Cool 10 minutes. Loosen cake from side of pan; remove pan. Cool completely. Spread Mocha Cream over top. Sift with cocoa just before serving. Store covered in refrigerator.

Makes 10 servings

Mocha Cream: Combine 1 cup (½ pint) cold whipping cream, 2 tablespoons powdered sugar, 1½ teaspoons instant coffee granules dissolved in 1 teaspoon water, and ½ teaspoon vanilla extract in medium bowl; beat until stiff. Makes about 2 cups.

❧ *tip* ❧

A flourless chocolate cake is a very rich cake leavened with eggs.

Four Way Fudgey Chocolate Cake

1¼ cups all-purpose flour
1 cup sugar
1 cup nonfat milk
⅓ cup HERSHEY'S Cocoa or HERSHEY'S Dutch Processed Cocoa
⅓ cup unsweetened applesauce
1 tablespoon white vinegar
1 teaspoon baking soda
½ teaspoon vanilla extract
Toppings (optional): Frozen light non-dairy whipped topping, thawed, REESE'S® Peanut Butter Chips, sliced strawberries, chopped almonds, raspberries

1. Heat oven to 350°F. Spray 9-inch square baking pan or 11×7×2-inch baking pan with vegetable cooking spray.

2. Stir together flour, sugar, milk, cocoa, applesauce, vinegar, baking soda and vanilla in large bowl; beat on low speed of mixer until blended. Pour batter into prepared pan.

3. Bake 30 to 35 minutes or until wooden pick inserted into center comes out clean. Cool completely in pan on wire rack.

4. Spoon whipped topping into pastry bag fitted with star tip; pipe stars in two lines to divide cake into four squares or rectangles. Using plain tip, pipe lattice design into one square; place peanut butter chips onto lattice. Place strawberries into another square. Sprinkle almonds into third square. Place raspberries into remaining square.

5. Serve immediately. Cover; refrigerate leftover cake. Store ungarnished cake, covered, at room temperature. *Makes 12 servings*

Southern Jam Cake

Cake
¾ cup butter or margarine, softened
1 cup granulated sugar
3 eggs
1 cup (12-ounce jar) SMUCKER'S® Seedless Blackberry Jam
2½ cups all-purpose flour
1 teaspoon baking soda
1 teaspoon ground cinnamon
1 teaspoon ground cloves
1 teaspoon ground allspice
1 teaspoon ground nutmeg
¾ cup buttermilk

Caramel Icing (optional)
2 tablespoons butter
½ cup firmly packed brown sugar
3 tablespoons milk
1¾ cups powdered sugar

Grease and flour tube pan. Combine ¾ cup butter and granulated sugar; beat until light and fluffy. Add eggs one at a time, beating well after each addition. Fold in jam.

Combine flour, baking soda, cinnamon, cloves, allspice and nutmeg; mix well. Add to batter alternately with buttermilk, stirring just enough to blend after each addition. Spoon mixture into prepared pan.

Bake at 350°F for 50 minutes or until toothpick inserted near center comes out clean. Cool in pan for 10 minutes. Remove from pan; cool completely.

In saucepan, melt 2 tablespoons butter; stir in brown sugar. Cook, stirring constantly, until mixture boils; remove from heat. Cool 5 minutes. Stir in milk; blend in powdered sugar. Frost cake.

Makes 12 to 16 servings

Baker's® One Bowl Chocolate Cake

Prep: 15 minutes
Bake: 35 minutes

> **6 squares BAKER'S® Semi-Sweet Baking Chocolate**
> **¾ cup (1½ sticks) butter or margarine**
> **1½ cups sugar**
> **3 eggs**
> **2 teaspoons vanilla**
> **2½ cups flour**
> **1 teaspoon baking soda**
> **¼ teaspoon salt**
> **1½ cups water**

HEAT oven to 350°F. Grease and flour 2 (9-inch) round cake pans.

MICROWAVE chocolate and butter in large microwavable bowl on HIGH 2 minutes or until butter is melted. Stir until chocolate is completely melted.

STIR sugar into chocolate mixture. Beat in eggs, one at a time, with electric mixer on low speed until completely mixed. Add vanilla. Add ½ cup of the flour, baking soda and salt. Beat in the remaining 2 cups flour alternately with water until well blended. Pour into prepared pans.

BAKE 35 minutes or until toothpick inserted into center comes out clean. Cool 10 minutes; remove from pans. Cool completely on wire racks. Fill and frost layers with fudge frosting.

Makes 12 servings

Martha Washington Buttermilk Chocolate Cake

Prep: 20 minutes
Bake: 40 minutes

> 4 squares BAKER'S®
>   Unsweetened Baking
>   Chocolate
> 2 cups sugar, divided
> 1½ cups buttermilk or sour
>   milk, divided
> 2 cups flour
> 1½ teaspoons CALUMET®
>   Baking Powder
> 1 teaspoon baking soda
> 1 teaspoon salt
> ¾ cup (1½ sticks) butter or
>   margarine
> 3 eggs
> 1 teaspoon vanilla

HEAT oven to 350°F.

MICROWAVE chocolate in medium microwavable bowl on HIGH 2 minutes or until chocolate is almost melted, stirring halfway through heating time. Stir until chocolate is completely melted. Stir in ½ cup of the sugar and ½ cup of the buttermilk. Cool.

MIX flour, baking powder, baking soda and salt in medium bowl. Beat butter in large bowl with electric mixer on medium speed to soften. Gradually add remaining 1½ cups sugar, beating until light and fluffy. Add eggs, 1 at a time, beating well after each addition. Blend in about ¼ of the flour mixture. Add the chocolate mixture and vanilla. Add remaining flour mixture alternately with remaining buttermilk, beating well after each addition. Pour into 2 greased and floured 9-inch cake pans.

BAKE 40 minutes or until cake springs back when lightly pressed. Cool cakes in pans 10 minutes. Remove from pans. Cool completely on wire racks. Frost as desired.

Makes 10 servings

Variation: Prepare as directed, substituting 2¼ cups sifted cake flour and 1½ cups plus 2 tablespoons buttermilk for the flour and milk.

Variation: Prepare as directed, substituting shortening for butter. Increase buttermilk to 1¾ cups.

Alternate Baking Pans: 3 (9-inch) round cake pans for 25 to 30 minutes; 2 (9-inch) square baking pans for 35 to 40 minutes; 4 (8-inch) round cake pans for about 25 minutes.

High Altitude Directions: Reduce sugar to 1⅔ cups, adding ⅓ cup to the melted chocolate, increase all-purpose flour to 2¼ cups, reducing baking powder to 1 teaspoon and add 1 additional tablespoon buttermilk. (Do not use sour milk.) Bake in 3 (9-inch) layer pans at 375°F for 25 to 30 minutes.

Gingerbread Cake with Lemon Sauce

Gingerbread Cake with Lemon Sauce

Cake

    ¼ **cup Butter Flavor CRISCO®**
      all-vegetable shortening or
      ¼ Butter Flavor CRISCO®
      Stick
    ¼ **cup firmly packed light**
      brown sugar
    ¼ **cup granulated sugar**
    1 **large egg, slightly beaten**
    ½ **cup buttermilk**
    ¼ **cup light molasses**
    1 **cup all-purpose flour**
    2 **teaspoons ground ginger**
    1 **teaspoon ground cinnamon**
    ½ **teaspoon baking soda**
    ¼ **teaspoon ground cloves**
    ¼ **teaspoon freshly grated**
      nutmeg
    ¼ **teaspoon salt**

Lemon Sauce

    ½ **cup granulated sugar**
    ¼ **cup unsalted butter**
    3 **tablespoons fresh lemon**
      juice
    1 **teaspoon vanilla**

1. Heat oven to 375°F. Lightly spray 8-inch square or round cake pan with CRISCO® No-Stick Cooking Spray; set aside.

2. For cake, combine shortening, brown sugar and ¼ cup granulated sugar in large bowl. Beat at medium speed with electric mixer until well blended. Beat in egg, buttermilk and molasses until well blended.

3. Combine flour, ginger, cinnamon, baking soda, cloves, nutmeg and salt in medium bowl. Add to creamed mixture; mix well. Pour batter into prepared pan.

4. Bake at 375°F for 20 to 25 minutes or until wooden pick inserted into center comes out clean. Cool in pan 15 minutes. Turn out onto cooling rack.

5. For Lemon Sauce, combine all ingredients in small saucepan. Bring to boil over medium-high heat, stirring constantly. Reduce heat to low and simmer 5 minutes or until sauce is slightly thickened. Serve sauce over each slice of cake.

Makes 6 to 8 servings

Hot Fudge Pudding Cake

Prep Time: 10 minutes
Bake Time: 35 minutes
Cool Time: 15 minutes

1¼ cups granulated sugar,
    divided
1 cup all-purpose flour
½ cup HERSHEY'S Cocoa,
    divided
2 teaspoons baking powder
¼ teaspoon salt
½ cup milk
⅓ cup butter or margarine,
    melted
1½ teaspoons vanilla extract
½ cup packed light brown
    sugar
1¼ cups hot water
    Whipped topping

1. Heat oven to 350°F.

2. Stir together ¾ cup granulated sugar, flour, ¼ cup cocoa, baking powder and salt. Stir in milk, butter and vanilla; beat until smooth. Pour batter into *ungreased* 9-inch square baking pan. Stir together remaining ½ cup granulated sugar, brown sugar and remaining ¼ cup cocoa; sprinkle mixture evenly over batter. Pour hot water over top. Do not stir.

3. Bake 35 to 40 minutes or until center is almost set. Let stand 15 minutes; spoon into dessert dishes, spooning sauce from bottom of pan over top. Garnish with whipped topping.

Makes about 8 servings

Sour Cream Pound Cake

3 cups sugar
1 cup (2 sticks) butter,
    softened
1 teaspoon vanilla
1 teaspoon lemon extract
6 eggs
3 cups cake flour
¼ teaspoon baking soda
1 cup dairy sour cream

Heat oven to 325°F. Butter and flour 10-inch tube pan. In large bowl, beat sugar and butter until light and fluffy. Add vanilla and lemon extract; mix well. Add eggs, one at a time, beating well after each addition. In medium bowl, combine flour and baking soda. Add to butter mixture alternately with sour cream, beating well after each addition. Pour batter into pan. Bake 1 hour and 20 minutes or until toothpick inserted near center comes out clean. Cool in pan 15 minutes; invert onto wire rack and cool completely. Store tightly covered.

Favorite recipe from **Southeast United Dairy Industry Association, Inc.**

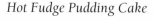
Hot Fudge Pudding Cake

Orange Dream Cake

Orange Dream Cake

Prep Time: 10 minutes
Bake Time: 40 minutes

 ¾ cup **MIRACLE WHIP® Salad Dressing**
 1 (two-layer) **yellow cake mix**
 1 envelope **DREAM WHIP® Whipped Topping Mix**
 ¾ cup **orange juice**
 3 **eggs**
 2 teaspoons **grated orange peel**
 1½ cups **powdered sugar**
 2 tablespoons **milk**
 1 tablespoon **multicolored sprinkles**

• BEAT salad dressing, cake mix, whipped topping mix, juice, eggs and peel at medium speed with electric mixer for 2 minutes. Pour into greased and floured 10-inch fluted tube pan.

• BAKE at 350°F for 35 to 40 minutes or until wooden toothpick inserted near center comes out clean. Let stand 10 minutes; remove from pan. Cool.

• STIR together powdered sugar and milk until smooth. Drizzle over cake. Decorate with sprinkles.

Makes 8 to 10 servings

Moist and Spicy Prune Cake

Cake

- 1 cup pitted, stewed prunes
- 2 cups all-purpose flour
- 1 teaspoon baking soda
- 1 teaspoon ground cinnamon
- ½ teaspoon ground cloves
- ½ teaspoon ground nutmeg
- ½ teaspoon ground allspice
- ¼ teaspoon salt
- 1½ cups granulated sugar
- 1 cup MOTT'S® Natural Apple Sauce
- 4 egg whites
- 2 tablespoons vegetable oil
- ½ cup low-fat buttermilk

Lemon Almond Icing

- 2 cups powdered sugar
- 1½ teaspoons lemon juice
- ¼ teaspoon almond extract

1. Preheat oven to 350°F. Spray 10-inch (12-cup) Bundt pan with nonstick cooking spray.

2. To prepare Cake, place prunes in food processor or blender; process until smooth.

3. In medium bowl, sift together flour, baking soda, cinnamon, cloves, nutmeg, allspice and salt.

4. In large bowl, whisk together granulated sugar, apple sauce, egg whites and oil.

5. Add flour mixture to apple sauce mixture alternately with buttermilk; stir until well blended. Add prunes; stir well. Pour batter into prepared pan.

6. Bake 60 minutes or until toothpick inserted near center comes out clean. Cool on wire rack 15 minutes before removing from pan. Place cake, fluted side up, on serving plate. Cool completely.

7. To prepare Lemon Almond Icing, in medium bowl, combine powdered sugar, lemon juice and almond extract until smooth. Add water, 1 teaspoon at a time, until of desired consistency. Drizzle over cooled cake. Cut into 14 slices.

Makes 14 servings

tip

Be sure to place the cake pan into the oven immediately. Cake batter should not sit before baking because the leavening begins working as soon as it is mixed with the liquid.

Cherry Glazed Chocolate Torte

Cherry Glazed Chocolate Torte

½ cup (1 stick) butter or
   margarine, melted
1 cup granulated sugar
1 teaspoon vanilla extract
2 eggs
½ cup all-purpose flour
⅓ cup HERSHEY'S Cocoa
¼ teaspoon baking powder
¼ teaspoon salt
1 package (8 ounces) cream
   cheese, softened
1 cup powdered sugar
1 cup frozen non-dairy
   whipped topping, thawed
1 can (21 ounces) cherry pie
   filling, divided

1. Heat oven to 350°F. Grease bottom of 9-inch springform pan.

2. Stir together butter, sugar and vanilla in large bowl. Add eggs; using spoon, beat well. Stir together flour, cocoa, baking powder and salt; gradually add to egg mixture, beating until well blended. Spread batter into prepared pan.

3. Bake 25 to 30 minutes or until cake is set. (Cake will be fudgey and will not test done.) Remove from oven; cool completely in pan on wire rack.

4. Beat cream cheese and powdered sugar in medium bowl until well blended; gradually fold in whipped topping, blending well. Spread over top of cake. Spread 1 cup cherry pie filling over cream layer; refrigerate several hours. With knife, loosen cake from side of pan; remove side of pan. Cut into wedges; garnish with remaining pie filling. Cover; refrigerate leftover dessert.

Makes 10 to 12 servings

Sour Cream Bundt Cake

Cinnamon Sugar
    6 tablespoons sugar
    2 tablespoons ground cinnamon

Cake
    2¾ cups all-purpose flour
    1 cup sugar
    1 package (4-serving size) vanilla flavor instant pudding and pie filling mix (not sugar-free)
    1 tablespoon plus 1 teaspoon baking powder
    ½ teaspoon salt
    1 cup (8 ounces) dairy sour cream
    ¾ CRISCO® Stick or ¾ cup CRISCO® all-vegetable shortening
    ¾ cup milk
    4 eggs
    2 teaspoons vanilla
    Reserved cinnamon sugar

1. Heat oven to 350°F. Grease 10-inch (12-cup) Bundt pan.

2. For cinnamon sugar, combine 6 tablespoons sugar and cinnamon in small bowl. Sprinkle in pan until generously coated. Reserve remaining cinnamon sugar.

3. For cake, combine flour, 1 cup sugar, pudding mix, baking powder and salt in large bowl. Combine at low speed of electric mixer. Add sour cream, shortening, milk, eggs and vanilla. Beat at medium speed 1 minute. Pour half of batter (about 3 cups) into pan. Sprinkle with reserved remaining cinnamon sugar. Cover with remaining batter.

4. Bake at 350°F for 1 hour to 1 hour 10 minutes or until toothpick inserted near center comes out clean. *Do not overbake.* Cool 20 minutes on wire rack before removing from pan. Place cake, fluted side up, on serving plate. Serve warm or at room temperature.
Makes 1 (10-inch) Bundt cake (12 to 16 servings)

✎ *tip* ✎

The best way to bake a cake is to place the cake on the center rack of the oven for proper heat circulation.

Western Golden Fruitcake

1 cup butter or margarine, softened
2 cups sugar
4 eggs
4 cups all-purpose flour
1½ teaspoons baking soda
1 cup buttermilk
½ cup freshly squeezed SUNKIST® orange juice
2 cups pecan or walnut halves
1 package (8 ounces) pitted dates, chopped
8 ounces candied cherries, halved
8 ounces candied pineapple chunks
Grated peel of 2 SUNKIST® fresh oranges
Fresh Orange or Lemon Glaze (recipes follow)

Preheat oven to 300°F.

In large bowl, cream together butter and sugar. Beat in eggs, 1 at a time. Sift together flour and baking soda. Add to creamed mixture alternately with buttermilk and orange juice, beating until smooth. Stir in nuts, dates, cherries, pineapple and orange peel. Divide batter; spoon 7½ cups into well-greased 10-inch Bundt or tube pan and spoon remaining 2½ cups batter into well-greased small 7½×3½×2¼-inch loaf pan. Bake both cakes 2 hours or until toothpick inserted near center comes out clean. Cool 10 minutes. Remove from pans; cool on wire racks. To serve, drizzle cakes with

Fresh Orange or Lemon Glaze and garnish with nut halves, if desired.

Fresh Orange Glaze: In small bowl, combine 1 cup confectioners' sugar, 1 teaspoon freshly grated orange peel and 1½ to 2 tablespoons freshly squeezed orange juice.

Fresh Lemon Glaze: In small bowl, combine 1 cup confectioners' sugar, 1 teaspoon freshly grated lemon peel and 1½ to 2 tablespoons freshly squeezed lemon juice.

tip

A fruit cake may be wrapped tightly in foil and kept in the refrigerator for up to 2 weeks or kept in the freezer for up to 2 months.

Easy Carrot Cake

Easy Carrot Cake

Prep Time: 15 minutes
Bake Time: 35 minutes

¹⁄₂ cup Prune Purée (recipe
    follows)
2 cups all-purpose flour
2 teaspoons ground cinnamon
1¹⁄₂ teaspoons baking soda
¹⁄₂ teaspoon salt
4 cups shredded DOLE®
    Carrots
2 cups sugar
¹⁄₂ cup DOLE® Pineapple Juice
2 eggs
2 teaspoons vanilla extract
Vegetable cooking spray

• Prepare Prune Purée; set aside.

• Combine flour, cinnamon, baking
soda and salt in medium bowl; set
aside.

• Beat together Prune Purée,
carrots, sugar, juice, eggs and vanilla
in large bowl until blended. Add
flour mixture; stir until well
blended.

• Spread batter into 13×9-inch
baking dish sprayed with vegetable
cooking spray.

• Bake at 375°F 30 to 35 minutes or
until toothpick inserted into center
comes out clean. Cool completely in
dish on wire rack. Dust with
powdered sugar and garnish with
carrot curls, if desired.

Makes 12 servings

Prune Purée: Combine 1¹⁄₃ cups
DOLE® Pitted Prunes, halved, and
¹⁄₂ cup hot water in food processor
or blender container. Process until
prunes are finely chopped, stopping
to scrape down sides occasionally.
(Purée can be refrigerated in airtight
container for up to 1 week.)

CHERISHED COOKIES & CANDY

Homemade cookies and candies have been loved by families for generations. No one can resist all-time favorite cookies like chocolate chip and brownies and candy like fudge and caramels.

Double Chocolate Oat Cookies (page 262)

Double Chocolate Oat Cookies

1 package (12 ounces) semisweet chocolate pieces, divided (about 2 cups)
½ cup (1 stick) margarine or butter, softened
½ cup granulated sugar
1 egg
¼ teaspoon vanilla
¾ cup all-purpose flour
¾ cup QUAKER® Oats (quick or old fashioned, uncooked)
1 teaspoon baking powder
¼ teaspoon baking soda
¼ teaspoon salt (optional)

Preheat oven to 375°F. Melt 1 cup chocolate pieces in small saucepan; set aside. Beat margarine and sugar until fluffy; add melted chocolate, egg and vanilla. Add combined flour, oats, baking powder, baking soda and salt; mix well. Stir in remaining chocolate pieces. Drop by rounded tablespoonfuls onto *ungreased* cookie sheets. Bake 8 to 10 minutes. Cool 1 minute on cookie sheets; remove to wire rack.

Makes about 3 dozen cookies

Peanut Butter Kisses

1¼ cups firmly packed light brown sugar
¾ cup creamy peanut butter
½ CRISCO® Stick or ½ cup CRISCO® all-vegetable shortening
3 tablespoons milk
1 tablespoon vanilla
1 egg
1¾ cups all-purpose flour
¾ teaspoon baking soda
¾ teaspoon salt
48 chocolate kisses, unwrapped

1. Heat oven to 375°F. Place sheets of foil on countertop for cooling cookies.

2. Combine brown sugar, peanut butter, shortening, milk and vanilla in large bowl. Beat at medium speed of electric mixer until well blended. Add egg. Beat just until blended.

3. Combine flour, baking soda and salt. Add to shortening mixture; beat at low speed until just blended. Form dough into 1-inch balls. Roll in granulated sugar. Place 2 inches apart on *ungreased* baking sheets.

4. Bake one baking sheet at a time at 375°F for 6 minutes. Press chocolate kiss into center of each cookie. Return to oven. Bake 3 minutes. *Do not overbake.* Cool 2 minutes on baking sheets. Remove cookies to foil to cool completely.

Makes about 3 dozen cookies

Peanut Butter Kisses

Spiced Date Bars

Ppep Time: 15 minutes
Bake Time: 30 minutes

½ **cup margarine, softened**
1 **cup packed brown sugar**
2 **eggs**
¾ **cup light sour cream**
2 **cups all-purpose flour**
1 **teaspoon baking soda**
1 **teaspoon ground cinnamon**
½ **teaspoon ground nutmeg**
1 **package (8 or 10 ounces)**
   DOLE® Chopped Dates or
   Pitted Dates, chopped
   Powdered sugar (optional)

• Beat margarine and brown sugar until light and fluffy. Beat in eggs, one at a time. Stir in sour cream.

• Combine dry ingredients. Beat into sour cream mixture; stir in dates. Spread batter evenly into greased 13×9-inch baking pan.

• Bake at 350°F 25 to 30 minutes or until toothpick inserted into center comes out clean. Cool completely in pan on wire rack. Cut into bars. Dust with powdered sugar.

Makes 24 bars

Applesauce Raisin Chews

1 **cup (2 sticks) margarine or**
   butter, softened
1 **cup firmly packed brown**
   sugar
1 **cup applesauce**
1 **egg**
1 **teaspoon vanilla**
2 **cups all-purpose flour**
1 **teaspoon baking soda**
1 **teaspoon ground cinnamon**
½ **teaspoon salt (optional)**
2½ **cups QUAKER® Oats (quick**
   or old fashioned,
   uncooked)
1 **cup raisins**

Heat oven to 350°F. Beat together margarine and sugar until creamy. Add applesauce, egg and vanilla; beat well. Add combined flour, baking soda, cinnamon and salt; mix well. Stir in oats and raisins. Drop by rounded tablespoonfuls onto *ungreased* cookie sheets. Bake 11 to 13 minutes or until light golden brown. Cool 1 minute on cookie sheets; remove to wire rack. Cool completely. Store in tightly covered container.

Makes about 4 dozen

Baker's® One Bowl Coconut Macaroons

Prep Time: 15 minutes
Bake Time: 20 minutes

> 1 package (14 ounces)
> BAKER'S® ANGEL FLAKE®
> Coconut (5⅓ cups)
> ⅔ cup sugar
> 6 tablespoons flour
> ¼ teaspoon salt
> 4 egg whites
> 1 teaspoon almond extract

HEAT oven to 325°F.

MIX coconut, sugar, flour and salt in large bowl. Stir in egg whites and almond extract until well blended.

DROP by teaspoonfuls onto greased and floured cookie sheets. Press 1 whole candied cherry or whole natural almond into center of each cookie, if desired.

BAKE 20 minutes or until edges of cookies are golden brown. Immediately remove from cookie sheets. Cool on wire racks.

Makes about 3 dozen cookies

Chocolate Dipped Macaroons:
Prepare Coconut Macaroons as directed. Cool. Melt 1 package (8 squares) Baker's® Semi-Sweet Baking Chocolate as directed on package. Dip cookies halfway into chocolate or drizzle tops of cookies with chocolate; let excess chocolate drip off.

Let stand at room temperature or refrigerate on wax paper-lined tray 30 minutes or until chocolate is firm.

White Chocolate Coconut Macaroons: Prepare Coconut Macaroons as directed, adding 3 squares Baker's® Premium White Baking Chocolate, chopped, to coconut mixture.

Citrus Macaroons: Prepare Coconut Macaroons as directed, adding 1 teaspoon grated orange or lemon peel to coconut mixture.

Chocolate Macaroons: Prepare Coconut Macaroons as directed, adding 2 squares Baker's® Semi-Sweet Baking Chocolate, melted, to mixture.

❧ *tip* ❧

Macaroons are a cookie with a crisp, yet chewy texture. A macaroon is traditionally made from egg whites and sugar and often flavored with coconut.

Best Brownies

½ cup (1 stick) butter or margarine, melted
1 cup sugar
1 teaspoon vanilla extract
2 eggs
½ cup all-purpose flour
⅓ cup HERSHEY'S Cocoa
¼ teaspoon baking powder
¼ teaspoon salt
½ cup chopped nuts (optional)
Creamy Brownie Frosting (recipe follows)

1. Heat oven to 350°F. Grease 9-inch square baking pan.

2. Stir together butter, sugar and vanilla in large bowl. Add eggs; beat well with spoon. Combine flour, cocoa, baking powder and salt; gradually add to butter mixture, beating until well blended. Stir in nuts. Spread into prepared pan.

3. Bake 20 to 25 minutes or until brownies begin to pull away from sides of pan. Cool; frost with Creamy Brownie Frosting. Cut into squares.

Makes about 16 brownies

Creamy Brownie Frosting

3 tablespoons butter or margarine, softened
3 tablespoons HERSHEY'S Cocoa
1 tablespoon light corn syrup or honey
½ teaspoon vanilla extract
1 cup powdered sugar
1 to 2 tablespoons milk

Beat butter, cocoa, corn syrup and vanilla in small bowl. Add powdered sugar and milk; beat to spreading consistency.

Makes about 1 cup frosting

Chunky Peanut Butter Cookies

½ cup chunky peanut butter
2 tablespoons reduced-calorie margarine
1⅓ cups packed brown sugar
2 egg whites
½ teaspoon vanilla
1⅛ cups all-purpose flour
¼ teaspoon baking soda

Preheat oven to 375°F. Spray cookie sheet with nonstick cooking spray. In large bowl, beat peanut butter and margarine with electric mixer on medium speed. Beat in sugar, egg whites and vanilla. Blend in flour and baking soda. Drop by teaspoonfuls, about 2 inches apart, onto cookie sheet. Press each cookie flat with back of fork. Bake 8 to 10 minutes.

Makes about 34 cookies

Favorite recipe from **The Sugar Association, Inc.**

From left to right: Best Brownies, Peanut Butter Chips and Jelly Bars (page 268)

Peanut Butter Chips and Jelly Bars

1½ cups all-purpose flour
½ cup sugar
¾ teaspoon baking powder
½ cup (1 stick) cold butter or margarine
1 egg, beaten
¾ cup grape jelly
1⅔ cups (10-ounce package) REESE'S® Peanut Butter Chips, divided

1. Heat oven to 375°F. Grease 9-inch square baking pan.

2. Stir together flour, sugar and baking powder in large bowl. With pastry blender or two knives, cut in butter until mixture resembles coarse crumbs. Add egg; blend well. Reserve half of mixture; press remaining mixture onto bottom of prepared pan. Spread jelly over crust. Sprinkle 1 cup peanut butter chips over jelly. Stir together reserved crumb mixture with remaining ⅔ cup chips; sprinkle over top.

3. Bake 25 to 30 minutes or until lightly browned. Cool completely in pan on wire rack. Cut into bars.

Makes about 16 bars

Oatmeal Hermits

3 cups QUAKER® Oats (quick or old fashioned, uncooked)
1 cup all-purpose flour
1 cup (2 sticks) butter or margarine, melted
1 cup firmly packed brown sugar
1 cup raisins
½ cup chopped nuts
1 egg
¼ cup milk
1 teaspoon ground cinnamon
1 teaspoon vanilla
½ teaspoon baking soda
½ teaspoon salt (optional)
¼ teaspoon ground nutmeg

Heat oven to 375°F. In large bowl, combine all ingredients; mix well. Drop by rounded tablespoonfuls onto *ungreased* cookie sheets. Bake 8 to 10 minutes. Cool 1 minute on cookie sheets; remove to wire cooling rack.

Makes about 3 dozen

Bar Cookies: Press dough into *ungreased* 15×10-inch jelly-roll pan. Bake about 17 minutes or until golden brown. Cool completely; cut into bars.

Basic Icebox Cookie Dough

1 cup butter or margarine, softened
1 cup sugar
1 egg
1 teaspoon vanilla
2½ cups all-purpose flour
1 teaspoon baking powder
½ teaspoon salt

Beat butter and sugar with electric mixer. Add egg and vanilla; mix well. Combine flour, baking powder and salt. Gradually add to butter mixture; mix well.

Makes 4½ cups dough

Maraschino Cherry Cookies: Add ½ cup chopped well-drained maraschino cherries to basic dough; divide dough in half. Form dough into 2 logs, 1½ inches in diameter. Wrap in waxed paper and refrigerate at least 6 hours. Cut into ¼-inch slices. Place on *ungreased* baking sheets. Bake at 375°F 8 to 10 minutes. Remove to cooling rack. Repeat with remaining dough. Makes 6 to 7 dozen cookies.

Maraschino Date Pinwheels: Combine 8 ounces cut-up pitted dates and ¼ cup water in small saucepan; bring to a boil. Reduce heat; simmer until thickened. Add ¾ cup chopped drained maraschino cherries; mix well and cool. Divide dough in half. Roll out each half to 12×10-inch rectangle on lightly floured surface. Spread half of cooled filling on each rectangle. Roll up beginning at long ends. Pinch ends of rolls to seal. Wrap in waxed paper and refrigerate at least 6 hours. Cut rolls into ¼-inch slices. Place 1 to 1½ inches apart on *ungreased* baking sheet. Bake at 375°F about 10 to 14 minutes or until lightly browned. Remove to cooling rack. Makes 6 to 7 dozen cookies.

Maraschino Thumbprint Cookies: Shape dough into balls, using 2 teaspoons dough for each cookie. Press thumb in center of each ball. Place whole well-drained maraschino cherry in center of each depression. Brush with beaten egg white. If desired, roll each ball in beaten egg white, then in finely chopped pecans before pressing with thumb and filling with cherry. Bake at 375°F 12 to 15 minutes. Remove to cooling rack. Makes 5 dozen cookies.

*Favorite recipe from **Cherry Marketing Institute***

Basic Icebox Cookies

Irresistible Peanut Butter Cookies

1¼ cups firmly packed light brown sugar

¾ cup JIF® Creamy Peanut Butter

½ Butter Flavor CRISCO® Stick or ½ cup Butter Flavor CRISCO® all-vegetable shortening

3 tablespoons milk

1 tablespoon vanilla

1 egg

1¾ cups all-purpose flour

¾ teaspoon baking soda

¾ teaspoon salt

1. Heat oven to 375°F. Place sheets of foil on countertop for cooling cookies.

2. Combine brown sugar, peanut butter, shortening, milk and vanilla in large bowl. Beat at medium speed of electric mixer until well blended. Add egg. Beat just until blended.

3. Combine flour, baking soda and salt. Add to creamed mixture at low speed. Mix just until blended.

4. Drop by rounded tablespoonfuls of dough 2 inches apart onto *ungreased* baking sheet. Flatten slightly in crisscross pattern with tines of fork.

5. Bake one baking sheet at a time at 375°F for 7 to 8 minutes, or until set and just beginning to brown. *Do not overbake.* Cool 2 minutes on baking sheet. Remove cookies to foil to cool completely.

Makes about 3 dozen cookies

Oatmeal Raisin Cookies

¼ cup (4 tablespoons) margarine, softened

1¼ teaspoons EQUAL® Measure (5 packets) *or* 3 tablespoons granulated sugar

¼ cup egg substitute *or* 2 egg whites

¾ cup unsweetened applesauce

¼ cup frozen unsweetened apple juice concentrate, thawed

1 teaspoon vanilla

1 cup all-purpose flour

1 teaspoon baking soda

½ teaspoon ground cinnamon

¼ teaspoon salt (optional)

1½ cups QUAKER® Oats (quick or old fashioned, uncooked)

⅓ cup raisins, chopped

Heat oven to 350°F. Lightly spray cookie sheets. Beat together margarine and EQUAL until creamy. Beat in egg substitute. Add applesauce, apple juice concentrate and vanilla; beat well. Blend in combined flour, baking soda, cinnamon and salt. Stir in oats and chopped raisins. Drop by rounded teaspoonfuls onto prepared cookie sheets. Bake 15 to 17 minutes or until cookies are firm to the touch and lightly browned. Cool 1 minute on cookie sheets; remove to wire rack. Cool completely.

Makes about 3 dozen

Irresistible Peanut Butter Cookies

Drop Sugar Cookies

2½ cups sifted all-purpose flour
½ teaspoon ARM & HAMMER® Baking Soda
¼ teaspoon salt
½ cup butter, softened
½ cup butter-flavored shortening
1 cup sugar
1 egg or ¼ cup egg substitute
1 teaspoon vanilla extract
2 teaspoons skim milk

Preheat oven to 400°F. Sift together flour, Baking Soda and salt; set aside. Beat butter and shortening in large bowl with electric mixer on medium speed until blended; add sugar gradually and continue beating until light and fluffy. Beat in egg and vanilla. Add flour mixture and beat until smooth; blend in milk. Drop dough by teaspoonfuls about 3 inches apart onto greased cookie sheets. Flatten with bottom of greased glass that has been dipped in sugar.

Bake 12 minutes or until edges are lightly browned. Cool on wire racks.

Makes about 5½ dozen cookies

Smucker's® Grandmother's Jelly Cookies

1½ cups sugar
1 cup butter or margarine, softened
1 egg
1½ teaspoons vanilla extract
3½ cups all-purpose flour
1 teaspoon salt
¾ cup SMUCKER'S® Red Raspberry, Strawberry or Peach Preserves

In large bowl, cream together sugar and butter until light and fluffy. Add egg and vanilla; beat well. Stir in flour and salt; mix well. Stir to make a smooth dough. (If batter gets too hard to handle, mix with hands.) Cover and refrigerate about 2 hours.

Preheat oven to 375°F. Lightly grease baking sheets. On lightly floured board, roll out half of dough to about ⅛-inch thickness. Cut out cookies with 2½-inch round cookie cutter. Roll out remaining dough; cut with 2½-inch cutter with hole in center. Place on baking sheets. Bake 8 to 10 minutes or until lightly browned. Cool about 30 minutes.

To serve, spread preserves on plain cookies; top with cookies with holes.

Makes about 3 dozen cookies

Hershey's Best Brownies

1 cup (2 sticks) butter or margarine
2 cups sugar
2 teaspoons vanilla extract
4 eggs
¾ cup HERSHEY'S Cocoa or HERSHEY'S Dutch Processed Cocoa
1 cup all-purpose flour
½ teaspoon baking powder
¼ teaspoon salt
1 cup chopped nuts (optional)

1. Heat oven to 350°F. Grease 13×9×2-inch baking pan.

2. Place butter in large microwave-safe bowl. Microwave at HIGH (100%) 2 to 2½ minutes or until melted. Stir in sugar and vanilla. Add eggs, one at a time, beating well with spoon after each addition. Add cocoa; beat until well blended. Add flour, baking powder and salt; beat well. Stir in nuts, if desired. Pour batter into prepared pan.

3. Bake 30 to 35 minutes or until brownies begin to pull away from sides of pan. Cool completely in pan on wire rack. Cut into bars.

Makes about 36 brownies

Pineapple Carrot Cookies

Prep Time: 30 minutes
Bake Time: 20 minutes per batch

2 cans (8 ounces each) DOLE® Crushed Pineapple
¾ cup margarine, softened
½ cup granulated sugar
½ cup packed brown sugar
1 egg
1 teaspoon vanilla extract
1 cup shredded DOLE® Carrots
1 cup chopped walnuts
1 cup DOLE® Seedless Raisins
1½ cups all-purpose flour
1 teaspoon ground cinnamon
½ teaspoon ground ginger
½ teaspoon baking powder
¼ teaspoon salt

• Preheat oven to 375°F.

• Drain crushed pineapple well; reserve juice, if desired.

• Beat margarine and sugars until light and fluffy. Beat in egg and vanilla. Beat in crushed pineapple, carrots, walnuts and raisins.

• Combine remaining ingredients; beat into pineapple mixture until well blended.

• Drop batter by heaping tablespoonfuls onto greased cookie sheets. Flatten tops with spoon. Bake 15 to 20 minutes.

Makes about 3 dozen cookies

Original Nestlé® Toll House® Chocolate Chip Cookies

2¼ cups all-purpose flour
1 teaspoon baking soda
1 teaspoon salt
1 cup (2 sticks) butter or margarine, softened
¾ cup granulated sugar
¾ cup packed brown sugar
1 teaspoon vanilla extract
2 large eggs
2 cups (12-ounce package) NESTLÉ® TOLL HOUSE® Semi-Sweet Chocolate Morsels
1 cup chopped nuts

PREHEAT oven to 375°F.

COMBINE flour, baking soda and salt in small bowl. Beat butter, granulated sugar, brown sugar and vanilla in large mixer bowl until creamy. Add eggs, one at a time, beating well after each addition. Gradually beat in flour mixture. Stir in morsels and nuts. Drop by rounded tablespoon onto *ungreased* baking sheets.

BAKE 9 to 11 minutes or until golden brown. Cool on baking sheets for 2 minutes; remove to wire racks to cool completely.
Makes about 5 dozen cookies

Pan Cookie Variation:
GREASE 15×10-inch jelly-roll pan. Prepare dough as directed. Spread into prepared pan. Bake 20 to 25 minutes or until golden brown. Cool in pan on wire rack. Makes 4 dozen bars.

Slice and Bake Cookie Variation:
PREPARE dough as directed. Divide in half; wrap in wax paper. Refrigerate for 1 hour or until firm. Shape each half into 15-inch log; wrap in wax paper. Refrigerate for 30 minutes.* Preheat oven to 375°F. Cut into ½-inch-thick slices; place on *ungreased* baking sheets. Bake for 8 to 10 minutes or until golden brown. Cool on baking sheets for 2 minutes; remove to wire racks to cool completely. Makes about 5 dozen cookies.*

May be stored in refrigerator for up to 1 week or in freezer for up to 8 weeks.

Original Nestlé® Toll House® Chocolate Chip Cookies

Oatmeal Scotchies™

1¼ cups all-purpose flour
1 teaspoon baking soda
½ teaspoon ground cinnamon
½ teaspoon salt
1 cup (2 sticks) butter or margarine, softened
¾ cup granulated sugar
¾ cup packed brown sugar
2 large eggs
1 teaspoon vanilla extract *or* grated peel of 1 orange
3 cups quick or old-fashioned oats
1⅔ cups (11-ounce package) NESTLÉ® TOLL HOUSE® Butterscotch Flavored Morsels

PREHEAT oven to 375°F.

COMBINE flour, baking soda, cinnamon and salt in small bowl. Beat butter, granulated sugar, brown sugar, eggs and vanilla in large mixer bowl. Gradually beat in flour mixture. Stir in oats and morsels. Drop by rounded tablespoons onto *ungreased* baking sheets.

BAKE 7 to 8 minutes for chewy cookies; 9 to 10 minutes for crisp cookies. Cool on baking sheets for 2 minutes; remove to wire racks to cool completely.

Makes about 4 dozen cookies

Pan Cookie Variation: Grease 15×10-inch jelly-roll pan. Spread dough into prepared pan. Bake for 18 to 22 minutes or until light brown. Cool completely in pan on wire rack. Makes 4 dozen bars.

Ranger Cookies

1 cup (2 sticks) margarine or butter, softened
1 cup granulated sugar
1 cup firmly packed brown sugar
2 eggs
1 teaspoon vanilla
2 cups all-purpose flour
1 teaspoon baking soda
½ teaspoon baking powder
½ teaspoon salt (optional)
2 cups QUAKER® Oats (quick or old fashioned, uncooked)
2 cups cornflakes
½ cup flaked or shredded coconut
½ cup chopped nuts

Heat oven to 350°F. Beat margarine and sugars until creamy. Add eggs and vanilla; beat well. Add combined flour, baking soda, baking powder and salt; mix well. Stir in oats, cornflakes, coconut and nuts; mix well. Drop dough by heaping tablespoonfuls onto *ungreased* cookie sheets. Bake 10 to 12 minutes or until light golden brown. Cool 1 minute on cookie sheets; remove to wire rack. Cool completely. Store tightly covered.

Makes 2 dozen large cookies

Oatmeal Scotchies™

Old-Fashioned Creamy Fudge

Prep Time: 20 minutes
Cook Time: 25 minutes
Cool Time: 2½ hours

> 2 cups sugar
> ¾ cup milk
> 2½ bars (1 ounce each) HERSHEY®S Unsweetened Baking Chocolate, broken into pieces
> 2 tablespoons light corn syrup
> ¼ teaspoon salt
> 2 tablespoons butter
> 1 teaspoon vanilla extract

1. Line 8-inch square pan with foil, extending foil over edges of pan. Lightly butter foil.

2. Stir together sugar, milk, baking chocolate, corn syrup and salt in heavy 2-quart saucepan. Cook over medium heat, stirring constantly, until mixture comes to full rolling boil. Cook, stirring occasionally, until mixture reaches 234°F on candy thermometer or until small amount of mixture dropped into very cold water forms a soft ball, which flattens when removed from water. (Bulb of candy thermometer should not rest on bottom of saucepan.)

3. Remove from heat. Add butter and vanilla. *Do not stir.* Cool at room temperature to 110°F (lukewarm). Beat with wooden spoon until fudge thickens and just begins to lose some of its gloss. Quickly spread into prepared pan.

4. Cool completely. Cut into squares. Store in tightly covered container at room temperature.

Makes about 3 dozen pieces or 1½ pounds

Note: For best results, do not double this recipe.

Old Fashioned Peanut Brittle

Prep Time: 10 minutes
Cook Time: 10 minutes
Cooling Time: 1 hour
Total Time: 1 hour and 20 minutes

> 1 cup sugar
> ½ cup light corn syrup
> ¼ cup water
> 1 cup PLANTERS COCKTAIL® Peanuts
> 2 tablespoons margarine
> 1 teaspoon vanilla extract
> 1 teaspoon baking soda

1. Cook and stir sugar, corn syrup and water in heavy bottomed 2-quart saucepan over high heat until sugar dissolves. Cook, without stirring, until mixture reaches 300°F (hard-crack stage), about 5 minutes.

2. Stir in peanuts, margarine, vanilla and baking soda. Quickly spread in thin layer on greased baking sheet; cool.

3. Break into pieces; store in airtight container for up to 2 weeks.

Makes 1 pound

Dreamy Divinity

3½ cups DOMINO® Granulated
    Sugar
⅔ cup water
⅔ cup light corn syrup
⅓ teaspoon salt
3 egg whites, beaten until stiff
1½ teaspoons vanilla extract
    Food coloring, candied
    cherries and chopped nuts
    (optional)

Combine sugar, water, corn syrup
and salt in saucepan. Heat, stirring
occasionally, until sugar dissolves.
Wipe down sugar crystals from side
of pan as necessary with pastry
brush dipped in water. Boil syrup
mixture, without stirring, until
mixture reaches 265°F or hard-ball
stage on candy thermometer.

Gradually beat hot syrup into beaten
egg whites. Add vanilla. Tint with
food coloring, if desired. Continue
beating until candy holds shape.
Drop by teaspoonfuls onto buttered
baking sheet or plate. Garnish with
cherries and nuts as desired. When
firm, store in airtight container.

Makes 50 pieces (1½ pounds)

Rocky Road Clusters

2 cups (12-ounce package)
    NESTLÉ® TOLL HOUSE®
    Semi-Sweet Chocolate
    Morsels
1 can (14 ounces) NESTLÉ®
    CARNATION® Sweetened
    Condensed Milk
2½ cups miniature
    marshmallows
1 cup coarsely chopped nuts
1 teaspoon vanilla extract

LINE baking sheets with waxed
paper.

COMBINE morsels and sweetened
condensed milk in large microwave-
safe bowl. Microwave on HIGH
(100%) power for 1 minute; stir.
Microwave at additional 10- to
20-second intervals, stirring until
smooth. Stir in marshmallows, nuts
and vanilla extract.

DROP by heaping tablespoonfuls in
mounds onto prepared baking
sheets. Refrigerate until firm.

Makes about 2 dozen candies

Classic Caramels

2 cups sugar
2 cups light corn syrup
1 cup half-and-half
1 cup unsalted butter
½ teaspoon salt
1 cup whipping cream
1 teaspoon vanilla

1. Line 8-inch square pan with heavy-duty foil, pressing foil into corners to cover completely and leaving 1-inch overhang on sides. Lightly butter foil.

2. Combine sugar, syrup, half-and-half, butter and salt in deep heavy 4- or 4½-quart saucepan. Bring to a boil over medium-high heat, stirring occasionally. Attach candy thermometer to side of pan, making sure bulb is submerged in sugar mixture but not touching bottom of pan. Continue boiling about 25 minutes or until sugar mixture reaches firm-ball stage (244° to 246°F) on candy thermometer, stirring frequently. Remove from heat and very gradually stir in cream.

3. Return to medium heat and cook about 15 minutes or until mixture reaches 248°F on candy thermometer, stirring frequently. Remove from heat; stir in vanilla. Immediately pour into prepared pan. (Do not scrape saucepan.) Cool at room temperature 3 to 4 hours until firm or cover with plastic wrap and let stand overnight. (Candy will be harder to cut if cooled overnight.)

4. Remove from pan by lifting caramels using foil handles. Place on cutting board; peel off foil. Cut into 1-inch strips; cut each strip into 1-inch squares with buttered knife or kitchen shears.

5. Wrap caramels individually in small squares of plastic wrap. Store in airtight container at room temperature up to 2 weeks.

Makes 64 caramels (about 2½ pounds)

Party Mints

Prep Time: 30 minutes
Stand Time: 8 hours

1 (14-ounce) can EAGLE® BRAND Sweetened Condensed Milk (NOT evaporated milk)
1 (32-ounce) package powdered sugar
½ teaspoon peppermint extract
Assorted colored granulated or crystal sugar

1. In medium mixing bowl, beat Eagle Brand and half of powdered sugar until blended. Gradually add remaining powdered sugar and peppermint extract, beating until stiff.

2. Shape mixture into ½-inch balls; roll in desired sugar and place on lightly greased cooling rack. Let stand 8 hours. Store covered at room temperature. *Makes 2½ pounds*

Classic Caramels

Fantasy Fudge

Prep Time: 10 minutes
Cook Time: 15 minutes
Total Time: 25 minutes

    3 cups sugar
    ¾ cup margarine or butter
    ⅔ cup evaporated milk
    1 (12-ounce) package
        BAKER'S® Semi-Sweet
        Chocolate Chunks
    4 cups JET-PUFFED® Miniature
        Marshmallows
    1 cup PLANTERS® Walnuts,
        chopped
    1 teaspoon vanilla extract

1. Heat sugar, margarine and milk in large heavy saucepan over medium heat to a boil, stirring constantly.

2. Continue boiling over medium heat 5 minutes or until candy thermometer reaches 234°F, stirring constantly to prevent scorching. Remove from heat.

3. Gradually stir in chocolate chunks until melted. Add remaining ingredients; mix well.

4. Pour into greased 9×9×2-inch or 13×9×2-inch pan. Cool at room temperature; cut into squares. Store in airtight container.

Makes 3 pounds

Tip: For ease in cutting fudge and cleaning pan, line pan with foil before preparing fudge; lightly grease foil. When fudge has cooled, lift from pan; cut into squares.

English Toffee

    1 cup butter or margarine
    1 cup granulated sugar
    1 cup BLUE DIAMOND®
        Chopped Natural
        Almonds, divided
    ⅓ cup semi-sweet real
        chocolate pieces

Combine butter and sugar in heavy skillet; cook, stirring, until boiling point is reached. Boil mixture over medium heat, stirring constantly, to soft crack stage, 270° to 280°F, or until a little mixture dropped in cold water becomes hard and brittle. Remove from heat and stir in ½ cup almonds. Pour into buttered 11×7-inch pan; let stand 10 minutes or until top is set. Sprinkle chocolate over top of candy. When chocolate has melted, smooth with spatula; sprinkle remaining almonds over chocolate. Let stand until set; break into bite-size pieces.

Makes about 1½ pounds

Carnation® Famous Fudge

1½ cups granulated sugar
⅔ cup (5 fluid-ounce can) NESTLÉ® CARNATION® Evaporated Milk
2 tablespoons butter or margarine
¼ teaspoon salt
2 cups miniature marshmallows
1½ cups (9 ounces) NESTLÉ® TOLL HOUSE® Semi-Sweet Chocolate Morsels
½ cup chopped pecans or walnuts (optional)
1 teaspoon vanilla extract

LINE 8-inch-square baking pan with foil.

COMBINE sugar, evaporated milk, butter and salt in medium, *heavy-duty* saucepan. Bring to a *full rolling boil* over medium heat, stirring constantly. Boil, stirring constantly, for 4 to 5 minutes. Remove from heat.

STIR in marshmallows, morsels, nuts and vanilla extract. Stir vigorously for 1 minute or until marshmallows are melted. Pour into prepared baking pan; refrigerate for 2 hours or until firm. Lift from pan; remove foil. Cut into pieces.

Makes about 2 pounds

For Milk Chocolate Fudge:
SUBSTITUTE 2 cups (11.5-ounce package) NESTLÉ® TOLL HOUSE® Milk Chocolate Morsels for Semi-Sweet Morsels.

For Butterscotch Fudge:
SUBSTITUTE 1⅔ cups (11-ounce package) NESTLÉ® TOLL HOUSE® Butterscotch Flavored Morsels for Semi-Sweet Morsels.

For Peanutty Chocolate Fudge:
SUBSTITUTE 1⅔ cups (11-ounce package) NESTLÉ® TOLL HOUSE® Peanut Butter & Milk Chocolate Morsels for Semi-Sweet Morsels and ½ cup chopped peanuts for pecans or walnuts.

tip

Store chocolate in a cool, dry place. If chocolate gets too warm, the cocoa butter rises to the surface and causes a grayish white appearance called a bloom. The bloom will not affect the chocolate's taste or cooking quality.

Double-Decker Fudge

1 cup REESE'S® Peanut Butter Chips

1 cup HERSHEY'S Semi-Sweet Chocolate Chips or HERSHEY'S MINI CHIPS™ Semi-Sweet Chocolate Chips

2¼ cups sugar

1 jar (7 ounces) marshmallow creme

¾ cup evaporated milk

¼ cup (½ stick) butter

1 teaspoon vanilla extract

Double-Decker Fudge

1. Line 8-inch square pan with foil, extending foil over edges of pan. Measure peanut butter chips into one medium bowl and chocolate chips into a second medium bowl.

2. Combine sugar, marshmallow creme, evaporated milk and butter in heavy 3-quart saucepan. Cook over medium heat, stirring constantly, until mixture boils; boil and stir 5 minutes. Remove from heat; stir in vanilla. Immediately stir one-half of the hot mixture (1½ cups) into peanut butter chips until chips are completely melted; quickly pour into prepared pan. Stir remaining one-half hot mixture into chocolate chips until chips are completely melted. Quickly spread over top of peanut butter layer.

3. Cool completely. Remove from pan; place on cutting board. Peel off and discard foil; cut into 1-inch squares. Store tightly covered.

Makes about 5 dozen pieces or about 2 pounds candy

Peanut Butter Fudge: Omit chocolate chips; place 1⅔ cups (10-ounce package) REESE'S® Peanut Butter Chips in large bowl. Cook fudge mixture as directed. Add to chips; stir until chips are completely melted. Pour into prepared pan; cool.

Chocolate Fudge: Omit peanut butter chips; place 2 cups (12-ounce package) HERSHEY'S Semi-Sweet Chocolate Chips or HERSHEY'S MINI CHIPS™ Semi-Sweet Chocolate in large bowl. Cook fudge mixture as directed. Add to chips; stir until chips are completely melted. Pour into prepared pan; cool.

Note: For best results, do not double this recipe.

Date-Oatmeal Cookies

Prep Time: 15 minutes
Bake Time: 12 minutes

1 cup all-purpose flour
1 cup DOLE® Chopped Dates
   or Pitted Prunes, chopped
¾ cup quick-cooking oats
1 teaspoon ground cinnamon
¾ teaspoon baking powder
⅔ cup packed brown sugar
1 medium ripe DOLE® Banana,
   mashed (½ cup)
¼ cup margarine, softened
1 egg
1 teaspoon vanilla extract
Vegetable cooking spray

• Combine flour, dates, oats, cinnamon and baking powder in bowl; set aside.

• Beat together sugar, banana, margarine, egg and vanilla until well blended. Add flour mixture; stir until ingredients are moistened.

• Drop dough by rounded teaspoonfuls, 2 inches apart, onto baking sheets sprayed with vegetable cooking spray.

• Bake at 375°F 10 to 12 minutes or until lightly brown. Remove cookies to wire rack; cool. Store in airtight container. *Makes 32 servings*

Double Almond Butter Cookies

Dough
2 cups butter, softened
2½ cups powdered sugar,
   divided
4 cups all-purpose flour
2 teaspoons vanilla

Filling
⅔ cup BLUE DIAMOND®
   Blanched Almond Paste
¼ cup packed light brown
   sugar
½ cup BLUE DIAMOND®
   Chopped Natural
   Almonds, toasted
¼ teaspoon vanilla

For dough, beat butter and 1 cup powdered sugar until smooth. Gradually beat in flour. Beat in 2 teaspoons vanilla. Chill dough ½ hour.

For filling, combine almond paste, brown sugar, almonds and ¼ teaspoon vanilla.

Preheat oven to 350°F. Shape dough around ½ teaspoon filling mixture to form 1-inch balls. Place on *ungreased* cookie sheets.

Bake 15 minutes. Cool on wire racks. Roll cookies in remaining 1½ cups powdered sugar or sift over cookies.

Makes about 8 dozen cookies

Chocolate Truffles

Prep Time: 10 minutes
Chill Time: 3 hours

> **3 cups (18 ounces) semi-sweet chocolate chips**
> **1 (14-ounce) can EAGLE® BRAND Sweetened Condensed Milk (NOT evaporated milk)**
> **1 tablespoon vanilla extract**
> **Coatings: finely chopped toasted nuts, flaked coconut, chocolate sprinkles, colored sugar, unsweetened cocoa, powdered sugar or colored sprinkles**

1. In heavy saucepan over low heat, melt chips with Eagle Brand. Remove from heat; stir in vanilla.

2. Chill 2 hours or until firm. Shape into 1-inch balls; roll in desired coating.

3. Chill 1 hour or until firm. Store covered at room temperature.

Makes about 6 dozen truffles

Microwave Directions: In 1-quart glass measure, combine chips and Eagle Brand. Microwave at HIGH (100% power) 3 minutes, stirring after 1½ minutes. Stir until smooth. Proceed as directed.

Amaretto Truffles: Substitute 3 tablespoons amaretto liqueur and ½ teaspoon almond extract for vanilla. Roll in finely chopped toasted almonds.

Orange Truffles: Substitute 3 tablespoons orange-flavored liqueur for vanilla. Roll in finely chopped toasted almonds mixed with finely grated orange peel.

Rum Truffles: Substitute ¼ cup dark rum for vanilla. Roll in flaked coconut.

Bourbon Truffles: Substitute 3 tablespoons bourbon for vanilla. Roll in finely chopped toasted nuts.

The Ultimate Caramel Apple

> **1 cup water**
> **1 cup sugar**
> **½ cup heavy cream**
> **6 Washington Red Delicious or Golden Delicious apples**
> **3 ounces white chocolate, finely chopped**
> **3 ounces semi-sweet chocolate, finely chopped**
> **¼ cup coarsely chopped natural pistachios**
> **Red hot cinnamon candies or other small candy**
> **Edible gold dragées**

1. In medium heavy saucepan, combine water and sugar. Over low heat, stir mixture gently until sugar is completely dissolved. Increase heat to medium-low; cook, without stirring, until mixture is dark amber. Remove from heat; slowly stir in heavy cream *Mixture will bubble up and spatter a bit.*

Set aside until barely warm and thickened.

2. Insert popsicle sticks or small wooden dowels into bottom center of apples. Use 10-inch-square piece styrofoam as stand for apples; cover top of styrofoam with waxed paper to catch caramel drippings.

3. Dip top half of each apple into thickened caramel. Stand caramel-topped apples on styrofoam, allowing caramel to run down sides; refrigerate to harden. Meanwhile, melt white chocolate in top of double boiler of gently simmering water; stir until smooth. Transfer melted chocolate to pastry bag fitted with small writing tip. Drizzle thin, random lines of melted chocolate over each apple. Repeat melting and drizzling with semi-sweet chocolate. Decorate each apple with pistachios, candies and gold dragées, if desired. Serve or refrigerate to serve later.

Makes 6 caramel apples

Favorite recipe from **Washington Apple Commission**

Penuche

1 pound (2¼ cups) firmly packed DOMINO® Light Brown Sugar
¾ cup milk
⅛ teaspoon salt
2½ tablespoons butter or margarine
1 teaspoon vanilla extract
½ cup chopped walnuts or pecans (optional)

Combine sugar, milk and salt in heavy saucepan. Heat, stirring occasionally, until sugar dissolves. Wipe down sugar crystals from side of pan as necessary with pastry brush dipped in water. Boil mixture, without stirring, until mixture reaches 238°F or soft-ball stage on candy thermometer. Remove from heat. Add butter; *do not stir.* Cool to 110°F or lukewarm, without stirring.

Add extract and nuts. Stir continuously until thick and creamy. Immediately turn into buttered 9×5-inch loaf pan. When firm, cut into squares. Store in airtight container.

Makes 24 pieces (1¼ pounds)

MEMORABLE PIES

Recreate fond memories with a luscious, fresh-baked pie— distinctively American and always delicious. Whether juicy berry, nutty pecan or creamy custard, there's a flavor and filling for every season.

Classic Lemon Meringue Pie (page 290)

Old Favorites taste NEW
cooked Crisco's digestible way

1. *Peachy Pie:* It's Crisco that makes its crust so tender and flaky. (And Crisco is the secret of light, fluffy cakes in speed time—and digestible fried foods, too.)

3. Yum—Crisco doughnuts! The outside is crisp, and the inside is digestible (because Crisco doesn't soak in!). Economy hint—deep-fry with the same Crisco again and again!

2. *Chicken Creole,* an easy meal-in-a-dish. In the pan-frying step use Crisco (to get digestible, fine-flavored fried foods). And, of course, use Crisco for speedier cakes and flakier pie crust.

Watch a man get sentimental over an old food favorite—such as pie or doughnuts. But—here's the catch!—if they are heavy or greasy, old favorites may be *unfairly* branded as indigestible.

My secret—and that of thousands of wo... ...ook only with pure digestible Cri... ...ay, this sweet, flu... fri... to...

1. PEACHY PIE *light fluffy Crisco makes light digestible pastry!*

8 to 10 yellow peaches	2 tablespoons
1 tablespoon lemon	flour
juice	⅛ teaspoon salt
¾ cup sugar	⅓ cup chopped
Digestible Crisco Pastry	almonds

Slice pared peaches. Add lemon juice. Mix dry ingredients, including almonds. Mix with peaches. Line pie plate with flaky *digestible* Crisco Pastry (see right). Brush bottom with melted Crisco. Add fruit. Roll out top crust ⅛ inch thick. Cut in strips and make criss-cross top. Bake in hot oven (450° F.) 10 minutes, then reduce to moderate (350° F.). Bake 20 to 25 min. longer.

Digestible Crisco Pastry: Sift 2 cups flour with 1 teaspoon salt. Cut in ⅔ cup of light digestible Crisco. Add 6 to 8 tablespoons cold water, using only enough to hold mixture together. Roll out on lightly floured board.

Taste Note: Crisco's creamy flavor improves fried foods . . . gives delicacy to cakes.

2. CREOLE CHICKEN DINNER *a meal-in-a-dish—digestible, thanks to Crisco*

1 roasting chicken	½ teaspoon paprika
or capon	¼ teaspoon pepper
5 tablespoons Crisco	3 teaspoons salt
2 onions, sliced	3 cups boiling water
2 raw carrots, diced	1 cup rice, washed
1 cup canned	and drained
tomatoes	Stuffed olives,
2 whole cloves	sliced

Clean chicken, cut into frying pieces, flour lightly. Melt Crisco (sweet and digestible) in heavy skillet and brown onions, then remove them. Use same Crisco to pan-fry chicken. Put chicken in center of large baking dish (with cover). Combine carrots, tomatoes, all seasonings and boiling water. Pour around chicken. Sprinkle in rice evenly around chicken. also fried onion. Cover. Bake in moderate oven (350° F.) until rice is dry and chicken tender, about an hour. Remove cover for last 5 minutes. In serving, rice may be piled into mounds and garnished with sliced olives.

Economy Note: Crisco's moderate price makes it ideal for fried foods, pies and cakes.

3. 24 DOUGHNUT DELIGHTS *not greasy—ever!—when fried in Crisco!*

3 tablespoons Crisco	¼ teaspoon
⅔ cup sugar	cinnamon
2 eggs	¼ teaspoon cloves
3½ cups flour	⅛ teaspoon mace
4 teaspoons baking	1 teaspoon salt
powder	⅔ cup milk

Beat creamy Crisco, sugar and eggs. Add sifted dry ingredients alternately with milk. Divide dough. Pat out one portion ½ inch thick on floured board and cut out doughnuts. Melt enough Crisco to fill deep flat-bottomed saucepan ⅔ full. Heat to 365°-375° F. (this heat browns inch-cube of bread in 1 min.). Drain fried doughnuts on absorbent paper. When cool, dip tops into glaze. Strain Crisco—re-use it for frying.

Vanilla Glaze: Blend 2 cups confectioners sugar, 1 tsp. vanilla, 3 tablespoons hot milk.

Chocolate Glaze: To above, add 1 sq. chocolate melted in 1 tblsp. boiling water.

Health Note: Light wholesome pastry and cakes when you use light digestible Crisco.

ONLY 10¢ for Winifred Carter's "Favorite Recipes." 98 tested recipes—33 colored pictures! Send name and address (with 10¢ in stamps) to Dept. XG-105, Box 837, Cincinnati, Ohio.

All Measurements Level. Recipes tested and approved by Good Housekeeping Institute.

Classic Lemon Meringue Pie

Crust
> **Classic CRISCO® Single Crust (page 294)**

Filling
- 1½ **cups sugar**
- ¼ **cup cornstarch**
- 3 **tablespoons all-purpose flour**
- ¼ **teaspoon salt**
- 1½ **cups hot water**
- 3 **egg yolks, beaten**
- 2 **tablespoons butter or margarine**
- 1½ **teaspoons grated lemon peel**
- ⅓ **cup plus 1 tablespoon fresh lemon juice**

Meringue
- ½ **cup sugar, divided**
- 1 **tablespoon cornstarch**
- ½ **cup cold water**
- 4 **egg whites**
- ¾ **teaspoon vanilla**

1. For crust, prepare and bake as directed. Cool. Heat oven to 350°F.

2. For filling, combine 1½ cups sugar, ¼ cup cornstarch, flour and salt in medium saucepan. Add 1½ cups hot water gradually, stirring constantly. Cook and stir on medium heat until mixture comes to a boil and thickens. Reduce heat to low. Cook and stir constantly 8 minutes. Remove from heat. Add about one third of hot mixture slowly to egg yolks. Mix well. Return mixture to saucepan. Bring mixture to a boil on medium-high heat. Reduce heat to low. Cook and stir 4 minutes. Remove from heat. Stir in butter and lemon peel. Add lemon juice slowly. Mix well. Spoon into baked pie crust.

3. For meringue, combine 2 tablespoons sugar, 1 tablespoon cornstarch and ½ cup cold water in small saucepan. Stir until cornstarch dissolves. Cook and stir on medium heat until mixture is clear. Cool.

4. Combine egg whites and vanilla in large bowl. Beat at high speed of electric mixer until soft peaks form. Beat in remaining 6 tablespoons sugar, 1 tablespoon at a time. Beat well after each addition. Combine meringue with cornstarch mixture and continue beating until stiff peaks form. Spread over filling, covering completely and sealing to edge of pie.

5. Bake at 350°F for 12 to 15 minutes or until meringue is golden. *Do not overbake.* Cool to room temperature before serving. Refrigerate leftover pie.

Makes 1 (9-inch) pie

Classic Cherry Pie

Crust

1 unbaked (9-inch) Classic CRISCO® Double Crust (page 294))

Filling

3 pounds pitted red tart cherries frozen with sugar, thawed*

1½ cups reserved cherry juice*

⅓ cup granulated sugar

⅓ cup firmly packed brown sugar

¼ cup cornstarch

½ teaspoon ground cinnamon

1½ tablespoons Butter Flavor CRISCO® Stick or 1½ tablespoons Butter Flavor CRISCO all-vegetable shortening

1 tablespoon vanilla

1 teaspoon almond extract

Glaze

Milk

Additional granulated sugar

Use 2 cans (1 pound each) red tart cherries packed in water in place of frozen. Reduce cherry liquid to 1 cup.

1. Prepare 9-inch double crust as directed. Heat oven to 425°F.

2. For filling, drain cherries in large strainer over bowl, reserving 1½ cups juice. Combine sugars, cornstarch and cinnamon in large saucepan. Stir in reserved 1½ cups cherry juice. Cook and stir on medium heat until mixture is thick and bubbly. Boil and stir 1 minute. Add cherries and cook 1 minute or until mixture comes to a boil. Remove from heat. Stir in 1½ tablespoons shortening, vanilla and almond extract. Spoon into unbaked pie crust. Moisten pastry edge with water.

3. Cover pie with top crust. Fold top edge under bottom crust; flute with fingers or fork. Cut slits in top crust to allow steam to escape.

4. For glaze, brush top crust with milk. Sprinkle with additional granulated sugar. Bake at 425°F for 15 minutes. *Reduce oven temperature to 350°F.*

5. Bake 25 minutes or until filling in center is bubbly and crust is golden brown. *Do not overbake.* Cool until barely warm or to room temperature before serving.

Makes 1 (9-inch) pie

Classic Cherry Pie

Chocolate Mudslide Frozen Pie

- 1 cup (6 ounces) NESTLÉ® TOLL HOUSE® Semi-Sweet Chocolate Morsels
- 1 teaspoon TASTER'S CHOICE® 100% Pure Instant Coffee
- 1 teaspoon hot water
- ¾ cup sour cream
- ½ cup granulated sugar
- 1 teaspoon vanilla extract
- 1 *prepared* 9-inch (9 ounces) chocolate crumb crust
- 1½ cups heavy whipping cream
- 1 cup powdered sugar
- ¼ cup NESTLÉ® TOLL HOUSE® Baking Cocoa
- 2 tablespoons NESTLÉ® TOLL HOUSE® Semi-Sweet Chocolate Mini Morsels

MELT *1 cup* morsels in small, *heavy-duty* saucepan over *lowest possible* heat. When morsels begin to melt, remove from heat; stir until smooth. Cool for 10 minutes.

COMBINE coffee granules and water in medium bowl. Add sour cream, granulated sugar and vanilla extract; stir until sugar is dissolved. Stir in melted chocolate until smooth. Spread into crust; chill.

BEAT cream, powdered sugar and cocoa in small mixer bowl until stiff peaks form. Spread or pipe over chocolate layer. Sprinkle with mini morsels. Freeze for at least 6 hours or until firm.   *Makes 8 servings*

Creamy Lemon Meringue Pie

- 3 eggs, separated
- 1 (14-ounce) can EAGLE® BRAND Sweetened Condensed Milk (NOT evaporated milk)
- ½ cup lemon juice from concentrate
  Few drops yellow food coloring (optional)
- 1 (8- or 9-inch) baked pastry shell or graham cracker crumb pie crust
- ¼ teaspoon cream of tartar
- ⅓ cup sugar

1. Preheat oven to 350°F. In medium mixing bowl, beat egg yolks; stir in Eagle Brand, lemon juice and food coloring, if desired. Pour into baked pastry shell.

2. In small mixing bowl, beat egg whites and cream of tartar until soft peaks form; gradually add sugar, beating until stiff but not dry. Spread meringue on top of pie, sealing carefully to edge of shell. Bake 12 to 15 minutes or until golden brown. Cool. Chill thoroughly. Refrigerate leftovers.

Makes one 8- or 9-inch pie

Chocolate Mudslide Frozen Pie

Classic Crisco® Crust

8-, 9- or 10-inch Single Crust
1⅓ **cups all-purpose flour**
½ **teaspoon salt**
½ **CRISCO® Stick or ½ cup CRISCO® Shortening**
3 **tablespoons cold water**

8- or 9-inch Double Crust
2 **cups all-purpose flour**
1 **teaspoon salt**
¾ **CRISCO® Stick or ¾ cup CRISCO® Shortening**
5 **tablespoons cold water**

10-inch Double Crust
2⅔ **cups all-purpose flour**
1 **teaspoon salt**
1 **CRISCO® Stick or 1 cup CRISCO® Shortening**
7 **to 8 tablespoons cold water**

1. Spoon flour into measuring cup and level. Combine flour and salt in medium bowl.

2. Cut in shortening using pastry blender (or 2 knives) until all flour is blended to form pea-size chunks.

3. Sprinkle with water, 1 tablespoon at a time. Toss lightly with fork until dough forms a ball.

For Single Crust Pies
1. Press dough between hands to form 5- to 6-inch "pancake." Flour rolling surface and rolling pin lightly. Roll dough into circle.

2. Trim 1 inch larger than upside-down pie plate. Loosen dough carefully.

3. Fold dough into quarters. Unfold and press into pie plate. Fold edge under. Flute.

For Baked Pie Crusts
1. For recipes using baked pie crust, heat oven to 425°F. Prick bottom and side thoroughly with fork (50 times) to prevent shrinkage.

2. Bake at 425°F for 10 to 15 minutes or until lightly browned.

For Unbaked Pie Crusts
1. For recipes using unbaked pie crust, follow baking directions given in each recipe.

For Double Crust Pies
1. Divide dough in half. Roll each half separately. Transfer bottom crust to pie plate. Trim edge even with pie plate.

2. Add desired filling to unbaked pie crust. Moisten pastry edge with water. Lift top crust onto filled pie. Trim ½ inch beyond edge of pie plate. Fold top edge under bottom crust. Flute. Cut slits in top crust to allow steam to escape. Bake according to specific recipe directions.

Key Lime Pie

Prep Time: 25 minutes
Bake Time: 45 minutes
Cool Time: 1 hour
Chill Time: 3 hours

> **3 eggs, separated**
> **1 (14-ounce) can EAGLE®
> BRAND Sweetened
> Condensed Milk (NOT
> evaporated milk)**
> **½ cup lime juice from
> concentrate**
> **2 to 3 drops green food
> coloring (optional)**
> **1 (9-inch) unbaked pastry
> shell**
> **½ teaspoon cream of tartar**
> **⅓ cup sugar**

1. Preheat oven to 325°F. In medium mixing bowl, beat egg yolks; gradually beat in Eagle Brand and lime juice. Stir in food coloring, if desired. Pour into pastry shell.

2. Bake 30 minutes. Remove from oven. *Increase oven temperature to 350°F.*

3. Meanwhile, for meringue, with clean mixer, beat egg whites and cream of tartar to soft peaks. Gradually beat in sugar, 1 tablespoon at a time. Beat 4 minutes or until stiff, glossy peaks form and sugar is dissolved.

4. Immediately spread meringue over hot pie, carefully sealing to edge of crust to prevent meringue from shrinking. Bake 15 minutes. Cool 1 hour. Chill at least 3 hours. Store covered in refrigerator.

Makes 8 servings

Key Lime Pie

Strawberry Cream Pie

> **2 cups crushed fresh
> strawberries**
> **3 tablespoons sugar**
> **½ cup sour cream**
> **1 tub (8 ounces) COOL WHIP®
> Whipped Topping, thawed**
> **1 prepared chocolate flavor
> crumb crust (6 ounces)**
> **Sliced fresh strawberries**

STIR crushed strawberries and sugar in large bowl. Stir in sour cream. Gently stir in whipped topping. Spoon mixture into crust.

REFRIGERATE 4 hours or until firm. Garnish with sliced strawberries.   *Makes 8 servings*

Triple Layer Butterscotch Pie

Prep Time: 15 minutes
Refrigerate Time: 3 hours

> 2 squares BAKER'S® Semi-Sweet Baking Chocolate, melted
> ¼ cup sweetened condensed milk
> 1 prepared chocolate flavor crumb crust (6 ounces or 9 inches)
> ¾ cup chopped pecans, toasted
> 1¾ cups cold milk
> 2 packages (4-serving size each) JELL-O® Butterscotch Flavor Instant Pudding & Pie Filling
> 1 tub (8 ounces) COOL WHIP® Whipped Topping, thawed, divided

POUR chocolate and sweetened condensed milk into bowl; stir until smooth. Pour into crust. Press nuts evenly onto chocolate in crust. Refrigerate 10 minutes.

POUR milk into large bowl. Add pudding mixes. Beat with wire whisk 1 minute or until well blended. (Mixture will be thick.) Spread 1½ cups of pudding over chocolate in crust. Immediately stir ½ of whipped topping into remaining pudding. Spread over pudding in crust. Top with remaining whipped topping.

REFRIGERATE 3 hours or until set. Garnish as desired.

Makes 8 servings

Planters® Perfect Pecan Pie

> 3 eggs
> 1 cup light corn syrup
> 1 cup sugar
> 2 tablespoons margarine or butter, melted
> 1 teaspoon vanilla extract
> ⅛ teaspoon salt
> 1 cup PLANTERS® Pecan Halves
> 1 (9-inch) unbaked pastry shell
> COOL WHIP® Whipped Topping and PLANTERS® Pecan Halves, for garnish

1. Beat eggs slightly. Stir in corn syrup, sugar, margarine, vanilla and salt until blended.

2. Stir in pecan halves; pour into pastry shell.

3. Bake at 400°F for 15 minutes. *Reduce temperature to 350°F; bake 25 to 30 minutes more or until lightly browned and completely puffed across top. Cool completely.*

4. Serve garnished with whipped topping and pecan halves, if desired.

Makes 8 servings

Triple Layer Butterscotch Pie

Libby's® Famous Pumpkin Pie

¾ **cup granulated sugar**
½ **teaspoon salt**
1 **teaspoon ground cinnamon**
½ **teaspoon ground ginger**
¼ **teaspoon ground cloves**
2 **large eggs**
1 **can (15 ounces) LIBBY'S®**
  100% Pure Pumpkin
1 **can (12 fluid ounces)**
  NESTLÉ® CARNATION®
  Evaporated Milk*
1 **_unbaked_ 9-inch (4-cup**
  volume) deep-dish pie
  shell
  Whipped Cream

*For lower fat/calorie pie, substitute CARNATION® Evaporated Lowfat Milk or Evaporated Fat Free Milk.

MIX sugar, salt, cinnamon, ginger and cloves in small bowl. Beat eggs in large bowl. Stir in pumpkin and sugar-spice mixture. Gradually stir in evaporated milk.

POUR into pie shell.

BAKE in preheated 425°F. oven for 15 minutes. *Reduce temperature to 350°F.;* bake 40 to 50 minutes or until knife inserted near center comes out clean. Cool on wire rack for 2 hours. Serve immediately or refrigerate. Top with whipped cream before serving.   *Makes 8 servings*

Note: Do not freeze, as this will cause the crust to separate from the filling.

Libby's® Famous Pumpkin Pie

Substitution: 1¾ teaspoons pumpkin pie spice may be substituted for the cinnamon, ginger and cloves; however, the taste will be slightly different.

For 2 Shallow Pies: Substitute two 9-inch (2-cup volume) pie shells. Bake in preheated 425°F. oven for 15 minutes. *Reduce temperature to 350°F.;* bake for 20 to 30 minutes or until pies test done.

Picture Perfect Creamy Banana Pie

Prep Time: 25 minutes
Chill Time: 4 hours

½ cup sugar, divided
1 envelope unflavored gelatine
2 tablespoons cornstarch
1¾ cups lowfat milk
2 eggs, separated
¼ cup margarine
2 teaspoons vanilla extract
3 DOLE® Bananas, divided
1 (9-inch) chocolate cookie crust

• Combine ¼ cup sugar with gelatine and cornstarch in medium saucepan. Stir in milk and slightly beaten egg yolks. Cook over medium heat, stirring, until mixture boils and thickens. Remove from heat. Stir in margarine and vanilla.

• Pour custard into large bowl. Cover surface with plastic wrap. Refrigerate 15 minutes.

• Place 2 bananas in blender or food processor container. Cover; blend until smooth. Stir into custard.

• Beat egg whites until foamy. Gradually add remaining sugar. Beat until stiff peaks form. Fold into custard mixture. Pour into prepared crust.

• Chill 4 hours or until firm. Garnish with whipped cream, if desired. Slice remaining banana. Arrange banana slices over top of pie.   *Makes 8 servings*

Strawberry Glazed Pie

Crust

Classic CRISCO® Single Crust (page 294)

Filling

3½ cups fresh strawberry halves (1 quart)
½ cup sugar
2 tablespoons cornstarch
⅛ teaspoon salt
6 tablespoons cold water
2 packages (3 ounces each) cream cheese, softened
2 tablespoons orange juice

1. For crust, prepare and bake as directed. Cool completely.

2. For filling, set aside 2 cups strawberry halves. Crush remaining 1½ cups strawberries with fork.

3. Combine sugar, cornstarch and salt in small saucepan. Add cold water gradually. Stir until smooth. Add crushed strawberries. Cook and stir on medium heat until mixture comes to a boil. Cook and stir 1 minute. Remove from heat. Cool by setting pan in bowl of ice water.

4. Beat cream cheese at medium speed of electric mixer until fluffy. Add orange juice gradually. Beat until smooth. Spread in bottom of baked pie crust. Arrange strawberry halves over cheese layer. Pour cooled strawberry mixture over strawberry halves. Refrigerate. Top each serving with dollop of whipped cream, if desired.

Makes 1 (9-inch) pie

French Apple Pie

Crust

   1 (9-inch) Classic CRISCO®
      Double Crust (page 294)

Nut Filling

   ¾ cup ground walnuts
   2 tablespoons packed brown
      sugar
   2 tablespoons beaten egg
   1 tablespoon milk
   1 tablespoon butter or
      margarine, softened
   ¼ teaspoon vanilla
   ¼ teaspoon lemon juice

Apple Filling

   5 cups sliced peeled Granny
      Smith apples (about
      1¾ pounds or 5 medium)
   1 teaspoon lemon juice
   ¾ cup granulated sugar
   2 tablespoons all-purpose
      flour
   1 teaspoon ground cinnamon
   1 teaspoon ground nutmeg
   ¼ teaspoon salt
   2 tablespoons butter or
      margarine

1. For crust, prepare 9-inch Classic Crisco® Double Crust. Press bottom crust into 9-inch pie plate. *Do not bake.* Heat oven to 425°F.

2. For nut filling, combine nuts, brown sugar, egg, milk, 1 tablespoon butter, vanilla and ¼ teaspoon lemon juice. Spread over bottom of unbaked pie crust.

3. For apple filling, place apples in large bowl. Sprinkle with 1 teaspoon lemon juice. Combine granulated sugar, flour, cinnamon, nutmeg and salt. Sprinkle over apples. Toss to mix. Spoon over nut filling. Dot with 2 tablespoons butter. Moisten pastry edge with water.

4. Cover pie with top crust. Trim to one-half inch beyond edge of pie plate. Fold top edge under bottom crust. Flute. Cut slits into top crust to allow steam to escape. Bake at 425°F for 50 minutes or until filling in center is bubbly and crust is golden brown. Cover crust edge with foil, if necessary, to prevent overbrowning. Cool until barely warm or at room temperature before serving.   *Makes 1 (9-inch) pie*

❧ *tip* ❧

If the pie dough is sticky and difficult to handle, refrigerate it until firm. Lightly flour the rolling pin and surface to prevent the dough from sticking.

French Apple Pie

1. Mix cream cheese and sugar with electric mixer until well blended. Fold in whipped topping, chopped cookies and green food coloring. Spoon into crust.

2. Refrigerate 3 hours or overnight.

3. Garnish with cookie halves. Refrigerate leftovers.

Makes 8 servings

Grasshopper Mint Pie

Grasshopper Mint Pie

Prep Time: 15 minutes
Chill Time: 3 hours

1 (8-ounce) package cream cheese, softened
⅓ cup sugar
1 (8-ounce) tub frozen whipped topping, thawed
1 cup chopped KEEBLER® Fudge Shoppe® Grasshopper Cookies
3 drops green food coloring
1 (6-ounce) READY CRUST® Chocolate Pie Crust
Additional KEEBLER® Fudge Shoppe® Grasshopper Cookies, halved, for garnish

Traditional Cherry Pie

4 cups frozen tart cherries
1⅓ cups granulated sugar
3 tablespoons quick-cooking tapioca or cornstarch
½ teaspoon almond extract
Pastry for double crust 9-inch pie
2 tablespoons butter or margarine

In medium bowl, combine cherries, sugar, tapioca and almond extract; mix well. (It is not necessary to thaw cherries before using.) Let cherry mixture stand 15 minutes.

Line 9-inch pie plate with pastry; fill with cherry mixture. Dot with butter. Cover with top crust, cutting slits for steam to escape.

Bake in preheated oven 400°F 50 to 55 minutes or until crust is golden brown and filling is bubbly.

Makes 6 to 8 servings

*Favorite recipe from **Cherry Marketing Institute***

Apple-Raisin Cobbler Pie

Apple-Raisin Cobbler Pie

Prep Time: 10 minutes
Baking Time: 35 minutes

> 2 (20-ounce) cans apple pie filling
> 1 cup raisins
> ¼ teaspoon ground nutmeg
> 1 (6-ounce) READY CRUST® Shortbread Pie Crust
> ⅓ cup all-purpose flour
> ¼ cup packed brown sugar
> 3 tablespoons butter or margarine, melted
> ¾ cup chopped walnuts

1. Preheat oven to 375°F.

2. Combine pie filling, raisins and nutmeg in large bowl. Spoon into crust. Combine flour and sugar in small bowl; stir in butter until crumbly. Stir in walnuts; sprinkle over filling.

3. Bake 35 to 45 minutes or until topping is golden.

Makes 8 servings

Chocolate Chiffon Pie

Prep Time: 20 minutes
Chill Time: 3 hours

> 2 (1-ounce) squares unsweetened chocolate, chopped
> 1 (14-ounce) can EAGLE® BRAND Sweetened Condensed Milk (NOT evaporated milk)
> 1 envelope unflavored gelatin
> ⅓ cup water
> ½ teaspoon vanilla extract
> 1 cup (½ pint) whipping cream, whipped
> 1 (6-ounce) chocolate or graham cracker crumb pie crust
> Additional whipped cream

1. In heavy saucepan over low heat, melt chocolate with Eagle Brand. Remove from heat.

2. Meanwhile, in small saucepan, sprinkle gelatin over water; let stand 1 minute. Over low heat, stir until gelatin dissolves.

3. Stir gelatin into chocolate mixture. Add vanilla. Cool to room temperature. Fold in whipped cream. Spread into crust.

4. Chill 3 hours or until set. Garnish with additional whipped cream. Store covered in refrigerator.

Makes 1 pie

Creamy Coconut Pie

Prep Time: 10 minutes
Freeze Time: 4 hours

> 1 (3-ounce) package cream cheese, softened
> 1 tablespoon sugar
> ½ cup milk
> 1⅓ cups sweetened flaked coconut
> 1 (8-ounce) tub COOL WHIP® Whipped Topping, thawed
> ½ teaspoon almond extract
> 1 (6-ounce) READY CRUST® Shortbread Pie Crust
> Toasted coconut, for garnish
> Maraschino cherries, for garnish

1. Beat cream cheese and sugar in medium bowl until fluffy. Gradually add milk; beat until smooth. Fold in coconut, whipped topping and extract. Spoon into crust.

2. Freeze 4 hours.

3. Garnish with toasted coconut and maraschino cherries. Let stand at room temperature to soften before serving.   *Makes 8 servings*

Chocolate Chiffon Pie

Buttered Pecan Pie

Crust
 1¼ **cups all-purpose flour**
 ¼ **cup confectioners' sugar**
 ¼ **cup plus 2 tablespoons finely chopped pecans**
 ⅛ **teaspoon salt**
 ½ **Butter Flavor CRISCO® Stick or ½ cup Butter Flavor CRISCO® all-vegetable shortening**
 3 **tablespoons ice water**

Filling
 3 **eggs**
 1 **cup butter pecan syrup or maple syrup**
 ⅔ **cup granulated sugar**
 1 **teaspoon vanilla**
 ¼ **teaspoon salt**
 ⅓ **cup butter or margarine, melted**
 1¼ **cups chopped pecans**

Decoration
 12 **pecan halves**

1. For crust, combine flour, confectioners' sugar, finely chopped nuts and ⅛ teaspoon salt in medium bowl. Cut in shortening using pastry blender (or 2 knives) until all flour is blended in to form pea-size chunks.

2. Sprinkle mixture with water, 1 tablespoon at a time. Toss lightly with fork until dough forms a ball. Press between hands to form 5- to 6-inch "pancake."

3. Roll and press crust into 9-inch pie plate. Do not flute. Do not bake. Heat oven to 350°F.

4. For filling, beat eggs in medium bowl until frothy. Add syrup, granulated sugar, vanilla and ¼ teaspoon salt. Beat until blended. Stir in melted butter and chopped nuts. Pour into unbaked pie crust.

5. For decoration, dip 6 nut halves in filling to coat. Arrange in center of pie to resemble flower. Press 6 scallops into crust edge using back of tablespoon. Place 1 nut half in each indentation. Press lightly. Cover edge of pie with foil to prevent overbrowning.

6. Bake at 350°F for 45 minutes. *Do not overbake.* Remove foil. Bake 5 minutes or until pie is almost set in center when shaken gently. Cool to room temperature before serving. Refrigerate leftovers.

Makes one 9-inch pie
(8 servings)

❧ *tip* ❧

Handle the dough quickly and lightly for a tender, flaky pie crust.

Frozen Peanut Butter Pie

Frozen Peanut Butter Pie

Prep Time: 20 minutes
Freeze Time: 4 hours

> **Chocolate Crunch Crust (recipe follows)**
> 1 **(8-ounce) package cream cheese, softened**
> 1 **(14-ounce) can EAGLE® BRAND Sweetened Condensed Milk (NOT evaporated milk)**
> ¾ **cup peanut butter**
> 2 **tablespoons lemon juice from concentrate**
> 1 **teaspoon vanilla extract**
> 1 **cup (½ pint) whipping cream, whipped**
> **Chocolate fudge ice cream topping**

1. Prepare Chocolate Crunch Crust. In large mixing bowl, beat cream cheese until fluffy; gradually beat in Eagle Brand and peanut butter until smooth. Stir in lemon juice and vanilla. Fold in whipped cream.

2. Spread in prepared crust. Drizzle topping over pie. Freeze 4 hours or until firm. Return leftovers to freezer.   *Makes one 9-inch pie*

Chocolate Crunch Crust: In heavy saucepan over low heat, melt ⅓ cup butter or margarine and 1 (6-ounce) package semi-sweet chocolate chips. Remove from heat; gently stir in 2½ cups oven-toasted rice cereal until completely coated. Press on bottom and up side to rim of buttered 9-inch pie plate. Chill 30 minutes.

Fresh Lemon Meringue Pie

1½ cups sugar
¼ cup plus 2 tablespoons cornstarch
½ teaspoon salt
½ cup cold water
½ cup fresh squeezed SUNKIST® lemon juice
3 egg yolks, well beaten
2 tablespoons butter or margarine
1½ cups boiling water
Grated peel of ½ SUNKIST® lemon
2 to 3 drops yellow food coloring (optional)
1 (9-inch) baked pie crust
Three-Egg Meringue (recipe follows)

In large saucepan, combine sugar, cornstarch and salt. Gradually blend in cold water and lemon juice. Stir in egg yolks. Add butter and boiling water. Bring to a boil over medium-high heat, stirring constantly. Reduce heat to medium and boil 1 minute. Remove from heat; stir in lemon peel and food coloring. Pour into baked pie crust. Top with Three-Egg Meringue, sealing well at edges. Bake at 350°F 12 to 15 minutes. Cool 2 hours before serving.

Makes 6 servings

Three-Egg Meringue

3 egg whites
¼ teaspoon cream of tartar
6 tablespoons sugar

In large bowl with electric mixer, beat egg whites with cream of tartar until foamy. Gradually add sugar and beat until stiff peaks form.

Oreo® Mud Pie

26 OREO® Chocolate Sandwich Cookies, divided
2 tablespoons margarine or butter, melted
1 pint chocolate ice cream, softened
2 pints coffee ice cream, softened
½ cup heavy cream, whipped
¼ cup PLANTERS® Walnuts, chopped
½ cup chocolate fudge topping

1. Finely crush 12 cookies; mix with margarine. Press crumb mixture onto bottom of 9-inch pie plate; stand remaining 14 cookies around edge of plate. Place in freezer 10 minutes.

2. Evenly spread chocolate ice cream into prepared crust. Scoop coffee ice cream into balls; arrange over chocolate layer. Freeze 4 hours or until firm.

3. To serve, top with whipped cream, walnuts and fudge topping.

Makes 8 servings

Fresh Lemon Meringue Pie

Classic Rhubarb Pie

Crust

> **Classic CRISCO® Double Crust (page 294)**

Filling

> **4 cups red rhubarb, cut into
> ½- to ¾-inch pieces**
> **1⅓ to 1½ cups sugar, to taste**
> **⅓ cup all-purpose flour**
> **2 tablespoons butter or
> margarine**

Glaze

> **1 tablespoon milk**
> **Sugar**

1. For crust, prepare crust as directed and press bottom crust into 9-inch pie plate leaving overhang. *Do not bake.* Heat oven to 400°F.

2. For filling, combine rhubarb and sugar in large bowl. Mix well. Stir in flour. Spoon into unbaked pie crust. Dot with butter. Moisten pastry edge with water.

3. Cover pie with woven lattice top.

4. For glaze, brush top crust with milk. Sprinkle with sugar. Cover edge with foil to prevent overbrowning. Bake at 400°F for 20 minutes. *Reduce oven temperature to 325°F.* Remove foil. Bake 30 minutes or until filling in center is bubbly and crust is golden brown (if using frozen rhubarb bake 60 to 70 minutes). *Do not overbake.* Cool until barely warm or to room temperature before serving.

Makes 1 (9-inch) pie

Classic Rhubarb Pie

Sweet Potato Pecan Pie

Prep Time: 30 minutes
Bake Time: 45 minutes

> **1 pound sweet potatoes or
> yams, cooked and peeled**
> **¼ cup (½ stick) butter or
> margarine, softened**
> **1 (14-ounce) can EAGLE®
> BRAND Sweetened
> Condensed Milk (NOT
> evaporated milk)**
> **1 egg**
> **1 teaspoon grated orange peel**
> **1 teaspoon ground cinnamon**
> **1 teaspoon vanilla extract**
> **½ teaspoon ground nutmeg**
> **¼ teaspoon salt**
> **1 (6-ounce) graham cracker
> crumb pie crust**
> **Pecan Topping (recipe
> follows)**

1. Preheat oven to 425°F. In large mixing bowl, beat hot sweet potatoes and butter until smooth. Add Eagle Brand and remaining ingredients except crust and Pecan Topping; mix well. Pour into crust.

2. Bake 20 minutes. Meanwhile, prepare Pecan Topping.

3. Remove pie from oven; *reduce oven temperature to 350°F.* Spoon Pecan Topping over pie.

4. Bake 25 minutes longer or until set. Cool. Serve warm or at room temperature. Garnish with orange zest twist, if desired. Refrigerate leftovers.   *Makes 1 pie*

Pecan Topping: In small mixing bowl, beat 1 egg, 2 tablespoons firmly packed light brown sugar, 2 tablespoons dark corn syrup, 1 tablespoon melted butter and ½ teaspoon maple flavoring. Stir in 1 cup chopped pecans.

Sweet Potato Pecan Pie

Chocolate Velvet Pie

1¾ **cups (11.5-ounce package) NESTLÉ® TOLL HOUSE® Milk Chocolate Morsels**
1 **package (8 ounces) cream cheese, softened**
1 **teaspoon vanilla extract**
1 **cup heavy whipping cream, whipped**
1 *prepared* **8-inch (6 ounces) chocolate crumb crust**
Sweetened whipped cream (optional)
Chocolate curls (optional)
Chopped nuts (optional)

MICROWAVE morsels in medium, microwave-safe bowl on MEDIUM-HIGH (70%) power for 1 minute; stir. Microwave at additional 10- to 20-seconds intervals, stirring until smooth. Cool to room temperature.

BEAT melted chocolate, cream cheese and vanilla extract in large mixer bowl until light in color. Fold in whipped cream. Spoon into crust. Refrigerate until firm. Top with sweetened whipped cream, chocolate curls and nuts.

                Makes 8 servings

Chocolate Bavarian Pie

1 envelope unflavored gelatin
1¾ cups milk, divided
⅔ cup sugar
6 tablespoons HERSHEY'S Cocoa
1 tablespoon light corn syrup
2 tablespoons butter (do *not* use margarine, spread or oil)
¾ teaspoon vanilla extract
1 cup (½ pint) cold whipping cream
1 baked 9-inch pie crust or crumb crust

1. Sprinkle gelatin over 1 cup milk in medium saucepan; let stand 2 minutes to soften.

2. Stir together sugar and cocoa. Add to mixture in saucepan. Add corn syrup. Cook, stirring constantly, until mixture comes to a boil. Remove from heat. Add butter; stir until melted. Stir in remaining ¾ cup milk and vanilla. Pour into large bowl. Cool; refrigerate until almost set.

3. Beat whipping cream in small bowl on high speed of mixer until stiff. Beat chocolate mixture on medium speed of mixer until smooth. On low speed, add half the whipped cream to chocolate mixture, beating just until blended. Pour into prepared crust. Refrigerate 3 hours or until firm. Just before serving, garnish with remaining whipped cream. Cover; refrigerate leftover pie.

Makes 6 to 8 servings

Pistachio Pie

Prep Time: 10 minutes
Chill Time: 2 to 3 hours

2 kiwis, peeled and sliced
1 (6-ounce) READY CRUST® Chocolate Pie Crust
1¾ cups cold milk
1 (4-serving-size) package pistachio flavored instant pudding and pie filling
Frozen non-dairy whipped topping, thawed, for garnish

1. Arrange kiwi slices to cover bottom of crust, reserving a few for garnish.

2. Combine milk and pudding mix in large bowl. Beat with electric mixer at low speed 1 minute or until well blended. Pour over kiwi and chill pie 2 to 3 hours.

3. Place reserved kiwi slices on top of pie and garnish with dollops of whipped topping.

Makes 8 servings

Peanut Butter Cup Cookie Ice Cream Pie

Peanut Butter Cup Cookie Ice Cream Pie

Prep Time: 15 minutes

- ½ **cup creamy peanut butter**
- ¼ **cup honey**
- 1 **quart (2 pints) vanilla ice cream, softened**
- 1 **cup KEEBLER® Chips Deluxe™ With Peanut Butter Cups Cookies, chopped**
- 1 **(6-ounce) READY CRUST® Chocolate Pie Crust**
- ½ **cup chocolate syrup**
  Whipped cream

1. Place large bowl in freezer. Mix peanut butter and honey in medium bowl. Place ice cream in bowl from freezer; add peanut butter mixture and cookies. Mix on low speed with electric mixer until blended.

2. Spoon half of ice cream mixture into crust. Spread chocolate syrup over ice cream mixture in crust. Spoon remaining ice cream mixture over chocolate syrup.

3. Garnish with whipped cream and additional chocolate syrup. Freeze leftovers.   *Makes 8 servings*

Cool 'n' Easy® Pie

⅔ cup boiling water
1 package (4-serving size)
    JELL-O® Brand Gelatin,
    any flavor
½ cup cold juice, any flavor
    Ice cubes
1 tub (8 ounces) COOL WHIP®
    Whipped Topping, thawed
1 prepared graham cracker
    crumb crust (6 ounces)
    Assorted fruit (optional)

STIR boiling water into gelatin in large bowl 2 minutes or until completely dissolved. Mix cold juice and ice to make 1 cup. Add to gelatin, stirring until slightly thickened. Remove any remaining ice.

STIR in whipped topping with wire whisk until smooth. Refrigerate 10 to 15 minutes or until mixture is very thick and will mound. Spoon into crust.

REFRIGERATE 4 hours or until firm. Just before serving, garnish with fruit, if desired. Store leftover pie in refrigerator.

Makes 8 servings

Black Raspberry Pie

Crust
    **Classic CRISCO® Double
        Crust (page 294)**

Filling
    4 cups fresh or frozen and
        partially thawed black
        raspberries
1¼ cups sugar
  ¼ cup cornstarch
  2 tablespoons butter or
      margarine, softened
    Dash salt

1. For crust, prepare as directed. Roll and press bottom crust into 9-inch pie plate. *Do not bake.* Heat oven to 350°F.

2. For filling, combine raspberries, sugar, cornstarch, butter and salt. Toss gently. Spoon into unbaked pie crust. Moisten pastry edge with water.

3. Roll top crust same as bottom. Lift onto filled pie. Trim ½ inch beyond edge of pie plate. Fold top edge under bottom crust. Flute. Cut slits in top crust to allow steam to escape.

4. Bake at 350°F for 1 hour or until filling in center is bubbly and crust is golden brown. *Do not overbake.* Cool to room temperature before serving.   *Makes 1 (9-inch) pie*

Hint: Try red raspberries if black raspberries are unavailable.

Cool 'n' Easy® Pie

1. Heat oven to 400°F.

2. For Filling, drain peaches, reserving 3 tablespoons syrup; set aside. Cut peaches into small pieces; place in large bowl. Combine cornstarch and 3 tablespoons sugar in medium bowl. Add 3 tablespoons reserved peach syrup; mix well. Add remaining sugar, eggs and buttermilk; mix well. Stir in ½ cup melted butter and vanilla. Pour over peaches; stir until peaches are coated. Pour filling into unbaked pie crust. Moisten pastry edge with water.

3. Cover pie with top crust. Fold top edge under bottom crust; flute with fingers or fork. Cut slits or designs in top crust to allow steam to escape.

4. For Glaze, brush top crust with 2 tablespoons melted butter. Sprinkle with additional sugar.

5. Bake at 400°F for 45 minutes or until filling in center is bubbly and crust is golden brown. *Do not overbake.* Cool to room temperature before serving.

Makes 1 (10-inch) pie

❧ *tip* ❧

To prevent a fruit pie from becoming soggy, fill the pie crust with the fruit filling just before baking.

Georgia Peach Pie

Georgia Peach Pie

Crust
 1 unbaked 10-inch Classic
  CRISCO® Double Crust
  (page 294)

Filling
 1 can (29 ounces) yellow cling
  peaches in heavy syrup
 3 tablespoons reserved peach
  syrup
 3 tablespoons cornstarch
 1 cup sugar, divided
 3 eggs
 ⅓ cup buttermilk
 ½ cup butter or margarine,
  melted
 1 teaspoon vanilla

Glaze
 2 tablespoons butter or
  margarine, melted
 Additional sugar

Hershey's Cocoa Cream Pie

**1 baked 9-inch pie crust or
graham cracker crumb
crust, cooled**
½ cup HERSHEY'S Cocoa
1¼ cups sugar
⅓ cup cornstarch
¼ teaspoon salt
3 cups milk
**3 tablespoons butter or
margarine**
**1½ teaspoons vanilla extract
Sweetened whipped cream**

1. Prepare crust; cool.

2. Stir together cocoa, sugar, cornstarch and salt in medium saucepan. Gradually add milk, stirring until smooth. Cook over medium heat, stirring constantly, until mixture comes to a boil; boil 1 minute.

3. Remove from heat; stir in butter and vanilla. Pour into prepared crust. Press plastic wrap directly onto surface. Cool to room temperature. Refrigerate 6 to 8 hours. Serve with sweetened whipped cream. Garnish as desired. Cover; refrigerate leftover pie.

Makes 6 to 8 servings

Hershey's Cocoa Cream Pie

Fluffy Lemon Berry Pie

Fluffy Lemon Berry Pie

Prep Time: 10 minutes
Chill Time: 3 hours

> **4 ounces cream cheese, softened**
> **1½ cups cold milk**
> **2 (4-serving size) packages JELL-O® Lemon Flavor Instant Pudding & Pie Filling**
> **1 (8-ounce) tub COOL WHIP® Whipped Topping, thawed**
> **1 (6-ounce) READY CRUST® Shortbread or Graham Cracker Pie Crust**
> **1 cup blueberries, raspberries or sliced strawberries**

1. Beat cream cheese in large bowl with wire whisk until smooth. Gradually beat in milk until well blended. Add pudding mixes. Beat 2 minutes or until smooth. Immediately stir in half of whipped topping.

2. Spoon into crust. Top with remaining whipped topping.

3. Refrigerate 3 hours or until set. Garnish with berries. Refrigerate leftovers. *Makes 8 servings*

My Best Apple Pie

Crust
> 1 cup all-purpose flour
> 1 cup whole wheat flour
> 1 teaspoon salt
> ½ teaspoon cinnamon
> ¾ CRISCO® Stick or ¾ cup CRISCO® all-vegetable shortening
> 5 tablespoons cold water

Filling
> 4 cups sliced peeled (¼-inch slices) Golden Delicious apples (about 1⅓ pounds or 4 medium)
> 3 cups sliced peeled (¼-inch slices) Granny Smith apples (about 1 pound or 3 medium)
> ¼ cup apple juice
> 2 tablespoons lemon juice
> ½ cup granulated sugar
> ½ cup firmly packed light brown sugar
> ¾ teaspoon cinnamon
> ½ teaspoon nutmeg
> 2 tablespoons plus 1½ teaspoons quick-cooking tapioca
> 1 teaspoon vanilla

1. For crust, combine all-purpose flour, whole wheat flour, salt and ½ teaspoon cinnamon in large bowl. Cut in shortening. See page 294 Classic Crisco® Crust Pie for remaining preparation. Roll and press bottom crust into 9-inch pie plate. Cover. *Do not bake.*

2. For filling, combine apples, apple juice and lemon juice in large saucepan. Cook and stir on high heat 5 minutes or until apples are slightly tender. Pour into large shallow dish. Place in refrigerator, uncovered, until cool, about 20 minutes.

3. Heat oven to 400°F.

4. Spoon apples and any liquid into large bowl. Add granulated sugar, brown sugar, ¾ teaspoon cinnamon, nutmeg, tapioca and vanilla. Toss to coat. Spoon into unbaked pie crust. Moisten pastry edge with water.

5. Roll top crust same as bottom. Lift onto filled pie. Trim ½ inch beyond edge of pie plate. Fold top edge under bottom crust. Flute. Cut slits in top crust to allow steam to escape.

6. Bake at 400°F for 15 minutes. *Reduce oven temperature to 350°F.* Bake 1 hour or until filling in center is bubbly and crust is golden brown. *Do not overbake.* Cool to room temperature before serving.

> *Makes 1 (9-inch) pie*

DESSERTS
& CHEESECAKES

*Great meals demand a memorable dessert to conclude
the perfect evening. Indulge in an exquisite cheesecake, a creamy
pudding, a fluffy mousse, a fruit-filled cobbler or a delicious
trifle—luscious desserts to satisfy every craving.*

Creamy Baked Cheesecake (page 322)

Charles Villiar Sparr, fifteen months old son of Mr. and Mrs. Charles Sparr of Prescott, Iowa.

Brown are his eyes and auburn his hair —and his little body is as sturdy as the most devoted mother could wish. "... his constant good health has made him full of vim and pep", Mrs. Sparr says.

Vigor—do you wish it for your boy?

SINCE her son, Villiar, is so healthy and active, both mentally and physically, it is not surprising that Mrs. Sparr is an enthusiast about Eagle Brand. For Eagle Brand has always been Villiar's food—and he has never had even the least of the usual ills of childhood.

When he was ten months old Villiar walked; at fifteen months—when this picture was taken—Villiar's mother began to teach him his A B C's! He has "keen intelligence", Mrs. Sparr reports, and "he learns exceedingly fast". Of course, her own thoughtful care has had much to do with the little boy's development, but she, herself, gives Eagle Brand the credit.

What mother doesn't want her child to be well and vigorous as to body, and quick as to mind? So much depends upon the food—and it is not necessary to experiment with your baby's food. Nurse him, of course, if it is possible—but if for any reason you cannot do this, don't take unnecessary risks. There are no doubts about the purity or the splendid results of Eagle Brand as an infant food. It has been the standard baby food for 64 years.

Eagle Brand is nothing but wholesome country milk blended with pure sugar. Mrs. Sparr is only one of the many thousands of mothers who have testified to its benefits. Doctors recommend it for babies who are puny and are losing weight. When other foods fail, Eagle Brand has proved itself again and again. It is easily digested; its purity and quality remain constant; it can be bought anywhere.

Do you want a cunning record book in which to keep your baby's history? Then write for "The Best Baby" and for chart and booklet about feeding. Both are free.

THE BORDEN COMPANY
Borden Building   New York

Borden's
THE NATION'S MILK

Eagle Brand
Condensed Milk
Evaporated Milk
Malted Milk
Milk Chocolate
Condensed Coffee

Established 1857

Trade Mark of THE BORDEN COMPANY
Reg. U. S. Pat. Off.
GAIL BORDEN
EAGLE BRAND
by which their PRESERVED MILK will hereafter be designated; and for additional protection against imposition, each label will bear the signature.
Gail Borden
THE BORDEN COMPANY
NEW YORK, U.S.A.

Borden's
EAGLE BRAND
Condensed Milk

Creamy Baked Cheesecake

Prep Time: 20 minutes
Bake Time: 55 to 60 minutes
Chill Time: 4 hours

- 1¼ cups graham cracker crumbs
- ¼ cup sugar
- ⅓ cup (⅔ stick) butter or margarine, melted
- 2 (8-ounce) packages cream cheese, softened
- 1 (14-ounce) can EAGLE® BRAND Sweetened Condensed Milk (NOT evaporated milk)
- 3 eggs
- ¼ cup lemon juice from concentrate
- 1 (8-ounce) container sour cream, at room temperature
- Raspberry Topping (recipe follows), if desired

1. Preheat oven to 300°F. In small mixing bowl, combine crumbs, sugar and butter; press firmly on bottom of *ungreased* 9-inch springform pan.

2. In large mixing bowl, beat cream cheese until fluffy. Gradually beat in Eagle Brand until smooth. Add eggs and lemon juice; mix well. Pour into prepared pan.

3. Bake 50 to 55 minutes or until set. Remove from oven; top with sour cream. Bake 5 minutes longer. Cool. Chill. Prepare Raspberry Topping, if desired, and serve with cheesecake. Store covered in refrigerator.

Makes 1 (9-inch) cheesecake

Raspberry Topping

Prep Time: 5 minutes

- 1 (10-ounce) package thawed frozen red raspberries in syrup
- ¼ cup red currant jelly or red raspberry jam
- 1 tablespoon cornstarch

1. Reserve ⅔ cup syrup from raspberries; set raspberries aside.

2. In small saucepan over medium heat, combine reserved syrup, jelly and cornstarch. Cook and stir until slightly thickened and clear. Cool. Stir in raspberries.

✤ *tip* ✤

A picture perfect cheesecake has a smooth top. One way to prevent cracking in the center of the cheesecake is to avoid overbeating the batter. Beat the mixture just until blended.

Ambrosial Fruit Dessert

Ambrosial Fruit Dessert

1 medium DOLE® Fresh Pineapple
1 medium orange, peeled, sliced
1 red apple, cored, sliced
1 cup seedless DOLE® Grapes
Fruit Glaze (recipe follows)
4 teaspoons flaked coconut

• Twist crown from pineapple. Cut pineapple in half lengthwise. Refrigerate one half for another use, such as fruit salad. Cut fruit from shell. Cut fruit crosswise into thin slices.

• Arrange fruits on 4 dessert plates. Drizzle with Fruit Glaze. Sprinkle with coconut.   *Makes 4 servings*

Fruit Glaze

¾ cup DOLE® Pineapple Orange Juice
2 tablespoons orange marmalade
1 tablespoon cornstarch
1 teaspoon rum extract
2 teaspoons grated lime peel

• Combine all ingredients, except lime peel, in saucepan. Cook, stirring, until sauce boils and thickens. Cool. Stir in lime peel.

Frozen Pumpkin Squares

Prep Time: 15 minutes
Freeze Time: 4 hours

    1 cup NABISCO® Old Fashioned Ginger Snaps, finely crushed
    ¼ cup finely chopped PLANTERS® Walnuts
    ¼ cup (½ stick) butter or margarine, melted
  1¼ cups cold milk
    2 packages (4-serving size each) JELL-O® Vanilla Flavor Instant Pudding & Pie Filling
    1 cup canned pumpkin
    1 teaspoon pumpkin pie spice
    1 tub (8 ounces) COOL WHIP® Whipped Topping, thawed, divided

MIX crumbs, walnuts and butter in small bowl. Reserve 2 tablespoons for garnish. Press onto bottom of foil-lined 8-inch square pan. Refrigerate.

POUR milk into large bowl. Add pudding mixes, pumpkin and spice. Beat with wire whisk 2 minutes or until well blended. Gently stir in 2¼ cups whipped topping. Spread over crust.

FREEZE 4 hours or until firm. Let stand at room temperature 10 minutes or until dessert can be easily cut. Cut into squares. Garnish with remaining whipped topping and sprinkle with reserved crumbs.

Makes 9 servings

Creamy Rice Pudding

Prep Time: 1 hour

  2½ cups water
    ½ cup uncooked long grain rice
    1 (3-inch) cinnamon stick *or* ¼ teaspoon ground cinnamon
    2 (¼-inch) pieces lemon peel
    Dash salt
    1 (14-ounce) can EAGLE® BRAND Sweetened Condensed Milk (NOT evaporated milk)
    Additional ground cinnamon

1. In medium saucepan combine water, rice, cinnamon stick, lemon peel and salt. Let mixture stand 30 minutes.

2. Bring mixture to a boil, stirring occasionally. Add Eagle Brand; mix well. Return to a boil; stir.

3. Reduce heat to medium. Cook, uncovered, stirring frequently, 20 to 25 minutes or until liquid is absorbed to top of rice.

4. Cool. (Pudding thickens as it cools.) Remove cinnamon stick and lemon peel. Sprinkle with additional cinnamon. Serve warm or chilled. Refrigerate leftovers.

Makes 4 to 6 servings

Frozen Pumpkin Square

Striped Delight

Prep Time: 20 minutes
Refrigerating Time: 4 hours
15 minutes

- 35 chocolate sandwich cookies, finely crushed (3 cups)
- 6 tablespoons butter or margarine, melted
- 1 package (8 ounces) PHILADELPHIA® Cream cheese, softened
- ¼ cup sugar
- 2 tablespoons cold milk
- 1 tub (12 ounces) COOL WHIP® Whipped Topping, thawed
- 3¼ cups cold milk
- 2 packages (4-serving size) JELL-O® Chocolate Flavor Instant Pudding & Pie Filling

MIX crushed cookies and butter in medium bowl. Press firmly into bottom of foil-lined 13×9-inch pan. Refrigerate 15 minutes.

BEAT cream cheese, sugar and 2 tablespoons milk in medium bowl with wire whisk until smooth. Gently stir in 1¼ cups whipped topping. Spread over crust.

POUR 3¼ cups milk into large bowl. Add pudding mixes. Beat with wire whisk 1 to 2 minutes. Pour over cream cheese layer. Let stand 5 minutes or until thickened. Drop remaining whipped topping by spoonfuls over pudding. Spread to cover pudding.

REFRIGERATE 4 hours or overnight. Cut into squares.

Makes 16 servings

Fresh Fruit with Citrus Glaze

Prep Time: 5 minutes
Cook Time: 5 minutes

- 2 cups DOLE® Pineapple, Pineapple Orange or Pine-Orange-Banana Juice
- 3 tablespoons sugar
- 1 tablespoon cornstarch
- 1 tablespoon lemon juice
- ½ teaspoon grated lemon peel
- 8 cups cut-up fresh fruit such as DOLE® Fresh Pineapple, Bananas, Strawberries, Red or Green Seedless Grapes, Cantaloupe, Oranges, Peaches, Nectarines or Kiwi
- Fresh mint leaves (optional)

• Combine pineapple juice, sugar, cornstarch, lemon juice and lemon peel in medium saucepan.

• Cook and stir over medium-high heat 5 minutes or until mixture comes to boil. Reduce heat to low; cook 2 minutes or until slightly thickened. Cool slightly. Sauce can be served warm or chilled.

• Arrange fruit in dessert dishes. Spoon glaze over fruit. Refrigerate any leftovers in air-tight container.

Makes 8 servings

Brownie Baked Alaska

Brownie Baked Alaskas

**2 purchased brownies
   (2½ inches square)**
**2 scoops fudge swirl ice cream
   (or favorite flavor)**
**⅓ cup semisweet chocolate
   chips**
**2 tablespoons light corn syrup
   or milk**
2 egg whites
¼ cup sugar

1. Preheat oven to 500°F. Place brownies on small cookie sheet; top each with scoop of ice cream and place in freezer.

2. Melt chocolate chips in small saucepan over low heat. Stir in corn syrup; set aside and keep warm.

3. Beat egg whites to soft peaks in small bowl. Gradually beat in sugar; continue beating until stiff peaks form. Spread egg white mixture over ice cream and brownies with small spatula (ice cream and brownies should be completely covered with egg white mixture).

4. Bake 2 to 3 minutes or until meringue is golden. Spread chocolate sauce on serving plates; place baked Alaskas over sauce.

Makes 2 servings

Easy Holiday Trifle

Prep Time: 20 minutes plus refrigerating

> **4 cups boiling water**
> **1 package (8-serving size)** *or* **2 packages (4-serving size each) JELL-O® Brand Orange Flavor Gelatin**
> **1 package (8-serving size)** *or* **2 packages (4-serving size each) JELL-O® Brand Cranberry Flavor Gelatin**
> **2 cups cold water**
> **1 package (10.75 ounces) frozen pound cake, thawed and cubed**
> **1 tub (8 ounces) COOL WHIP® Whipped Topping, thawed**
> **2 cups sliced strawberries (optional)**

STIR 2 cups boiling water into each flavor of gelatin in separate bowls at least 2 minutes until completely dissolved. Stir 1 cup cold water into each bowl. Pour into separate 13×9-inch baking pans. Refrigerate 3 hours or until firm. Cut each pan into ½-inch cubes.

PLACE cranberry gelatin cubes in 3½-quart serving bowl or trifle bowl. Layer with cake cubes, ½ of whipped topping and strawberries. Cover with orange gelatin cubes. Garnish with remaining whipped topping.

REFRIGERATE at least 1 hour or until ready to serve.

Makes 12 to 15 servings

How To Serve: This recipe can also be made in individual glasses as parfaits. Proceed as directed, alternating gelatin cubes, cake cubes, strawberries and whipped topping.

Famous Chocolate Refrigerator Roll

Prep Time: 30 minutes
Chill Time: 4 hours
Total Time: 4 hours and 30 minutes

> **1 teaspoon vanilla extract**
> **2 cups heavy cream, whipped, *or* 1 (8-ounce) container COOL WHIP® Whipped Topping, thawed**
> **1 (9-ounce) package NABISCO® Famous Chocolate Wafers**
> **Chocolate curls, for garnish**

1. Stir vanilla into whipped cream or topping.

2. Spread ½ tablespoon whipped cream or topping on each wafer. Begin stacking wafers together and stand on edge on serving platter to make 14-inch log.

3. Frost with remaining whipped cream or topping. Chill for 4 to 6 hours.* To serve, garnish with chocolate curls; slice roll at 45° angle.

Makes 12 servings

*Or, freeze until firm; cover with plastic wrap. Thaw in refrigerator for 1 hour before serving.

Easy Holiday Trifle

Philadelphia® 3-Step® Cheesecake

Prep Time: 10 minutes
Cook Time: 40 minutes

> **2 packages (8 ounces each) PHILADELPHIA® Cream Cheese or PHILADELPHIA® Neufchâtel Cheese, ⅓ Less Fat than Cream Cheese, softened**
> **½ cup sugar**
> **½ teaspoon vanilla**
> **2 eggs**
> **1 HONEY MAID® Graham Cracker Pie Crust (6 ounces)**

1. BEAT cream cheese, sugar and vanilla with electric mixer on medium speed until well blended. Add eggs, 1 at a time, mixing on low speed after each addition just until blended.

2. POUR into crust.

3. BAKE at 350°F, 40 minutes or until center is almost set. Cool. Refrigerate 3 hours or overnight.

Makes 8 servings

Fruit Topped: Top chilled cheesecake with sliced assorted fresh fruit. Drizzle with 2 tablespoons strawberry *or* apple jelly, heated, if desired.

Chocolate Chip: Stir ½ cup miniature semi-sweet chocolate chips into batter. Sprinkle with additional ¼ cup chips before baking.

Pumpkin: Beat ½ cup canned pumpkin, ½ teaspoon ground cinnamon and dash *each* ground cloves and nutmeg in with cream cheese.

Lemon: Stir 1 tablespoon fresh lemon juice and ½ teaspoon grated lemon peel into batter.

Chocolate: Stir 4 squares BAKER'S® Semi-Sweet Baking Chocolate, melted, into batter.

Crème de Menthe: Stir 4 teaspoons green crème de menthe into batter. Substitute OREO® Pie Crust for HONEY MAID® Graham Cracker Pie Crust.

❧ *tip* ❧

To help ensure a picture perfect cheesecake with a smooth top, avoid jarring the cake during baking and cooling.

Mud Slides

2 cups cold milk
1 package (4-serving size) JELL-O® Chocolate Flavor Instant Pudding & Pie Filling
14 chocolate sandwich cookies, finely crushed (about 1½ cups)
2 cups thawed COOL WHIP® Whipped Topping

Mud Slide

LINE bottoms and sides of 2 loaf pans with wet paper towels. Tilt 2 (12-ounce) glasses in each pan.

POUR milk into 1-quart container with tight-fitting lid. Add pudding mix; cover tightly. Shake vigorously at least 45 seconds; pour evenly into glasses.

GENTLY stir 1¼ cups cookies into whipped topping with wire whisk in medium bowl until blended. Spoon evenly over pudding in glasses; sprinkle with remaining ¼ cup cookies.

REFRIGERATE until ready to serve.

Makes 4 servings

Fresh Nectarine-Pineapple Cobbler

Prep Time: 20 minutes
Bake Time: 45 minutes

1½ cups DOLE® Fresh Pineapple, cut into chunks
3 cups sliced ripe DOLE® Fresh Nectarines or Peaches
½ cup sugar
2 tablespoons all-purpose flour
½ teaspoon ground cinnamon
1 cup buttermilk baking mix
½ cup low-fat milk

• Combine pineapple chunks, nectarines, sugar, flour and cinnamon in 8×8-inch glass baking dish; spread fruit evenly in dish.

• Stir together baking mix and milk in small bowl until just combined. Pour over fruit.

• Bake at 400°F 40 to 45 minutes or until fruit is tender and crust is browned. *Makes 8 servings*

Rice Pudding

3 cups 2% low-fat milk
1 large stick cinnamon
1 cup uncooked rice*
2 cups water
½ teaspoon salt
  Peel of orange or lemon
¾ cup sugar
¼ cup raisins
2 tablespoons dark rum

*Recipe based on regular-milled long grain white rice.

Heat milk and cinnamon in small saucepan over medium heat until milk is infused with flavor of cinnamon, about 15 minutes. Combine rice, water, and salt in 2- to 3-quart saucepan. Bring to a boil; stir once or twice. Place orange peel on top of rice. Reduce heat; cover and simmer 15 minutes or until rice is tender and liquid is absorbed. Remove and discard orange peel. Strain milk and stir into cooked rice. Add sugar and simmer 20 minutes or until thickened, stirring often. Add raisins and rum; simmer 10 minutes. Serve hot. To reheat, add a little milk to restore creamy texture.   *Makes 6 servings*

Hint: Use medium or short grain rice for rice pudding for a creamier consistency.

Favorite recipe from **USA Rice Federation**

Philadelphia® 3-Step® Luscious Lemon Cheesecake

Prep Time: 10 minutes plus refrigerating
Bake Time: 40 minutes

2 packages (8 ounces each) PHILADELPHIA® Cream Cheese, softened
½ cup sugar
1 tablespoon fresh lemon juice
½ teaspoon grated lemon peel
½ teaspoon vanilla
2 eggs
1 HONEY MAID® Graham Pie Crust (6 ounces)

1. **BEAT** cream cheese, sugar, juice, peel and vanilla with electric mixer on medium speed until well blended. Add eggs; mix just until blended.

2. **POUR** into crust.

3. **BAKE** at 350°F for 40 minutes or until center is almost set. Cool. Refrigerate 3 hours or overnight. Garnish with thawed COOL WHIP® Whipped Topping and lemon slices.
   Makes 8 servings

Rice Pudding

Cherry Crisp

1 (21-ounce) can cherry pie filling
½ teaspoon almond extract
½ cup all-purpose flour
½ cup firmly packed brown sugar
1 teaspoon ground cinnamon
3 tablespoons butter or margarine, softened
½ cup chopped walnuts
¼ cup flaked coconut
Ice cream or whipped cream (optional)

Cherry Crisp

Pour cherry pie filling into *ungreased* 8×8×2-inch baking pan. Stir in almond extract.

Place flour, brown sugar and cinnamon in medium mixing bowl; mix well. Add butter; stir with fork until mixture is crumbly. Stir in walnuts and coconut. Sprinkle mixture over cherry pie filling.

Bake in preheated 350°F oven 25 minutes or until golden brown on top and filling is bubbly. Serve warm or at room temperature. If desired, top with ice cream or whipped cream.

Makes 6 servings

Note: This recipe can be doubled. Bake in two 8×8×2-inch baking pans or one 13×9×2-inch pan.

Favorite recipe from **Cherry Marketing Institute**

Original Banana Pudding

¾ cup sugar, divided
⅓ cup all-purpose flour
Dash salt
3 eggs, separated
2 cups milk
½ teaspoon vanilla extract
35 NILLA® Wafers
5 bananas, sliced (about 3½ cups)

1. Mix ½ cup sugar, flour and salt in top of double boiler. Blend in 3 egg yolks and milk. Cook, uncovered, over boiling water, stirring constantly 10 to 12 minutes or until thickened. Remove from heat; stir in vanilla.

2. Spread small amount of custard on bottom of 1½-quart round casserole; cover with layer of wafers and layer of sliced bananas. Pour ⅓ of custard over bananas.

3. Continue to layer wafers, bananas and custard to make 3 layers of each, ending with custard.

4. Beat reserved egg whites in small bowl with electric mixer at high speed until soft peaks form; gradually add remaining ¼ cup sugar, beating until mixture forms stiff peaks. Spoon on top of custard, spreading to cover entire surface and sealing well to edges.

5. Bake at 350°F for 15 to 20 minutes or until browned. Garnish with additional banana slices if desired. Serve warm or cold.

Makes 8 servings

Quick Banana Pudding: Prepare 2 (4-serving size) packages instant vanilla pudding & pie filling according to package directions. Layer prepared pudding with wafers and bananas as above. Cover; refrigerate at least 3 hours. Garnish with 2 cups prepared whipped topping and additional banana slices.

Pudding in a Cloud

Preparation Time: 15 minutes
Refrigerating Time: 2 hours

> **2 cups COOL WHIP® Whipped Topping, thawed**
> **2 cups cold milk**
> **1 package (4-serving size) JELL-O® Instant Pudding & Pie Filling, any flavor**

SPOON whipped topping evenly into 6 dessert dishes. Using back of spoon, make depression in center; spread whipped topping up side of each dish.

POUR milk into medium bowl. Add pudding mix. Beat with wire whisk 2 minutes. Let stand 5 minutes. Spoon pudding into center of whipped topping.

REFRIGERATE until ready to serve
Makes 6 servings

Fruit 'n Juice Squares

Prep Time: 15 minutes
Refrigerate Time: 3¾ hours

- 1½ cups boiling water
- 1 package (8-serving size) or 2 packages (4-serving size each) JELL-O® Brand Strawberry or Cranberry Flavor Gelatin
- 1 cup cold orange juice
  Ice cubes
- 1 tub (8 ounces) COOL WHIP® Whipped Topping, thawed, divided
- 1 can (8¾ ounces) fruit cocktail, drained

STIR boiling water into gelatin in large bowl at least 2 minutes until completely dissolved. Mix cold juice and ice cubes to make 1¼ cups. Add to gelatin, stirring until slightly thickened (consistency of unbeaten egg whites). Remove any remaining ice. Refrigerate 45 minutes.

RESERVE 1 cup gelatin; set aside. Stir ½ of whipped topping into remaining gelatin until smooth. Pour mixture into 8-inch square pan. Refrigerate about 5 minutes until set but not firm (should stick to finger when touched and should mound). Stir fruit into reserved gelatin and carefully spoon over creamy layer in pan.

REFRIGERATE 3 hours or until firm. Cut into squares and garnish with remaining whipped topping.

Makes 9 servings

Cherry Dream

- 5 cups loosely packed angel food cake cubes (about 10 ounces or ½ of large angel food cake)
- 1 (21-ounce) can cherry pie filling
- 1¾ cups (4 ounces) frozen non-dairy whipped topping, thawed
  Fresh mint, for garnish

Sprinkle cake cubes in bottom of 9-inch square baking pan. Fold cherry pie filling into whipped topping in medium bowl. Spoon cherry mixture evenly over cake cubes. Let chill, covered, several hours or overnight. Garnish each serving with sprig of mint.

Makes 8 servings

*Favorite recipe from **Cherry Marketing Institute***

Fruit 'n Juice Square

New York Cheesecake

Prep Time: 15 minutes plus refrigerating
Bake Time: 1 hour

> 1 cup graham cracker crumbs
> 3 tablespoons sugar
> 3 tablespoons butter or margarine, melted
> 5 packages (8 ounces each) PHILADELPHIA® Cream Cheese, softened
> 1 cup sugar
> 3 tablespoons flour
> 1 tablespoon vanilla
> 3 eggs
> 1 cup BREAKSTONE'S® or KNUDSEN® Sour Cream

MIX crumbs, 3 tablespoons sugar and butter; press onto bottom of 9-inch springform pan. Bake at 350°F for 10 minutes.

MIX cream cheese, 1 cup sugar, flour and vanilla with electric mixer on medium speed until well blended. Add eggs, 1 at a time, mixing on low speed after each addition, just until blended. Blend in sour cream.

BAKE 1 hour or until center is almost set. Run knife or metal spatula around rim of pan to loosen cake; cool before removing rim of pan. Refrigerate 4 hours or overnight. *Makes 12 servings*

Chocolate New York Cheesecake: Substitute 1 cup chocolate wafer cookie crumbs for graham cracker crumbs. Blend 8 squares BAKER'S® Semi-Sweet Chocolate, melted and slightly cooled, into batter. Continue as directed.

Festive Stuffed Dates

Prep Time: 25 minutes

> 1 box (8 ounces) DOLE® Whole Pitted Dates
> 1 package (3 ounces) reduced-fat cream cheese, softened
> ¼ cup powdered sugar
> 1 tablespoon grated orange peel

• Make slit in center of each date. Combine cream cheese, powdered sugar and orange peel. Fill centers of dates with cream cheese mixture. Refrigerate.

• Dust with additional powdered sugar just before serving, if desired.
Makes about 27 stuffed dates

Luscious Cold Chocolate Soufflés

Luscious Cold Chocolate Soufflés

1 envelope unflavored gelatin

¼ cup cold water

2 tablespoons reduced-calorie tub margarine

1½ cups cold nonfat milk, divided

½ cup sugar

⅓ cup HERSHEY'S Cocoa or HERSHEY'S Dutch Processed Cocoa

2½ teaspoons vanilla extract, divided

1 envelope (1.3 ounces) dry whipped topping mix

1. Measure lengths of foil to fit around 6 small soufflé dishes (about 4 ounces each); fold in thirds lengthwise. Tape securely to outsides of dishes to form collars, allowing collars to extend 1 inch above rims of dishes. Lightly oil insides of foil.*

2. Sprinkle gelatin over water in small microwave-safe bowl; let stand 2 minutes to soften. Microwave at HIGH (100%) 40 seconds; stir thoroughly. Stir in margarine until melted; let stand 2 minutes or until gelatin is completely dissolved.

3. Stir together 1 cup milk, sugar, cocoa and 2 teaspoons vanilla in small bowl. Beat on low speed of mixer while gradually pouring in gelatin mixture. Beat until well blended.

4. Prepare topping mix as directed on package, using remaining ½ cup milk and remaining ½ teaspoon vanilla; carefully fold into chocolate mixture until well blended. Spoon into prepared soufflé dishes, filling ½ inch from tops of collars. Cover; refrigerate until firm, about 3 hours. Carefully remove foil. Garnish as desired.   *Makes 6 servings*

Six (6-ounce) custard cups may be used in place of soufflé dishes; omit foil collars.

Chocolate Mousse

Chocolate Mousse

1 teaspoon unflavored gelatin
1 tablespoon cold water
2 tablespoons boiling water
½ cup sugar
¼ cup HERSHEY₅S Cocoa
1 cup cold whipping cream
1 teaspoon vanilla extract

1. Sprinkle gelatin over cold water in small bowl; let stand 1 minute to soften. Add boiling water; stir until gelatin is completely dissolved and mixture is clear. Cool slightly.

2. Stir together sugar and cocoa in medium bowl; add whipping cream and vanilla. Beat at medium speed, scraping bottom of bowl occasionally, until mixture is stiff; pour in gelatin mixture and beat until well blended. Spoon into serving dishes. Refrigerate about 30 minutes.

Makes 4 (½-cup) servings

Chocolate Mousse Filled Croissants: Prepare Chocolate Mousse according to directions. Cut 6 bakery croissants horizontally in half. Spread about ⅓ cup mousse onto each bottom half; replace with top half of croissant. Refrigerate about 30 minutes. Makes 6 servings.

Chocolate Mousse Parfaits: Prepare Chocolate Mousse according to directions. Alternately spoon mousse and sliced fresh fruit into parfait glasses. Refrigerate about 1 hour. Makes 5 to 6 servings.

Peach Melba Dessert

Preparation Time: 20 minutes
Refrigerating Time: 6 hours

1½ cups boiling water, divided
2 packages (4-serving size) JELL-O® Brand Raspberry Flavor Sugar Free Low Calorie Gelatin Dessert or JELL-O® Brand Raspberry Flavor Gelatin Dessert, divided
1 container (8 ounces) BREYERS® Vanilla Lowfat Yogurt
1 cup raspberries, divided
1 can (8 ounces) peach slices in juice, undrained
Cold water

STIR ¾ cup boiling water into 1 package of gelatin in large bowl at least 2 minutes or until completely dissolved. Refrigerate about 1 hour or until slightly thickened (consistency of unbeaten egg whites). Stir in yogurt and ½ cup raspberries. Reserve remaining raspberries for garnish. Pour gelatin mixture into serving bowl. Refrigerate about 2 hours or until set but not firm (gelatin should stick to finger when touched and should mound).

MEANWHILE, drain peaches, reserving juice. Add cold water to reserved juice to make 1 cup; set aside. Stir remaining ¾ cup boiling water into remaining package gelatin in large bowl at least 2 minutes until completely dissolved. Stir in measured juice and water. Refrigerate about 1 hour or until slightly thickened (consistency of unbeaten egg whites).

RESERVE several peach slices for garnish; chop remaining peaches. Stir chopped peaches into slightly thickened gelatin. Spoon over gelatin layer in bowl. Refrigerate 3 hours or until firm. Top with reserved peach slices and raspberries.   *Makes 8 servings*

Peach Melba Dessert

Raspberry Almond Trifles

Prep Time: 20 minutes
Chill Time: 2 hours

>   **2 cups whipping cream**
>   **¼ cup plus 1 tablespoon raspberry liqueur or orange juice, divided**
>   **1 (14-ounce) can EAGLE® BRAND Sweetened Condensed Milk (NOT evaporated milk)**
>   **2 (3-ounce) packages ladyfingers**
>   **1 cup seedless raspberry jam**
>   **½ cup sliced almonds, toasted**

1. In large mixing bowl, beat whipping cream and 1 tablespoon liqueur until stiff peaks form. Fold in Eagle Brand; set aside.

2. Layer bottom of 12 (4-ounce) custard cups or ramekins with ladyfingers. Brush with some remaining liqueur. Spread half of jam over ladyfingers. Spread evenly with half of cream mixture; sprinkle with half of almonds. Repeat layers with remaining ladyfingers, liqueur, jam, cream mixture and almonds. Cover and chill 2 hours. Store covered in refrigerator.

Makes 12 servings

Raspberry Swirl Cheesecakes

Prep Time: 15 minutes
Bake Time: 25 minutes
Chill Time: 4 hours

> 1½ **cups fresh or thawed lightly sweetened loose-pack frozen red raspberries**
> 1 **(14-ounce) can EAGLE® BRAND Sweetened Condensed Milk (NOT evaporated milk), divided**
> 2 **(8-ounce) packages cream cheese, softened**
> 3 **eggs**
> 2 **(6-ounce) chocolate crumb pie crusts**
> **Chocolate and white chocolate leaves (recipe follows), if desired**
> **Fresh raspberries, if desired**

1. Preheat oven to 350°F. In blender container, blend 1½ cups raspberries until smooth; press through sieve to remove seeds. Stir ⅓ cup Eagle Brand into sieved raspberries; set aside.

2. In large mixing bowl, beat cream cheese, eggs and remaining Eagle Brand. Spoon into crusts. Drizzle with raspberry mixture. With table knife, gently swirl raspberry mixture through cream cheese mixture.

3. Bake 25 minutes or until center is nearly set when shaken. Cool; chill at least 4 hours. Garnish with chocolate leaves and fresh raspberries, if desired. Store leftovers covered in refrigerator. *Makes 16 servings (2 cheesecakes)*

Chocolate Leaves: Place 1 (1-ounce) square semi-sweet or white chocolate in microwave-safe bowl. Microwave at HIGH (100% power) 1 to 2 minutes, stirring every minute until smooth. With small, clean paintbrush, paint several coats of melted chocolate on undersides of nontoxic leaves, such as mint, lemon or strawberry. Wipe off any chocolate from top sides of leaves. Place leaves, chocolate sides up, on waxed paper-lined baking sheet or on curved surface, such as rolling pin. Refrigerate leaves until chocolate is firm. To use, carefully peel leaves away from chocolate.

✄ *tip* ✄

Cheesecakes must be thoroughly chilled before serving. They can be stored several days in the refrigerator and even frozen successfully without the toppings.

Saucy Bake

Saucy Bake

Preparation Time: 30 minutes
Baking Time: 1 hour

> 1 package (2-layer size) yellow or devil's food cake mix or cake mix with pudding in the mix
> 2 cups water
> 2 cups milk
> 2 packages (4-serving size) JELL-O® Chocolate Flavor Instant Pudding & Pie Filling
> ⅓ cup sugar
> ¼ to ½ teaspoon ground cinnamon

HEAT oven to 350°F.

PREPARE cake mix as directed on package. Pour batter into greased 13×9-inch baking pan. Pour water and milk into large bowl. Add pudding mixes, sugar and cinnamon. Beat with electric mixer on low speed 1 to 2 minutes or until well blended. Pour over cake batter in pan.

BAKE 1 hour or until cake tester inserted into center comes out clean. Garnish as desired. Serve warm.   *Makes 15 servings*

Southern Banana Pudding

Preparation Time: 30 minutes
Baking Time: 15 minutes

> 1 package (4-serving size)
>   JELL-O® Vanilla or Banana
>   Cream Flavor Cook &
>   Serve Pudding & Pie
>   Filling (not Instant)
> 2½ cups milk
> 2 egg yolks, well beaten
> 30 to 35 vanilla wafers
> 2 large bananas, sliced
> 2 egg whites
>   Dash salt
> ¼ cup sugar

HEAT oven to 350°F.

STIR pudding mix into milk in medium saucepan. Add egg yolks. Stirring constantly, cook on medium heat until mixture comes to full boil. Remove from heat.

ARRANGE layer of cookies on bottom and up side of 1½-quart baking dish. Add layer of banana slices; top with ⅓ of pudding. Repeat layers twice, ending with pudding.

BEAT egg whites and salt in medium bowl with electric mixer on high speed until foamy. Gradually add sugar, beating until stiff peaks form. Spoon meringue mixture lightly onto pudding, spreading to edge of dish to seal.

BAKE 10 to 15 minutes or until meringue is lightly browned. Serve warm or refrigerate until ready to serve. *Makes 8 servings*

Brownie Pie à la Mode

> 1 pint vanilla ice cream,
>   slightly softened
> 1 (15½-ounce) package
>   brownie mix
> ½ cup chopped walnuts
> ½ cup SMUCKER'S® Chocolate
>   Fudge Topping
> 2 tablespoons flaked coconut

Spoon ice cream into chilled 2-cup bowl or mold, packing it firmly with back of spoon. Cover with plastic wrap or aluminum foil; freeze at least 1 hour or until firm.

Prepare brownie mix according to package directions; stir in walnuts. Pour into greased 9-inch pie plate. Bake as directed on package. Cool completely on wire rack.

To serve, remove ice cream from freezer. Dip bowl in lukewarm water for 5 seconds. Cut around edge of ice cream with knife and invert onto center of brownie pie. Pour fudge topping over ice cream; sprinkle with coconut. Let stand 5 to 10 minutes at room temperature for easier slicing. *Makes 8 servings*

Southern Banana Pudding

JUST-FOR-FUN COLLECTION

Surprise everyone with the extras. Enhance any meal
or event with special beverages, sweet or spicy sauces, tangy
condiments or fun foods for kids. Find creative and tasty recipes
that add pizazz to snacktime and mealtime.

Sinfully Rich Nonfat Fudge Sauce (page 348)

Sinfully Rich Nonfat Fudge Sauce

½ cup sugar
¼ cup **HERSHEY'S Cocoa or HERSHEY'S Dutch Processed Cocoa**
1 tablespoon plus 1 teaspoon cornstarch
½ cup evaporated nonfat milk
2 teaspoons vanilla extract
   Assorted fresh fruit (optional)
   Cake (optional)
   Frozen nonfat yogurt (optional)

1. Stir together sugar, cocoa and cornstarch in small saucepan; stir in evaporated milk. Cook over low heat, stirring constantly with whisk, until mixture boils. Continue cooking and stirring until sauce is smooth and thickened. Remove from heat. Stir in vanilla.

2. Serve warm or cold with fresh fruit, cake or yogurt, if desired. Cover; refrigerate leftover sauce.

Makes 7 servings

Festive Citrus Punch

1 can (6 ounces) frozen Florida grapefruit juice concentrate, thawed
1 can (6 ounces) frozen pineapple juice concentrate, thawed
1 cup water
3 tablespoons honey
2 tablespoons grenadine syrup (optional)
1 bottle (1 liter) ginger ale, chilled
   Mint sprigs for garnish
   Ice cubes

Combine grapefruit juice, pineapple juice, water and honey in punch bowl or large pitcher. Stir in grenadine, if desired. Stir until well combined.

Just before serving, slowly pour ginger ale down side of punch bowl. Stir gently to combine. Garnish, if desired. Serve over ice in chilled glasses.

Makes about 18 (4-ounce) servings

Favorite recipe from **Florida Department of Citrus**

Spiced Red Wine with Grape Ice Ring

Spiced Red Wine

Grape Ice Ring (recipe
    follows)
½ cup sugar
½ cup water
1 bottle (750 ml) Burgundy
    wine, chilled
2 cups white grape juice,
    chilled
1 cup peach schnapps, chilled

Prepare Grape Ice Ring.

Combine sugar and water in small saucepan. Bring to a boil. Boil, stirring constantly, until sugar dissolves. Cool to room temperature. Cover; refrigerate until chilled, about 2 hours.

Combine wine, grape juice, schnapps and sugar syrup in punch bowl. Float Grape Ice Ring in punch.

Makes 14 servings

Grape Ice Ring

2 pounds assorted seedless
    grapes (Thompson, Red
    Empress, etc.)
Lemon leaves* (optional)

*These nontoxic leaves are available in florist shops.

Fill 4-cup ring mold with water to within ¾ inch of top. Freeze until firm, about 8 hours or overnight. Arrange clusters of grapes and leaves on ice; fill with water to top of mold. Freeze until solid, about 6 hours. To unmold, dip bottom of mold briefly in hot water.

Makes 1 ring

Hot Cocoa

½ cup sugar
¼ cup HERSHEY'S Cocoa
   Dash salt
⅓ cup hot water
 4 cups (1 quart) milk
¾ teaspoon vanilla extract
   Miniature marshmallows or
   sweetened whipped cream
   (optional)

1. Stir together sugar, cocoa and salt in medium saucepan; stir in water. Cook over medium heat, stirring constantly, until mixture comes to a boil. Boil 2 minutes, stirring constantly. Add milk; heat to serving temperature, stirring constantly. *Do not boil.*

2. Remove from heat; add vanilla. Beat with rotary beater or whisk until foamy. Serve topped with marshmallows or sweetened whipped cream, if desired.
Makes 5 (8-ounce) servings

Spiced Cocoa: Add ⅛ teaspoon ground cinnamon and ⅛ teaspoon ground nutmeg with vanilla. Serve with cinnamon stick, if desired.

Mint Cocoa: Add ½ teaspoon mint extract *or* 3 tablespoons crushed hard peppermint candy *or* 2 to 3 tablespoons white crème de menthe with vanilla. Serve with peppermint candy stick, if desired.

Citrus Cocoa: Add ½ teaspoon orange extract *or* 2 to 3 tablespoons orange liqueur with vanilla.

Swiss Mocha: Add 2 to 2½ teaspoons powdered instant coffee with vanilla.

Canadian Cocoa: Add ½ teaspoon maple extract with vanilla.

Cocoa Au Lait: Omit marshmallows or sweetened whipped cream. Spoon 2 tablespoons softened vanilla ice cream on top of each cup of cocoa at serving time.

Slim-Trim Cocoa: Omit sugar. Substitute nonfat milk for milk. Proceed as above. Stir in sugar substitute with sweetening equivalence of ½ cup sugar with vanilla.

Quick Microwave Cocoa: To make one serving, in microwave-safe cup or mug, combine 1 heaping teaspoon HERSHEY'S Cocoa, 2 heaping teaspoons sugar and dash of salt. Add 2 teaspoons cold milk; stir until smooth. Fill cup with milk. Microwave at HIGH (100%) 1 to 1½ minutes or until hot. Stir to blend.

Hot Spiced Tea

4 cups freshly brewed tea
¼ cup honey
4 cinnamon sticks
4 whole cloves
4 lemon or orange slices
  (optional)

Combine tea, honey, cinnamon sticks and cloves in large saucepan; simmer 5 minutes. Serve hot. Garnish with lemon slices, if desired.   *Makes 4 cups*

Favorite recipe from **National Honey Board**

Real Old-Fashioned Lemonade

Juice of 6 SUNKIST® lemons
  (1 cup)
¾ cup sugar or to taste
4 cups cold water
1 SUNKIST® lemon, cut into
  cartwheel slices
Ice cubes

In large pitcher, combine lemon juice and sugar; stir to dissolve sugar. Add remaining ingredients; blend well.   *Makes about 6 cups*

Pink Lemonade: Add a few drops of red food coloring or grenadine syrup.

Honeyed Lemonade: Substitute honey to taste for the sugar.

Holiday Mulled Cider

Preparation Time: 10 minutes
Cooking Time: 15 minutes

6 cups apple cider
3 cups orange juice
2 cups water
½ cup freshly squeezed lemon
  juice
¾ cup firmly packed DOMINO®
  Light Brown Sugar
3 sticks cinnamon
12 whole cloves
¼ teaspoon ground cardamom
¼ teaspoon ground ginger
⅛ teaspoon ground nutmeg
  Lemon slices

Combine all ingredients except lemon slices in 4-quart saucepan. Bring to a boil. Reduce heat to low; continue heating for 15 minutes to blend spices. Remove cinnamon sticks and cloves. Serve in mugs garnished with lemon slices.

Makes 12 servings

Bloody Marys

Prep Time: 5 minutes
Chill Time: 30 minutes

- 1 quart tomato juice
- ½ cup vodka
- 2 tablespoons *Frank's® RedHot®* Cayenne Pepper Sauce
- 2 tablespoons *French's®* Worcestershire Sauce
- 2 tablespoons prepared horseradish
- 1 tablespoon lemon juice
- 1 teaspoon celery salt

Combine all ingredients in large pitcher; refrigerate. Serve over ice.

Makes 4 servings

tip

Serve party beverages in clear glass pitchers or bowls to show off the beautiful colors of the juices and add a festive touch to the table decorations.

Celebration Punch

- 1 can (46 fluid ounces) DEL MONTE® Pineapple Juice, chilled
- 1 can (46 fluid ounces) apricot nectar, chilled
- 1 cup orange juice
- 1 cup rum (optional)
- ¼ cup fresh lime juice
- 2 tablespoons grenadine
  Ice cubes

1. Combine all ingredients in punch bowl.

2. Garnish with pineapple wedges and lime slices, if desired.

Makes 16 (6-ounce) servings

Holiday Wassail

- 1 gallon MOTT'S® Apple Juice
- 1 quart orange juice
- 1 can (16 ounces) frozen pineapple juice, thawed
- 2 cups lemon juice
- 1 cup sugar
- 2 cinnamon sticks
- 2 teaspoons cloves

Place all ingredients in non-aluminum pan; stir and heat to boiling. Simmer for 1 hour. Serve hot. *Makes 24 servings*

Bloody Marys

Piña Colada Punch

5 cups DOLE® Pineapple Juice, divided
1 can (15 ounces) real cream of coconut
1 liter lemon-lime soda
2 limes
1½ cups light rum (optional)
Ice cubes
Mint sprigs

• Chill all ingredients.

• Blend 2 cups pineapple juice with cream of coconut in blender. Combine puréed mixture with remaining 3 cups pineapple juice, soda, juice of 1 lime, rum and ice. Garnish with 1 sliced lime and mint.
Makes 15 servings

❧ *tip* ❧

Prepare delicious fruit beverages with and without alcohol to include the tastes of all your guests.

Peach Bellinis

4 fresh California peaches, peeled and coarsely chopped
½ cup sugar
2 tablespoons lemon juice
¾ cup water
1 bottle (750 ml) chilled sweet sparkling wine
Mint sprigs (optional)

Combine fruit, sugar, lemon juice and water in blender or food processor. Process until smooth.* To serve, pour about ¼ cup peach purée into 6- or 8-ounce stemmed glass. Slowly fill glass with sparkling wine. Stir to blend. Garnish with mint. *Makes 10 servings*

*If made ahead, cover and refrigerate for up to 3 hours. When ready to serve, continue as directed.

*Favorite recipe from **California Tree Fruit Agreement***

Piña Colada Punch

Smucker's® Orange Chili Barbecue Sauce

Prep Time: 5 minutes
Cook Time: 1 to 2 minutes

- 1 cup SMUCKER'S® Sweet Orange Marmalade
- 1 cup tomato sauce or crushed tomatoes packed in tomato purée
- 2 tablespoons chili powder
- 2 tablespoons red wine vinegar
- 1 teaspoon ground cumin
- 1 teaspoon chopped garlic
- ½ teaspoon salt
- ¼ teaspoon ground red pepper or hot pepper sauce (for spicier sauce)

Combine all ingredients in small saucepan; mix well. Heat until sauce comes to a boil, stirring constantly. Simmer 1 minute. Use immediately or cool and store in refrigerator for future use.

Use sauce as a marinade and baste for baked or grilled chicken, ribs, beef or pork. *Makes 6 servings*

Microwave Directions: Combine all ingredients in a microwave-safe bowl; mix well. Cover with plastic wrap and heat on HIGH (100% power) for 2 minutes. Stir; cover and heat for 1 minute.

Smucker's® Lemon Apricot Marinade

Prep Time: 5 minutes

- ½ cup SMUCKER'S® Apricot Preserves
- ¼ cup pitted green olives, sliced into quarters
- Juice and grated peel of 1 large lemon (about 3 tablespoons juice and 1 tablespoon peel)
- 1 teaspoon freshly ground black pepper
- ¼ teaspoon salt

Combine all ingredients in small bowl and mix well. Use marinade for grilling and basting shrimp, salmon, swordfish or chicken.
Makes 6 servings

❧ *tip* ❦

If you want to serve extra marinade as a sauce with grilled meats, it is best to reserve a portion of the marinade for the sauce or double the recipe reserving one portion for the marinade and one for the sauce.

Tangy Orange Red Pepper Relish

4 large red bell peppers, roasted, skinned and coarsely chopped *or* 1 (15-ounce) jar roasted red peppers, drained
2 tablespoons cider vinegar
1 clove garlic
½ cup SMUCKER'S® Sweet Orange Marmalade
1 tablespoon cornstarch
2 tablespoons cold water
1 teaspoon hot pepper sauce

In food processor or blender, place red peppers, vinegar and garlic; purée into smooth paste. Add marmalade; blend. Pour relish into small saucepan.

Dissolve cornstarch in cold water; stir into relish. Simmer over high heat 5 minutes or until slightly thickened. Remove from heat; stir in hot pepper sauce. Pour relish into serving bowl; cool.
Makes 1½ cups relish

Note: To skin red peppers, cut in half and remove seeds. Place cut-side-down on broiler pan. Broil for 10 minutes or until skin is charred. When cool, peel skin from peppers.

Note: Serve this relish with grilled hot dogs or with your favorite grilled meats, poultry or fish.

Velveeta® Golden Sauce

Prep Time: 5 minutes
Cook Time: 10 minutes

½ pound (8 ounces) VELVEETA® Pasteurized Prepared Cheese Product, cut up
¼ cup milk

Stir VELVEETA and milk in saucepan on low heat until smooth. Serve over hot cooked pasta or vegetables. *Makes 1 cup*

Microwave Directions: Microwave VELVEETA and milk in 1½-quart microwavable bowl on HIGH 2½ to 4½ minutes or until smooth, stirring every minute. Serve as directed.

Fruit Pizza

1 (20-ounce) package
   refrigerated sugar cookie
   dough
1 (8-ounce) package cream
   cheese, softened
1 cup powdered sugar
   Assorted fresh fruit
   (strawberries, bananas,
   kiwi fruit, blueberries,
   mandarin oranges, etc.)
½ cup SMUCKER'S® Apricot
   Preserves or Sweet Orange
   Marmalade
1 tablespoon water

Cut dough into 1-inch slices and place on *ungreased* cookie sheet or pizza pan. Bake 17 to 19 minutes or until light golden brown around edges. Cool.

Combine cream cheese and sugar; mix well. Spread over cookies. Decorate with sliced fruit. (Dip banana slices in lemon juice to prevent browning.) Combine preserves and water; mix well. Drizzle over fruit topping. Serve immediately or refrigerate until serving time.   *Makes 9 servings*

Chocolate Leaves

   Semisweet chocolate
      (squares or bars), shaved
      or chopped
   Shortening

Supplies
   Nontoxic leaves, such as
      rose, lemon or camellia
   Small, clean paintbrush or
      pastry brush

1. Place chocolate in measuring cup. Add shortening. (Use 1 teaspoon shortening for every 2 ounces chocolate.) Fill saucepan one-quarter full (about 1 inch deep) with warm (not hot) water. Place measuring cup in water to melt chocolate, stirring frequently until smooth. (Be careful not to get any water into chocolate.) Remove measuring cup from saucepan. Let chocolate cool slightly.

2. Wash leaves; dry well with paper towels. Brush melted chocolate onto underside of each leaf with paintbrush or pastry brush, coating leaf thickly and evenly. Repeat brushing with second coating of chocolate, if desired, for sturdier leaf. Carefully wipe off any chocolate that may have run onto front of leaf.

3. Place leaves, chocolate side up, on waxed paper. Let stand in cool, dry place until chocolate is firm. (Do not chill in refrigerator.)

4. When chocolate is firm, carefully peel leaves away from chocolate; chill until ready to use.

Chocolate-Dipped Strawberries

½ cup semisweet chocolate chips
1 teaspoon shortening
10 to 12 fresh strawberries, cleaned

1. Place chocolate chips and shortening in small microwavable bowl. Microwave at HIGH 1½ to 3 minutes or until smooth when stirred, stirring after each minute. (Or, place in top of double boiler. Heat over boiling water until chocolate is smooth when stirred.)

2. Dip strawberries into chocolate. Place on waxed paper-lined baking sheet; let stand until chocolate is set.

❧ *tip* ❧

When you buy fresh strawberries, choose fruit that is fresh, clean and bright red with stems attached. To clean, wash berries with stems on just before preparing and pat berries dry with paper towels to keep from getting soggy.

Ice Cream Cookie Dessert

1 (1¼-pound) package chocolate sandwich cookies
1 stack (18 cookies) chocolate fudge mint cookies
½ gallon vanilla or mint chocolate chip ice cream, softened
2 cups (two 12-ounce jars) SMUCKER'S® Hot Fudge Topping
1 (12-ounce) carton whipped topping, thawed

Crush cookies until fine. Reserve 1 cup of crumbs for topping. Press remaining cookie crumbs in 13×9-inch pan. Spoon ice cream on top of crumbs and freeze.

Heat hot fudge topping as directed on jar; spread over ice cream. Freeze for 1 hour.

Spread with whipped topping; top with reserved cookie crumbs. Freeze until ready to serve.

Makes 12 to 16 servings

Old-Fashioned Pop Corn Balls

**2 quarts popped JOLLY TIME®
Pop Corn**
1 cup sugar
⅓ cup light or dark corn syrup
⅓ cup water
¼ cup butter or margarine
½ teaspoon salt
1 teaspoon vanilla

Keep popped pop corn warm in 200°F oven while preparing syrup. In 2-quart saucepan, stir together sugar, corn syrup, water, butter and salt. Cook over medium heat, stirring constantly, until mixture comes to a boil. Continue cooking without stirring until temperature reaches 270°F on candy thermometer or until small amount of syrup dropped into very cold water separates into threads which are hard but not brittle. Remove from heat. Add vanilla; stir just enough to mix through hot syrup. Slowly pour over popped pop corn, stirring to coat well. Cool just enough to handle. With JOLLY TIME® Pop Corn Ball Maker or buttered hands, shape into balls.
*Makes 12 medium-sized
pop corn balls*

Original Ranch® Oyster Crackers

Original Ranch® Oyster Crackers

**1 box (16 ounces) oyster
crackers**
¼ cup vegetable oil
**1 packet (1 ounce) HIDDEN
VALLEY® Original Ranch®
Salad Dressing &
Seasoning Mix**

Place crackers in gallon-size Glad® Zipper Storage Bag. Pour oil over crackers; seal bag and toss to coat. Add salad dressing & seasoning mix; seal bag and toss again until coated. Bake on *ungreased* baking sheet at 250°F. for 15 to 20 minutes or until crackers are golden brown.
Makes 8 cups

"M&M's"® Family Party Mix

2 tablespoons butter or margarine*

¼ cup honey*

2 cups favorite grain cereal *or* 3 cups granola

1 cup coarsely chopped nuts

1 cup thin pretzel pieces

1 cup raisins

2 cups "M&M's"® Chocolate Mini Baking Bits

For a drier mix, eliminate butter and honey. Simply combine dry ingredients and do not bake.

Preheat oven to 300°F. In large saucepan over low heat, melt butter; add honey until well blended. Remove from heat and add cereal, nuts, pretzel pieces and raisins, stirring until all pieces are evenly coated. Spread mixture onto *ungreased* cookie sheet and bake about 10 minutes. *Do not overbake.* Spread mixture onto waxed paper and allow to cool completely. In large bowl combine mixture and "M&M's"® Chocolate Mini Baking Bits. Store in tightly covered container.

Makes about 6 cups snack mix

Original Ranch® Snack Mix

8 cups KELLOGG'S® CRISPIX®* cereal

2½ cups small pretzels

2½ cups bite-size Cheddar cheese crackers (optional)

3 tablespoons vegetable oil

1 packet (1 ounce) HIDDEN VALLEY® Original Ranch® Salad Dressing & Seasoning Mix

Kellogg's® and Crispix® are registered trademarks of Kellogg Company.

Combine cereal, pretzels and crackers in gallon-size Glad® Zipper Storage Bag. Pour oil over mixture. Seal bag and toss to coat. Add salad dressing & seasoning mix; seal bag and toss again until coated.

Makes 10 cups

Snack Mix

Funny Face Sandwich Melts

Prep Time: 10 minutes
Cook Time: 1 minute

> 2 super-size English muffins,
>   split and toasted
> 8 teaspoons *French's*® Sweet &
>   Tangy Honey Mustard
> 1 can (8 ounces) crushed
>   pineapple, drained
> 8 ounces sliced smoked ham
> 4 slices Swiss cheese or white
>   American cheese

1. Place English muffins, cut side up, on baking sheet. Spread each with *2 teaspoons* mustard. Arrange one-fourth of the pineapple, ham and cheese on top, dividing evenly.

2. Broil until cheese melts, about 1 minute. Decorate with mustard and assorted vegetables to create your own funny face.

Makes 4 servings

❧ *tip* ☙

This sandwich is also easy to prepare in the toaster oven.

Creamy JELL-O® Jigglers®

Prep Time: 15 minutes
Refrigerating Time: 3 hours

> 2½ cups boiling water
> 2 packages (8-serving size) *or*
>   4 packages (4-serving size)
>   JELL-O® Brand Gelatin
>   Dessert, any flavor
> 1 cup cold milk
> 1 package (4-serving size)
>   JELL-O® Vanilla Flavor
>   Instant Pudding & Pie
>   Filling

STIR boiling water into gelatin in large bowl at least 3 minutes until completely dissolved. Cool 30 minutes at room temperature.

POUR milk into medium bowl. Add pudding mix. Beat with wire whisk 1 minute. Quickly pour into gelatin. Stir with wire whisk until well blended. Pour into 13×9-inch pan.

REFRIGERATE 3 hours or until firm. Dip bottom of pan in warm water about 15 seconds. Cut into decorative shapes with cookie cutters all the way through gelatin or cut into 1-inch squares. Lift from pan.   *Makes about 24 pieces*

Funny Face Sandwich

Breakfast Blossoms

1 (12-ounce) can buttermilk biscuits (10 biscuits)
¾ cup SMUCKER'S® Strawberry Preserves
¼ teaspoon ground cinnamon
¼ teaspoon ground nutmeg

Grease ten 2½- or 3-inch muffin cups. Separate dough into 10 biscuits. Separate each biscuit into 3 even sections or leaves. Stand 3 sections evenly around side and bottom of cup, overlapping slightly. Press dough edges firmly together.

Combine preserves, cinnamon and nutmeg; place tablespoonful in center of each cup.

Bake at 375°F for 10 to 12 minutes or until lightly browned. Cool slightly before removing from pan. Serve warm.   *Makes 10 rolls*

❧ *tip* ❧

Keep a can of prepared biscuits in the refrigerator for an easy, warm breakfast treat.

Soft Pretzels

1 tablespoon granular dry yeast
⅔ cup lukewarm water
1 tablespoon canola oil
2 tablespoons granulated sugar
½ teaspoon salt
1 egg, lightly beaten, divided
2¼ cups all-purpose flour, divided
2 teaspoons baking soda
Sesame seeds

In bowl of food processor with a metal blade, dissolve yeast in lukewarm water. Add canola oil, sugar, salt, half beaten egg and 1¼ cups flour. Process 20 seconds. Let rise in processor bowl 30 minutes. Add remaining flour and process until ball forms.

Turn dough out onto lightly floured board. Knead 1 to 2 minutes. Cut dough into 8 or 10 equal pieces.

Roll each piece into 16-inch rope. Dissolve baking soda in 2 cups water. Dip dough ropes into baking soda solution. Form into pretzel shape. Seal ends.

Preheat oven to 400° F. Place pretzels on lightly oiled baking sheet. Let rise slightly, but not until doubled in bulk, about 15 minutes. Brush with remaining beaten egg. Sprinkle with sesame seeds.

Bake about 15 minutes. Cool on wire rack.   *Make 8 to 10 pretzels*

Favorite recipe from **Canada's Canola Industry**

Pudding Chillers

Prep Time: 10 minutes
Freeze Time: 5 hours

> **2 cups cold milk**
> **1 package (4-serving size)**
> **JELL-O® Instant Pudding**
> **& Pie Filling, any flavor**
> **6 (5-ounce) paper cups**

POUR milk into medium bowl. Add pudding mix. Beat with wire whisk 2 minutes. Spoon into cups. Insert wooden pop stick into each for a handle.

FREEZE 5 hours or overnight until firm. To remove pop from cup, place bottom of cup under warm running water for 15 seconds. Press firmly on bottom of cup to release pop. (Do not twist or pull pop stick.)

Makes 6 pops

Rocky Road: Use JELL-O® Chocolate Flavor Instant Pudding & Pie Filling and stir in ½ cup miniature marshmallows and ¼ cup each BAKER'S® Semi-Sweet Real Chocolate Chunks and chopped peanuts.

Toffee Crunch: Use JELL-O® Vanilla Flavor Instant Pudding & Pie Filling and stir in ½ cup chopped chocolate-covered toffee bars.

Cookies & Cream: Use JELL-O® Vanilla Flavor Instant Pudding & Pie Filling and stir in ½ cup chopped chocolate sandwich cookies.

Pudding Chillers

Coconut Honey Pop Corn Balls

> **3 quarts popped JOLLY TIME®**
> **Pop Corn**
> **¾ cup coconut**
> **⅓ cup honey**
> **½ teaspoon ground cinnamon**
> **Dash of salt**
> **3 tablespoons butter or**
> **margarine**

Preheat oven to 250°F. Line shallow pan with foil. Place popped pop corn in pan. Keep pop corn warm in oven. Spread coconut in shallow baking pan; toast coconut, stirring once, about 8 to 10 minutes. Combine honey, cinnamon and salt in small saucepan. Heat to boiling; boil 2½ minutes, stirring constantly. Add butter; stir until melted. Pour honey mixture over pop corn. Add coconut. Toss well. Cool just enough to handle. With JOLLY TIME® Pop Corn Ball Maker or buttered hands, shape into balls.

Makes about 10 pop corn balls

Fruity Gelatin Pops

Prep Time: 10 minutes
Freeze Time: 7 hours

> 1 cup boiling water
> 1 package (4-serving size) JELL-O® Brand Gelatin Dessert, any flavor
> ⅓ cup sugar
> 1⅓ cups cold juice, any flavor
> 6 (5-ounce) paper cups

STIR boiling water into gelatin and sugar in medium bowl at least 2 minutes until completely dissolved. Stir in cold juice. Pour into cups. Freeze about 2 hours or until almost firm. Insert wooden pop stick into each for handle.

FREEZE 5 hours or overnight until firm. To remove pop from cup, place bottom of cup under warm running water for 15 seconds. Press firmly on bottom of cup to release pop. (Do not twist or pull pop stick.) Store leftover pops in freezer up to 2 weeks.   *Makes 6 pops*

Outrageous Orange Pops: Use 1 cup boiling water, JELL-O® Brand Orange Flavor Gelatin Dessert, ⅓ cup sugar and 1⅓ cups orange juice.

Fruity Strawberry Pops: Use 1 cup boiling water, JELL-O® Brand Strawberry Flavor Gelatin Dessert, ⅓ cup sugar, ⅔ cup cold water and ⅔ cup puréed strawberries.

Lemonade Pops: Use 1 cup boiling water, JELL-O® Brand Lemon Flavor Gelatin Dessert, ⅓ cup sugar, 1 cup cold water and 2 tablespoons lemon juice.

Iced Tea Pops: Use 1 cup boiling water, JELL-O® Brand Lemon Flavor Gelatin Dessert, 2 tablespoons sugar and 1½ cups pre-sweetened iced tea.

JELL-O® Juicy Jigglers®

Refrigerating Time: 3 hours

> 2½ cups boiling juice (Do not add cold water)
> 2 packages (8-serving size) *or* 4 packages (4-serving size) JELL-O® Brand Gelatin Dessert, any flavor

STIR boiling juice into gelatin in large bowl at least 3 minutes until completely dissolved. Pour into 13×9-inch pan.

REFRIGERATE 3 hours or until firm (does not stick to finger when touched). Dip bottom of pan in warm water about 15 seconds. Cut into decorative shapes with cookie cutters all the way through gelatin or cut into 1-inch squares. Lift from pan.

Makes about 24 pieces

Fruity Gelatin Pops

ACKNOWLEDGMENTS

The publisher would like to thank the companies and organizations listed below for the use of their recipes and photographs in this publication.

A.1.® Steak Sauce

Arm & Hammer Division, Church & Dwight Co., Inc.

Barilla America, Inc.

BC-USA, Inc.

BelGioioso® Cheese, Inc.

Blue Diamond Growers®

Bob Evans®

California Tree Fruit Agreement

California Wild Rice Advisory Board

Campbell Soup Company

Canada's Canola Industry

Cherry Marketing Institute

CHIPS AHOY!® Chocolate Chip Cookies

Clamato® is a registered trademark of Mott's, Inc.

COLLEGE INN® Broth

Colorado Potato Administrative Committee

ConAgra Foods®

Del Monte Corporation

Delmarva Poultry Industry, Inc.

Dole Food Company, Inc.

Domino® Foods, Inc.

Duncan Hines® and Moist Deluxe® are registered trademarks of Aurora Foods Inc.

Eagle® Brand

Equal® sweetener

Fleischmann's® Original Spread

Fleischmann's® Yeast

Florida Department of Citrus

The Golden Grain Company®

Grandma's® is a registered trademark of Mott's, Inc.

Grey Poupon® Dijon Mustard

Hebrew National®

Heinz U.S.A.

Hershey Foods Corporation

The Hidden Valley® Food Products Company

Hillshire Farm®

Hormel Foods, LLC

JOLLY TIME® Pop Corn

Keebler® Company

Kellogg Company

The Kingsford Products Company

Kraft Foods Holdings

Lawry's® Foods, Inc.

© Mars, Incorporated 2002

McIlhenny Company (TABASCO® brand Pepper Sauce)

Minnesota Cultivated Wild Rice Council

Mott's® is a registered trademark of Mott's, Inc.

Nabisco Biscuit and Snack Division

National Chicken Council / US Poultry & Egg Association

National Honey Board

National Pork Board

National Turkey Federation

Nestlé USA

NILLA® Wafers

OREO® Chocolate Sandwich Cookies

Perdue Farms Incorporated

PLANTERS® Nuts

The Quaker® Oatmeal Kitchens

Reckitt Benckiser

RED STAR® Yeast, a product of Lasaffre Yeast Corporation

Riviana Foods Inc.

Sargento® Foods Inc.

The J.M. Smucker Company

Southeast United Dairy Industry Association, Inc.

StarKist® Seafood Company

The Sugar Association, Inc.

Sunkist Growers, Inc.

Tyson Foods, Inc.

Unilever Bestfoods North America

USA Rice Federation

Washington Apple Commission

Wisconsin Milk Marketing Board

Index

METRIC CONVERSION CHART

VOLUME MEASUREMENTS (dry)

⅛ teaspoon = 0.5 mL
¼ teaspoon = 1 mL
½ teaspoon = 2 mL
¾ teaspoon = 4 mL
1 teaspoon = 5 mL
1 tablespoon = 15 mL
2 tablespoons = 30 mL
¼ cup = 60 mL
⅓ cup = 75 mL
½ cup = 125 mL
⅔ cup = 150 mL
¾ cup = 175 mL
1 cup = 250 mL
2 cups = 1 pint = 500 mL
3 cups = 750 mL
4 cups = 1 quart = 1 L

VOLUME MEASUREMENTS (fluid)

1 fluid ounce (2 tablespoons) = 30 mL
4 fluid ounces (½ cup) = 125 mL
8 fluid ounces (1 cup) = 250 mL
12 fluid ounces (1½ cups) = 375 mL
16 fluid ounces (2 cups) = 500 mL

WEIGHTS (mass)

½ ounce = 15 g
1 ounce = 30 g
3 ounces = 90 g
4 ounces = 120 g
8 ounces = 225 g
10 ounces = 285 g
12 ounces = 360 g
16 ounces = 1 pound = 450 g

DIMENSIONS

1/16 inch = 2 mm
⅛ inch = 3 mm
¼ inch = 6 mm
½ inch = 1.5 cm
¾ inch = 2 cm
1 inch = 2.5 cm

OVEN TEMPERATURES

250°F = 120°C
275°F = 140°C
300°F = 150°C
325°F = 160°C
350°F = 180°C
375°F = 190°C
400°F = 200°C
425°F = 220°C
450°F = 230°C

BAKING PAN SIZES

Utensil	Size in Inches/Quarts	Metric Volume	Size in Centimeters
Baking or Cake Pan (square or rectangular)	8×8×2	2 L	20×20×5
	9×9×2	2.5 L	23×23×5
	12×8×2	3 L	30×20×5
	13×9×2	3.5 L	33×23×5
Loaf Pan	8×4×3	1.5 L	20×10×7
	9×5×3	2 L	23×13×7
Round Layer Cake Pan	8×1½	1.2 L	20×4
	9×1½	1.5 L	23×4
Pie Plate	8×1¼	750 mL	20×3
	9×1¼	1 L	23×3
Baking Dish or Casserole	1 quart	1 L	—
	1½ quart	1.5 L	—
	2 quart	2 L	—